"If you want to love more, learn more, and laugh more, read this magnificent book. Cynthia Brian will put a bounce in your step!
    –Roger Crawford, author of *How High Can You Bounce?*

"This wonderful book reminds us that we have the power to create the life we dream of. Follow Cynthia's simple steps and you won't be able to wipe the smile off your face."
    –Marcia Wieder, author of *Making Your Dreams Come True*

"This thoughtful and inspiring book will nurture your heart and nourish your mind."
    –Nido R. Qubein, Chairman, National Speakers Foundation

"Cynthia Brian lives her life in an inspiring way. Her stories have touched my life and her spirit has rubbed off. I'm glad she wrote this book and I believe you will be also."
    –Patrick Combs, author of *Major in Success*

"*Be the Star You Are!* is for anyone who wants to truly live a rich life. Cynthia Brian shows you how to live with passion, go for your dreams, and have fun!"
    –David L. Bach, author of *Smart Women Finish Rich*

"What's the best way to become the star you are? Ask one! And, in my book, that's Cynthia Brian!"
    –T. Scott Gross, author of *Borrowed Dreams* and *Absolutely Outrageous Service*

"Cynthia Brian has created a magical book that will help you discover your talents and help you reach far beyond your wildest dreams."
    –Roger Dawson, author of *Secrets of Power Negotiating*

"Cynthia is a star–now you can join her! Just read the book; her stories will inspire you to go as far and as high as you can."
    –John Kremer, author of *Celebrate Today* and *1001 Ways to Market Your Book*

"*Be the Star You Are!* is a moving, motivating, and entertaining book, chock-full of strategies and tactics that you can use right now to bring out your very best!"
    –Orvel Ray Wilson, CSP, author of *Guerrilla Marketing and Guerrilla Negotiating*

"*Be the Star You Are!* is written directly from Cynthia Brian's heart and soul. Reading this book is like being on center stage with the best lighting, the best director, a winning script in your hands, and feeling the confidence you already are a star."

–Carol Adrienne, author of *The Purpose of Your Life*

"I respect an author who practices what she preaches. Cynthia Brian loves life and lives it to the fullest. This comprehensive treasury of wisdom will inspire you to do the same."

–Les Hewitt, President, Achievers Canada, and coauthor of *The Power of Focus*

"Read *Be the Star You Are!* and discover your own dazzling light. Cynthia guides us through our own 99 gifts and reminds us that we have the power to energize our lives in every precious moment."

–Brian D. Biro, author of *Beyond Success* and *The Joyful Spirit*

"*Be the Star You Are!* has a wonderfully inspiring message: Live fully and laugh heartily. Read, enjoy, and be awakened to the potentials of your unique soul."

–Dr. Ray Moody, author of *Life After Life* and *The Last Laugh*

"Cynthia Brian will encourage, inspire, inform, and motivate you. It's a promise! Each story, each personal message is unique and special. All you need to do is unwrap the 99 gifts she delivers. *Be the Star You Are!* is a powerful package."

–Connie Goldman, NPR radio producer/host and author of *Tending the Earth, Mending the Spirit*

"Cynthia Brian provides 99 steps to help you get closer to your divine self and share the blessings that have been bestowed upon you."

–Gerald G. Jampolsky, M.D., author of *Love Is Letting Go of Fear* and *Shortcuts to God*

"Cynthia Brain's no-nonsense advice comes straight from the heart. *Be the Star You Are!* is a breath of fresh air."

–Noah St. John, author of *Permission to Succeed*

"Inspiration is a like a bath–it wears off after a while. That's why so many people crave truly inspirational books and that's why *Be the Star You Are!* is such a treasure. If you're looking for a lift, if you want to see how other people just like you have overcome the same kinds of challenges you're facing, you can't do better than reading Cynthia Brian's new book."

–Keith Ellis, author of *The Magic Lamp:*
Goal Setting for People Who Hate Setting Goals

"Cynthia Brian not only talks the talk, but also actually walks the walk! I highly recommend this book! Read it, reread it, and implement the strategies she shares and you too will be a star!"

–Willie Jolley, author of *It Only Takes a Minute to Change Your Life*

"Your light will shine bright when you read this book. *Be the Star You Are!* is overflowing with inspiring stories that lighten your heart, clear your mind, and tune you into a fulfilling life."

–Dr. Richard Bellamy, author of *12 Secrets for Manifesting Your Vision, Inspiration,*
and Purpose and *How to Make Your Dreams Come True!*

"Cynthia Brian is a light for love and healing in the world. Her book *Be the Star You Are!* inspires readers to discover their radiance, empowering them to realize their full potential for love and joy."

–David Simon, M.D. Medical Director, The Chopra Center for Well Being,
and author of *Vital Energy*

"*Be the Star You Are!* will open your eyes and your hearts to who you really are! It only takes one person to change the world–what are you waiting for? Cynthia Brian will inspire you to not only achieve your heart's desire, but also to have fun doing it!"

–Ivan Burnell, author of *The Power of Positive Doing* and *Say "YES" to Life!*

"Cynthia Brian is one of the most sparkling stars I have ever met. She is the perfect author to bring us these tremendously interesting and uplifting stories. I suggest you buy a carton of these jewel books–they make perfect gifts!"

–Dottie Walters CSP, international speaker, author, consultant, publisher/editor:
Sharing Ideas magazine, President, Walters International Speakers Bureau

"A *power* message for all!"

–Andy Lakey, author and artist

"You can live the dream as the song says, 'Be the Star You Are!, light the flame that burns, deep within your heart, where the real you yearns.' All you have to do is read this inspirational book, go for it, and fly."

–Frankie Laine, legendary entertainer and songwriter

"Cynthia Brian is more than a star–she's a bright comet flashing across the firmament. Her presence and creative energy are testimony to the success of these principles."

–Arlene Bernstein, author of *Growing Season:*
A Healing Journey into the Heart of Nature

"Be the Star You Are! is a bright, passionate, and delightful road map to joyful self-expression! Cynthia Brian has taken the riches of her experience and extracted the best for you to make your own career and life shine. Run with the ball and win!"

–Alan Cohen, author of *My Father's Voice* and
The Dragon Doesn't Live Here Anymore

"*Be the Star You Are!* sets a strong foundation for your life by guiding you through the steps for creating a fulfilling and empowering life. You are reminded of the simple yet important gifts of each act we participate in."

–Loren Slocum, author of *No Greater Love*

"Cynthia Brian's joy, generosity, and energy are absolutely infectious! *Be the Star You Are!* is a marvelous gift to the world. Keep up the wonderful work!"

–Patty Aubery, President, *Chicken Soup for the Soul*® Enterprises, and author of *Chicken Soup for the Survivor's Soul* and *Chicken Soup for the Expectant Mother's Soul*

"Cynthia Brian's enthusiasm is catching. In *Be the Star You Are!*, Brian shares her personal journey with wit and depth while motivating us all to be our best."

—Francesca De Grandis, author of *Be a Goddess! A Guide to Celtic Spells* and
Wisdom for Self-Healing, Prosperity, and Great Sex

BE THE STAR YOU ARE!

BE THE STAR YOU ARE!

99 GIFTS FOR LIVING, LOVING, LAUGHING, AND LEARNING TO MAKE A DIFFERENCE

CYNTHIA BRIAN

CELESTIAL ARTS
Berkeley / Toronto

Celestial Arts
P.O. Box 7123
Berekely, CA 94707
www.tenspeed.com
A Heart & Star Book

Book and cover design by Campana Design
Cover photo by Norbert Brein-Kozakewycz
Photo on back flap by Ken Rice

Be the Star You Are!™ is a trademark of the author
Starstyle is a registered trademark

Distributed in Australia by Simon and Schuster Australia, in Canada by Ten Speed Press Canada, in New Zealand by Southern Publishers Group, in South Africa by Real Books, in Southeast Asia by Berkeley Books, and in the United Kingdom and Europe by Airlift Books.

A portion of the proceeds from this book benefit the positive programming media library charity, *Be the Star You Are!*®, a 501(c)(3) organization. For more information, visit www.bethestaryouare.org or call 877-944-STAR. PO Box 376, Moraga, CA 94556

Library of Congress Cataloging-in-Publication Data

Brian, Cynthia.
    Be the star you are! : 99 gifts for living, loving, laughing, and learning to make a difference / by Cynthia Brian.
        p. cm.
    Includes bibliographical references.
    ISBN 1-58761-008-6
    1. Self-actualization (Psychology)   I. Title.
    BF637.S4 .B74 2001
    158—dc21
                                                    00-065913

First printing, 2001
Printed in Canada

1 2 3 4 5 — 05 04 03 02 01

DEDICATION

This book is dedicated with gratitude to my incredible parents, Al and Alice Abruzzini, who gave me roots; to my husband, Brian, who helped me grow; and to our children, Justin David and Heather Brittany, who allowed me to blossom. You are my everlasting garden, my sun, my moon, and my stars.

I also dedicate this book to all the "Beloved" Davids who travel through my days supporting me in thinking big and shooting for the stars.

With endless love, appreciation, and admiration to all.

ACKNOWLEDGMENTS

If I had been asked as a child whether I would become an author when I grew up, I probably would have responded with "What would I write?" Although I always loved creative writing, it wasn't until my dad died that I realized I had anything worth saying to the world. Many individuals illuminate our paths, offering leadership, love, and learning, but sometimes we don't understand what gifts they have bestowed upon us until they have gone. I am deeply grateful to the many guides and teachers that have traveled the roads with me, providing me with the stories you are about to read. Some were family, friends, students, clients, cast, crew, and guests. Many were complete strangers. All made a difference in my life.

In the course of writing this book, I have been privileged to listen to, learn from, work with, and be loved by many people. I wish to acknowledge my great gratitude to the following individuals:

My heartfelt thanks to my husband, Brian, and my children, Justin and Heather, who patiently endured the struggles, challenges, frustrations, and joys that are all part of the writing process. You are the glue that binds my life in reality. I love you dearly, and I couldn't have completed this book without your support and encouragement.

To my dad, Al Abruzzini, my personal angel and greatest champion, I now understand the meaning of your dying words: "My end is your beginning." Throughout my writings I have felt your heavenly presence. You were my foundation and pillar of strength in life, you remain so in death. Thank you, Daddy.

To Dr. Bernie Siegel, the miracle worker, my adopted "Big Daddy," I am proud to be your California "Chosen Daughter." Thank you for your constant encouragement and for being there when we needed you most. Your earthiness, laughter, and kindness are the torch that keep many lives illuminated.

If it wasn't for renowned author Roger Crawford, you would not be reading this book. His generosity on a plane ride from Denver, sharing information with me on how to get published, became my first chapter. Thanks, Roger, for telling me that my stories were bookworthy.

Thank you Lynn Carey, esteemed newspaper columnist, for your encouragement in journaling the struggle of my father's life.

Merci, merci à ma grammar-mère, Eleanor Dugan, my fellow francophile, friend, and editor, for your belief in the value of this manuscript. Your humor, style, and energy kept me going on the right road, even though it was sometimes bumpy. I can't count how many times you said this was a winning book, and I appreciate every word. Everyone deserves an Eleanor in her corner! I am so glad Roger introduced us.

To my soulful literary agent, Ed Silver, who was unceasingly enthusiastic about this project. He felt the spirit of the book when he first read the proposal and knew in his heart that he wanted to promote it. Ed, you are the kind of agent every author needs!

To my publisher, Ten Speed Press/Celestial Arts and, specifically, Vice President at Large, Jo Ann Deck. We were destined to meet, and it is no coincidence that our fathers both died on December 8. This book was orchestrated in heaven. My gratitude, Jo Ann Germaine, for our lovely lunch meetings, our walks in the secret garden, and your loving direction. It's been a pleasure to work together. To Annie Nelson, my excellent editor, who has been gracious with suggestions and enthusiastic about every aspect of the book, what a joy you are! Your attention to detail and your eagerness to create a work of art are the reasons this book is so eloquent and elegant. Thank you to Gonzalo Ferreyra, Mark Anderson, and Kristen Casemore, whose combined marketing and publicity expertise will surely make this book a best-seller. Thank you to Nancy Campana of Campana Design, whose brilliant design talents shine brightly on these pages. Thank you to my great friend Marcia Welch for inviting me to the Gracenet event where I met Nicole Geiger of Tricycle Press who subsequently introduced me to Jo Ann in the Celestial Arts division. The circle of synchronicities continues in this book of hearts and stars.

Many thanks to Jack Canfield, Mark Victor and Patty Hansen, Patty and Jeff Aubery, and Mark and Chrissy Donnelly for believing in my abilities and bringing me on board as a coauthor for *Chicken Soup for the Gardener's Soul*. I am honored to be included in the illustrious family of the renowned *Chicken Soup for the Soul* series. My admiration and appreciation to my coauthors of *Chicken Soup for the Gardener's Soul*. To all the amazing celebrities, authors, filmmakers, and extraordinary people I have had the great honor to interview as guests on my television and radio programs, I am grateful for your insights and expertise. You bring positive messages to a world that craves them. And to my fabulous crews who have worked with me over the years on television and radio, thank you for your dedication to positive programming and for making me look good! Gracious gratitude to the numerous incredible people who generously endorsed this book, giving it wings to soar. You are the bright stars in my galaxy.

Many others have been instrumental in the development of this book. Their constant confidence in the messages of my mission was positive fuel for my fire. To the dedicated volunteers of the positive programming non-profit organization, *Be the Star You Are!,* specifically the dream team— Patricia Hallberg, our invaluable distribution coordinator; Kim Carlson, our Web master and newsletter designer extraordinaire; Sara La France, our gallant grant writer; Michele Phillips, our responsive enthusiastic office assistant; and Rebecca Schmidt, an unconditional proponent of *Be the Star You Are!* since its inception—my appreciation. You truly are stars in my book. Kudos and gratitude to the legendary singer Frankie Laine and producer/writer Deane Hawley for creating the theme song to *Be the Star You Are!* It is truly a musical mission statement. Thanks to my *Starstyle* clients and acting students for their enthusiasm for this project, even when it meant less time for them. A special thanks to everyone at Business Radio 1220 A.M., KBZS in San Francisco and all my dedicated listeners who were the focus group for these stories. Every week I shared a chapter on the air and heard your responses to my stories. Great job, everybody; this is the book you asked for!

Many people from Ireland have played important roles in my life. I am proud to be an honorary Irishwoman and wish to thank my Irish comrades for their friendship. To my mentor and dear friend, Father Patrick McGrath, who was always available to discuss any issue. Our family is blessed to have you in our lives. Much of who I am is a reflection of your spiritual influence. Sister Mary Germaine, my first-grade teacher, although we've only spent a few days together, we are soulmates and our energies cross the oceans. You hold a special place in my heart. To the Sisters of the Holy Faith and my grammar school teachers at Holy Spirit School, you instilled in me a passion for the English language and written word. I can still recite my copulative verbs and all my prepositions! To Nora Daly Nordan, my first "foreign" pen pal and lifelong writing buddy, you have inspired me greatly. Thank you also to the entire Daly clan, who have been my family away from home many times during my travels.

To my other special European relationships, Family Cornips in Holland, the Van Balens in Belgium, and all my relatives in Switzerland, I owe many memories to you.

To my collegiate best friends, Eileen Goodis Strom and Janet Wells Kahane, we will always be "The Three MsKeteers." You are not only incredible women, but amazing professionals bringing intelligence and graceful leadership to the global marketplace as presidents of your companies. I am proud to be your friend. Thank you to Norbert Brein-Kozakewycz for shooting my gorgeous photograph for the cover of this book and for doing such a great job with headshots over the years for myself and my clients; to Ken Rice, Russ Fischella, and George Hall, my garden, entertainment, and design photographers; Paul Bogle, my dream weaver; Barbara Gabriel, my forever focus partner; Jerry Ackerman, my screenplay colleague and *Starstyle* webmaster; Tony Berman, Richard Idell, and Jennifer Marone, my caring legal eagles; David Loveall, my unsurpassed healer; David Marten, my greatest advocate; Eric Koenig, my wireless genius; Autry Henderson, my angelic advisor; and T.J. Van Buren, my head cheerleader. You are all the greatest!

My thanks to the print media for their auspicious reviews and to the producers of radio and TV programs across America who have helped promote this work of love. Your interest in my book and my work is greatly appreciated.

Special thanks to all my dear friends and to my grand extended family— my grandparents, aunts, uncles, cousins, nieces, nephews, in-laws, and out-laws who have played the costarring roles in my life performance. My highest praise and adoration to you for all the fun times, inspiration, and great stories.

I would be remiss if I didn't thank all God's creatures that have nurtured and blessed me throughout my life. Many animals, furred, feathered, and finned, have taught me about the gifts you are about to explore.

Sincerest thanks to my incredible brothers, Fred on the farm and David in heaven, and to my terrific sisters, Debbie and Patty. You epitomize the best of kin, and I am blessed to have you as my siblings. And most of all, my earnest gratitude to my parents, Al and Alice Abruzzini, who imbued me with a love of the land, an appreciation for family, and the meaning of integrity in all relationships. Your unconditional love and confidence in my aptitudes blessed me with a profoundly healthy self-esteem. Everything I have learned about life and mending the spirit are presents from you, my amazing parents.

Thank you to God, the angels, and the saints for the many opportunities born of faith that I have been granted and for keeping my light burning bright even in times of darkness. My prayers have been answered, and I am genuinely grateful.

And finally, thank you to *you,* my readers, for choosing this book. You are holding a beacon of illuminating love in your hands, and my wish is that you will develop and recount your own stories of a lifetime. May the sun shine in your garden and the stars shine in your heart.

Be the Star You Are; share and enjoy!

Cynthia Brian

Contents

INTRODUCTION TO THE 99 GIFTS 1

THE GIFT OF

Abundance	7	Communication	59
Acceptance	10	Community	63
Action	13	Conviction	69
Adventure	15	Cooperation	72
Affection	17	Courage	75
Affirmation	20	Creativity	78
Appreciation	22	Curiosity	82
Aptitude	24	Daring	85
Asking	26	Dedication	89
Attitude	29	Delight	92
Awareness	32	Destiny	95
Balance	34	Determination	100
Beauty	39	Devotion	104
Being	41	Differences	107
Breathing	44	Direction	112
Celebration	47	Dreams	115
Challenge	50	Enthusiasm	119
Change	53	Exercise	122
Choice	56	Fairness	126

Faith	128	Moderation	238
Feedback	131	Motivation	241
Forgiveness	133	Opportunity	245
Friendship	137	Optimism	249
Fun	141	Passion	253
Generosity	145	Patience	258
Giving	148	Perseverance	262
Grace	152	Planning	265
Gratitude	155	Playfulness	268
Growth	158	Prayer	272
Happiness	162	Purpose	275
Harmony	167	Reflection	277
Healing	170	Rejection	281
Health	175	Responsibility	285
Honesty	179	Rest	288
Hope	182	Risk	291
Hosannas	186	Serendipity	294
Humor	190	Simplicity	297
Imagination	192	Solitude	301
Improvisation	195	Spontaneity	303
Ingenuity	198	Success	306
Inspiration	201	Surrender	309
Interdependence	206	Survival	311
Joy	210	Transformation	315
Knowledge	214	Truth	319
Leadership	217	Understanding	323
Lifelines	221	Visualization	327
Listening	223	Winning	332
Love	226	Wisdom	336
Magic	229	You	339
Miracles	231		

RECOMMENDED READING   341

DO YOU DARE TO CARE?   345

ABOUT THE AUTHOR   349

FOREWORD

This book contains much wisdom. I recommend everyone read it because most of us are not truly educated about how to deal with life's difficulties. Unfortunately the majority of people learn from their losses, illnesses, and tragedies and not from their parents, teachers or religions. Read this book so that you can become strong enough to not break under life's pressures.

I have written a book called *Prescriptions for Living* and I made a comment in it that I must also make about this book. There is nothing new in it. That is a compliment not a criticism. I didn't say anything was missing, I said it contained nothing new. I say this because this book contains the wisdom of the sages. The age-old messages and themes that can lead us to heal our lives are contained here, but rather than centuries-old myths and parables you may have trouble understanding, you will find modern stories and events that are easy to learn from and apply to your life. Read on and learn as I have that there are paths to wholeness that you can be guided to by others. If you have a skilled coach, the lessons don't have to be painful. You do, however, have to show up for practice. Every performer who becomes a star knows that. As Lily Tomlin says, "How do you get to Carnegie Hall? Practice, practice, practice."

This book shares many gifts with you. For many of us life seems devoid of gifts, but you will begin to find them in your life when someone is there to point them out. As Cynthia tells us, we are all stars made in God's likeness. The guilt, shame, and blame most of us grow up with come from those we meet after we are born. Let this book and Cynthia's words heal those wounds and help you to see you are a star and a child of God. Let this book do for you what the ugly duckling had to do for himself. Let it reflect your beauty. I often ask people how they would introduce themselves to God. What would you say now? Ask yourself the same question when you are done reading Cynthia's book.

We all have choices and need to know how to make the wise choices for ourselves and our lives. We need to learn how to live unique and authentic lives. Cynthia will help you find your path and way through life. She is what we all need, an excellent guide and coach. Each one of us is an actor.

Studies show our body chemistry is altered by the role we choose to play. Let Cynthia be your acting coach so your life is filled with joy and love and nourishes and supports your body and your ability to heal. You have a lifetime to rehearse, so read on and get started now.

For years I have entitled my workshops "The Art of Healing," a term Cynthia uses also, and it is what you will learn in this book. The stories will teach you about acceptance and the importance of connections. The role animals and children play in our lives and what they can teach us. You will learn that we prepare our futures unconsciously and consciously. Reading this book will change your future as you choose to live a healthier, more empowered life. You will learn that decisions should not only be based upon what you think, but what you feel.

Listen to your body and live your life. You are not put here to live other people's choices and lose your life, but to follow your path and feel the joy of the day as you contribute in your unique way to the world. A nice by-product will be a longer, healthier life.

I don't want to rewrite the book in this foreword, which would be easy for me to do because I agree with it, so I will stop here. The greatest compliment I can give a book is to say that it made me laugh and cry. When I am touched in that way I know I am reading the truth and it has affected me. This book did both, which is why I am recommending it, writing a foreword for it, and hoping you will all read it and learn from it about life's great truths. Remember you are like a blank canvas. So get to work and create a living masterpiece, *yourself!*

—BERNIE SIEGEL, M.D.

Introduction
to the 99 Gifts

Y ou were not created equal. And you wouldn't want to be! You are something far better than equal. You are *unique.*

No one has ever walked the earth with your exact combination of inborn and acquired strengths, weaknesses, skills, foibles, talents, frailties, and experiences. The synergy of all these forces is what makes you strictly one of a kind, an original. And this mixture is the source of your power, providing all the raw materials you need to become a star.

I challenge you to become the star you already are. This book will make you aware of the many gifts you now possess. I won't promise you that living the life you've always dreamed of is easy. In fact, it can be darn hard work. But this book is chock-full of the possibilities already within your grasp, offered to you in the form of personal anecdotes, useful tips, and stimulating exercises. Use it as your road map.

Some of my stories and commentary will be unexpected, out of the ordinary, and definitely different. When you do the accompanying exercises, use your imagination, open your heart and mind, and express yourself. My purpose is to expose you to the myriad ways you can become your best self while discovering and enjoying your star power. I'll provide the guidance. You provide the guts. Together we'll discover the gifts.

My own experiences have given me the skills to help you discover and focus your distinctive abilities. Personally, I am a woman, wife, mother, lover, animal aficionado, world traveler, master gardener, and chief cook and bottle washer. Professionally, for twenty-five years, I've been in the entertainment industry as an actor, model, producer, writer, director, casting director, consultant, coach, and mother of children working in show business. I also host two national cable television series: *Starstyle—Live Your Dreams!* (which is about following your heart and pursuing your passion) and *Starstyle—The Business of Show Business (How to Get Going and Stay Going in Acting and Modeling While Avoiding the Scams)*. I created these shows and my weekly radio show, *Starstyle—Be the Star You Are!*, because I feel it is important to provide role models and help people live more meaningful business and personal lives.

Coaching children in acting is another of my specialties. My aim has always been to encourage, inspire, motivate, and protect these imaginative young beings placed in my care. Their innate spontaneity and sense of self-worth constantly amazes and impresses me. If only we could find a way to keep this energy as adults, I thought. So I devised ways for my adult acting students to regain this vital exuberance.

What does acting have to do with everyday life? Everything! Acting reflects life and life is reflected in acting. The same techniques and exercises that I use to teach acting and self-esteem are useful for anyone in almost any situation. My background and training are in acting, but my *life* experiences are what make me an authority to write about identifying and developing your star qualities.

I have made mistakes, endured failures, and suffered rejections, but each time I fell down, I got back up, learned my lesson, and transformed that lesson into a gift. These gifts can help you increase joy, peace, love, harmony, and success in your own life.

Happiness and success depend on your determination and dedication to create your own present and future. I come from a long line of hardworking farmers and grew up a goal-oriented, hardworking superachiever who honors every scar and every accomplishment.

With five mouths to feed, my parents couldn't afford to buy us new clothes for high school or offer us a college education. We had to figure out our own strategies for achieving our dreams. From age nine to eighteen, I carefully saved every penny I earned from raising chickens and selling their eggs for thirty to fifty cents a dozen to finance my college degrees. I worked as a field laborer for neighboring farmers, picking and cutting fruit. This paid twenty cents for each fifty-pound box. My grandparents bought me a sewing machine when I was a child (which I still use regularly), and I learned to sew, making all my own clothes and most of our household furnishings until well into my adult years. When I first wanted to travel, I worked for the airlines so that I could get passes, or I sought out discount coupons. Where there is a will, there is a way. And I've always had will. I'm proud of my upbringing and glad I had to earn my way in the world. It was an investment in the ethics of work. It feels good to look back and know that I am where I am today because of the choices I've made throughout a lifetime.

We each design our own lifestyles!

Although most of the self-help books on the market today tout the message that if one is on "his or her path," the road should be easy. I heartily disagree. Living the dream, becoming successful, and building integrity mean you show up and are willing to put in the time, energy, effort, and hard work necessary to achieve your goals. I have had some extraordinary experiences, met incredible people, found myself in exotic lands for little or no cost, and enjoyed amazing opportunities, all because I was willing to take risks, ask questions, fall down, make mistakes, and follow through on promises. You can do it too!

One tool that has helped me immensely that I use in my acting classes is storytelling. Storytelling is as old as humankind and a strong tradition in my large Italian family. I have always felt that I learned more swiftly and easily by listening to true tales of trailblazers, so my instruction method is to teach by sharing examples of my real-life experiences.

Throughout the ages, wise storytellers have reawakened the inner spirits of their listeners and inspired them to explore new territories. Stories allow us to dream and give us the courage to act upon our dreams. Stories help us discover and remember meaningful information. A story informs us by synthesizing complex issues, ambiguous situations, and opposing forces. Stories can challenge conventional wisdom, showing us people who deviate from traditional practices and produce breakthrough results.

My goal is to offer you tantalizing new possibilities for excellence through the stories in this book. The stories in this book are all true. They happened to me, my family, or my good friends. Through these experiences—good, bad, sad, or exalting—we learned a lesson in living. My hope is that these stories won't end with the telling, but will inspire your own ideas and insights so you go on to live your own stories, based on your unique gifts.

It doesn't matter whether your stories come from growing up in a loving family or from a difficult childhood. Today you are taking a giant step toward creating positive life experiences because you are now the writer, producer, director, and *star* of your own life. You *can* live your dreams.

We have been told that we are created in the image and likeness of God. God is great, God is magnificent, and, therefore, we are great and magnificent. We are worthy. We are enough. We are all stars.

Let's get started. The future stars in all my acting classes must agree to follow three simple rules. They are mandatory. I also insist that you, my readers, abide by them.

Still here? Okay.

THE THREE RULES FOR BEING A STAR AND LIVING YOUR DREAM:

1. You must smile.
2. You must have fun.
3. You must be willing to be wild and crazy.

That's it. Those are my rules. Not hard to obey if you have the guts to stretch, reach out, and risk making a fool of yourself. That's exactly what you must do to find your inner fire and live your dream. When you follow these three rules, you'll encounter a new, more authentic you. You'll be real, listening to your heart and following your inner wisdom to success. How, you may ask, will these rules help me be the star that I am or want to be? Very simply.

SMILE

When you smile, it is difficult to be sad. When you are smiling, the little things in life won't get you down for long. A smile brightens the lives of those you meet and their joy bounces back to you. A smile helps you see the world in a positive light, which increases your enthusiasm and creativity. A smile exudes confidence and helps you deflect negative interactions.

HAVE FUN

Every moment is more satisfying when you decide to be playful. Having fun is adjusting your attitude so even life's emergencies can be met with grace and be seen in perspective. If you choose to be in a good mood and laugh at life, you'll go with the flow and live in the moment more frequently without being flustered or bothered by any curve balls thrown at you.

BE WILD AND CRAZY

This is the most important rule, the one that can make the difference between living Thoreau's "life of quiet desperation" or becoming the star you already are. Being wild and crazy means taking measured risks and putting yourself in potentially uncomfortable situations that may be beneficial. Ask for what you want and don't be afraid to fail, knowing that your biggest failure may lead to your greatest success. Learn to laugh at yourself and stretch beyond your wildest imagination. Stop playing it safe and strive for excellence. Do the unexpected, reaching for the stars and expecting to land on them!

With these three important, mandatory rules, you are ready for the journey to your best you!

Do you dare to accept?

There's a saying in show business, often heard after a disastrous dress rehearsal: "It will be *all right on the night*." The comforting idea is that you've already gotten past every catastrophe that could happen, so the actual performance will be flawless.

Life is our performance. Unfortunately, it offers no dress rehearsals. You're "on stage" all the time—no stopping and starting over. You can improve greatly over time, but you get just one shot at each scene, so you want your performance to be as excellent as possible. You want to be the star of your own production!

Fortunately, although life comes without dress rehearsals, it *does* offer many opportunities for *preparation*. Stanislavksi, the Russian theatrical genius, wrote a classic actors' handbook called *An Actor Prepares*. Stanislavski's system is based on the art of living every moment of a part, seeking truth, dignity, and style in acting while appreciating the quality of the play itself, understanding the intentions of the author and director, and interpreting the intentions of fellow actors. Can you think of a better description of life?

My book is about preparing you to star in your own life while igniting the flame that is already inside you...my version of the Stanislavski system for living authentically.

My aim, as always, is to encourage, inspire, inform, and motivate. You are one of a kind, you are you, you have the power to love yourself and become the person you want to be. You're ready to become the star of your own life when you recognize, use, and enhance your God-given gifts.

Start anywhere. In fact, I encourage you to open the book wherever it falls and know that what you read there is meant for you today. You'll find ninety-nine lessons that I call gifts—informative, inspirational, funny—each with a practical, playful preparation exercise. Use what works for you and incorporate it into your life. This book is like having me as your personal growth coach anytime, anywhere.

Go ahead. Try it. You won't be disappointed.

Lights! Camera! Action!

ABUNDANCE

I grew up on a farm, the eldest of five children. Our parents taught us certain values: hard work, loyalty to family and friends, responsibility, and keeping your word. We learned to be independent and self-sufficient. Although we had few possessions and even less money, we were content in our simple, natural surroundings. I can't imagine a better upbringing for a child.

Our playground was vineyards, hills, and dales. Our companions were horses, cows, sheep, chickens, ducks, rabbits, dogs, and cats. As we hiked the mountains and paddled the creeks, we pretended we were explorers discovering new worlds. We had caves to hide in. The mustard fields were our doll houses. We drove tractors, plowed fields, and picked fruit until our hands were raw. The nearest neighbor children lived two miles away, so our life was mostly within our family.

Every season brought new adventures and excitement—preparing the vegetable garden in spring, going on camping trips in the summer, hay rides and harvest festivals in the fall, and enjoying the warming fires and holiday magic of winter. Life on the farm was fun, challenging, hard work, and full of promise.

We didn't have fancy clothes…a pair of Levis, a pair of boots, a couple of shirts, a school uniform, and a good Sunday church outfit. Twice a year, at Christmas and Easter, our Auntie Cleo would take us shopping and buy us a new outfit. These were thrilling excursions. I learned to sew in high school so I could have a bigger wardrobe and, since I was the oldest, my sisters inherited my hand-me-downs. We always felt a sense of abundance, surrounded by delicious, home-grown food, a close-knit family, plenty of trees, and land to roam. We were truly rich in spirit if not in money.

From my first awareness, I knew I was important. I grew up believing that I had the power to achieve anything I ever wanted, as long as I was willing to work diligently to get it. It never occurred to me that I could or should be handed something free simply because I wanted it.

Yes, I am definitely an optimist. My glass is always half full, even when it's filled with bitter medicine. My life has been a rose garden, albeit with lots of thorns and tragedies. As a child, I almost died of encephalitis. Many people I have loved died at early ages from accidents or illness. My youngest brother, David, was crushed by an overturned tractor when he was sixteen. My gentle grandfather was killed while mowing his lawn when an elm tree inexplicably toppled over on a windless day. And my dad, who is my hero, died after battling a rare cancer, just after he retired.

Because of these experiences and many more, I have learned that our greatest failing is *not* to take action, *not* to sing our song. I admit that living expansively and exuberantly isn't always easy. Sorrow and pain make us want to contract and withdraw, not expand and excel. We live well only when we embrace this paradox—the very fragility, pathos, and unpredictability of life make every moment precious.

My aim is to persuade, push, and compel you to live every minute fully and consciously. We never know how many chances we'll have to "get it right." Life is finite. If I am driven in my mission, it's because of my own agony in dealing with loss. What I have learned is that pain, suffering, emptiness, and loneliness are an important part of the human experience. Everyone—rich or poor, weak or powerful—endures these emotions. We are here on earth to learn, to laugh, to cry, to feel love and pain, to be. Most important, we are here to live and make a difference. Part of getting it right is getting it wrong. We are not the same, but we are all one.

Abundance is not about acquiring a luxury house, a fancy car, expensive clothes, and a jet-set lifestyle. Abundance is about feeling that there is enough in life for everyone. My early years taught me that a sense of abundance goes far beyond material things. It spans our spiritual life, emotional stability, intellectual stimulation, and physical closeness to the earth. Having abundance means having fresh air to breathe, clean water to drink, food in our stomachs, a roof overhead, somewhere to walk and feel the beauty of nature, someone to love and someone who loves you in return, laughter, learning, and the wealth of health. As children we were taught to be happy for another's success and to believe that there is abundance in all things. If someone else can achieve greatness, so can I. So can you.

We are rarely lacking in abundance, just the ability to understand the meaning of simple abundance. The world is a place of emotional and spiritual plenty. *Abbondanza,* as my mother always said in Italian. Notice and be grateful for everything you have. Abundance is everyone, everywhere, everything.

EXERCISE

Abbondanza

☆ *Shut your eyes. Imagine in vivid detail everything you feel you really need to have a fulfilled life. Your list will be unique to you, but it may include loving relationships, children, animals, a home to live in, food on the table, clothing, a car, enjoyable work, and so forth. Once you see yourself surrounded by everything you need, add some of the things you want.*

☆ *Open your eyes, get out your pen, and make three columns: "What I need," "What I want," and "What I have."*

☆ *Then every day, write down the things that you give thanks for: sunrises, beautiful gardens, a pillow to lay your head on. Recognize the abundance around you. Tell yourself frequently, "I have abundance in all things. There is enough to go around."*

Work hard, dream hard,
laugh hard,
live abundantly.

The Gift of

ACCEPTANCE

My husband is never on time. No matter what time he says he will meet me, he is always at least half an hour late. When we were first married and I was happily playing the role of a dutiful hausfrau, he would call to say he was on his way home and to have dinner waiting. Three hours later, when the meal was inedible, he'd arrive. Because of his tardiness, we missed appointments, planes, and dinner parties. People commented negatively about our behavior. I'm punctual by nature, and I hated my husband's excuses. My emotions ranged from hurt to frustration, anger, and disbelief. Each time, he'd promise to do better.

Of course, I thought I could change him. I thought if he "really loved me" he would change and do what I wished he would do, which was be on time. Arguments were frequent. Finally, I realized that if we were to remain married, I would need to find a way to accept his behavior. Without condoning his lateness, I decided to accept it. He would change only when he chose to change, not through anything I could do.

Nevertheless, the kids and I decided to try one more idea; we gave him a clock engraved with the words "On-time Brian." We thought that a positive reinforcement might be more effective than constantly haranguing him about being late. That same day, I began driving my own car to events so I'd arrive on time. I no longer nag. He alone must accept the consequences of his lateness. As soon as I accepted his lateness and got on with my own plans on my own schedule, his lateness diminished. We've been married twenty-five years now, and acceptance is one of the keys to our survival. I realized that I needed not only to accept Brian the way he is, but to accept my response to his actions. Self-acceptance is as difficult as accepting another person. It was necessary for me to see how my negative reactions to his lateness could ruin an evening or a trip together. Because I am usually a prompt person, I took the position that "prompt" was the "right" way to be and expected everyone else to follow suit. The secret is in accepting both the positive and negative attributes of ourselves and others while we strive for improvement. Brian and I both contributed to the problem while undermining our joy until we both took full responsibility for our own actions, reactions, and interactions.

Acceptance facilitated change.

Acceptance is about doing the best you can in the situation you are in with the skills you possess. Self-accepting people are empowered to be honest and sincere. They do not fear that someone will discover their flaws because they acknowledge and accept their own flaws.

Acceptance is not the same as settling for second best. Acceptance is striving for the best and then not agonizing about the outcome. We can never change other people, we can only change ourselves and our reactions to circumstances. We can learn to accept, without necessarily condoning, that which we cannot change.

Life is never perfect. Many of us are still playing "parent" tapes long after we have become adults. We still listen to what our parents predicted about our behavior and future. These messages were not always direct. Children learn by seeing and feeling. For example, if you noticed a sibling got lavish praise for his or her skill at sports while you received only modest compliments about good grades or being a talented artist or musician, you might have deduced that sports were more important than academic achievement or creative endeavors. You might have assumed that you and your accomplishments were not as good or as important as your sibling's. You made a mental "tape" about yourself that can replay the rest of your life. Competition and comparison, even unintentional, are deadly games in which everybody loses.

Trying to be "perfect" is setting yourself up for failure. The only perfect being is God. Strive instead for excellence. Enjoy life to the fullest...prudently. When you get in your car, buckle your seat belt and drive the speed limit.

Improving on Imperfections

Acceptance is Life 101. Get yourself a notebook or journal. It can be as simple or fancy as you wish. Ask yourself the following questions and record the answers in your journal. There are no right or wrong answers, just awareness about who you are and how you can learn the gift of acceptance.

☆ *Do I like spending time with myself?*

☆ *Is my body in the best shape I can achieve?*

☆ *Do I accept my imperfections and still strive for excellence?*

☆ *Am I seeking knowledge on a daily basis?*

☆ *Do I accept my foibles and mistakes, learning and growing from them? Or am I beating myself up because I believe I have failed?*

☆ *Do I accept others the way they are, not allowing their idiosyncrasies to color my world?*

☆ *If I was someone else, could I accept me for who I am?*

True self-acceptance begins with an honest evaluation of our limitations, dreams, and aspirations.

We can't change anyone else—
only reject or accept their limitations.
We can change ourselves—
after we accept our limitations.

Cynthia Brian

ACTION

Going into action makes life happen. When my son, Justin, was twelve, he and a few friends at summer camp decided to search for the "big swing tree" they had heard about while sitting around the campfire. It was against camp rules to depart from the marked trails, but, being young and inquisitive, they did, trespassing as they went.

Sure enough, they found the fabled tree. It stood beside a ravine, an ancient oak with a huge chain dangling from one of its branches. One by one, the kids dragged the chain up the bank and swung out over the ravine. After my son had swung a few times, he handed the chain to the boy behind him. The child ran up the hill and, with an exuberant leap, swung out over the ravine.

There was a loud crack, the limb broke, and the boy fell twenty-five feet onto the rocks below. The others stood frozen in horror. Then they scrambled down the rocks to find him unconscious, bones protruding through his skin, blood everywhere.

No one knew what to do, but Justin reacted quickly. He sent the others to get help. Then he stripped off his jacket and wrapped the unconscious boy to keep him warm and prevent shock. He used pressure to stop the bleeding, and, as the boy regained consciousness and began moaning, Justin cradled his head gently, reassuring him.

Justin had no formal first aid training, but he had been on several fire calls with my dad's volunteer fire department and had heard what to do in such an emergency. For an hour and a half he remained calm. When rescue workers arrived, they credited Justin with saving the boy's life and keeping him from going into shock.

During the crisis, Justin went into action as a reaction to circumstances. But he didn't stop there. When he returned from camp, he *acted,* implementing a CPR and first aid course for kids in our county. He even organized fund-raisers to pay the costs. At age twelve, he understood that all achievement starts with action.

You can dream all you want, talk all you want, write all you want, but until you do something, nothing happens. No one will jump on your bandwagon until you have one rolling. To achieve your dream, you must first dream it, then write the plan, acquire the skills, and go into action.

EXERCISE

Lights! Camera! Action!

All acting is reacting. For any action there is an immediate reaction, whether good or bad. Living and acting are the same. Fear keeps people from acting. For this exercise, work with a friend or family member. One person performs an action, for example, laughing hysterically for no reason or giving a pat on the back. The other reacts to this action without stopping to analyze. Whatever the actor does, the reactor must portray a realistic reaction. How does your partner respond? With what words or body movements? Don't try to be funny. Be honest. Work from the heart. Change positions so each of you experiences both the action and reaction. When it's your turn to act, notice what responses your actions get. Are they what you expected?

This is a very powerful exercise to help you identify your ability to go into action. Pretend the camera is rolling, the lights are on you, and the director has shouted, "Action!"

Tomorrow never comes. Act now.

Cynthia Brian

The Gift of

ADVENTURE

I've confronted wild animals in Africa, paddled down the Amazon, hitchhiked through Europe, and trekked in Machu Picchu, but the adventure that had the most impact on my life was a simple one—in fact, an experience that most people wouldn't consider an adventure at all.

When my daughter, Heather, was four, she required serious surgery. As I prepared her, I explained in simple terms that she and I were about to have an adventure together. We talked about why she needed the surgery, what the anesthesia would be like, how she would feel after the procedure, and how our adventure would unfold. We would "camp out" in the hospital, read books, sing songs, play make-believe, tell stories, draw, and paint. And we would be together for every moment of the adventure. While I secretly feared the impending surgery and its outcome, she was looking forward to it as a great experience, counting down the days to our big adventure.

We packed up my sleeping bag and pillow, sweat suit, and office supplies, all the toys, books, and tapes she enjoyed, and we took off. After we set up our camp in her room, she was wheeled off down the hall for long, arduous surgery.

Although Heather was in pain during her recovery, we turned a difficult time into an exciting bonding experience. As I had promised, I never left her for the next two weeks except to take a shower in her bathroom, and only then when her father or grandmother was by her side.

We turned every detail of her recovery into a discovery. We did all the things we had planned: reading, storytelling, playing house, painting, singing, dressing up. We raced down the hallways in her wheelchair. Heather's preschool science teacher, Evelyn, "snuck" a couple of favorite animals into the hospital for Heather's enjoyment.

One was a talking parrot, which truly entertained the nurses and other children.

We visited other patients, bringing them surprises to make them feel better. At a young age, Heather was learning compassion for others worse off than she was. Her own discomfort seemed to dissipate while she talked to them and encouraged them to get well. Heather realized how fortunate she was to have a mom and dad who loved her and were with her.

Because of this intense, loving adventure, Heather and I developed a powerful bond that will never be broken. She knows I'm there for her and will never abandon her, no matter what. Whenever we drive past the hospital, she still says, "There's my hospital," and we still talk about all our "adventures" during those two eventful weeks.

To expand who you are, look for the adventure in *all* things. Life is an involuntary bungee jump. You can shut your eyes tight, cringe, and shriek in terror, hoping it will all be over soon. Or you can open yourself to the experience, savoring every sensation and crying out with joy and exhilaration.

Celebrate your aliveness, your health, your humanness. There is no time to feel sorry for yourself when you recognize that someone somewhere would gladly trade places with you. Make every day an adventure, in this body, in this time, and in this place.

EXERCISE

Be Alive

Jot down three situations in your life that could be interpreted as adventures. What did you do well? If you had them to do over again, would you do anything differently?

"Adventure is worthwhile in itself."
—*Amelia Earhart, American aviator*

Cynthia Brian

The Gift of
AFFECTION

My maternal grandmother, Juanita Abruzzini, was a passionate animal lover. She had a herd of horses, several dogs, some wild animals, and aviaries filled with exotic birds. She and Grandpa Fred rode in fine western regalia in parades around California and often hitched their horses up to buggies and appeared in movies. Grandma was a true-blue cowgirl. She was so renowned for her work with horses that she was hired to train famous horses for the film industry.

Perhaps I inherited my love of the animal kingdom from Grandma and passed this passion on to my son and daughter. Grandma taught me how to communicate with these furred and feathered friends.

When my sisters and I were young, Grandma and Grandpa gave Dad three horses: a chestnut quarter horse named Taffy that my sister Patty claimed; a dappled, gray Appaloosa named Shadow that Debbie wanted; and a small, white Arabian colt for me. I immediately named her Bambi, after my favorite movie character. I vividly remember the three of us girls going up to the horse pasture when we were ready to ride like cowgirls. We'd shout, "Bambi! Taffy! Shadow!" They'd hear us and come running. Bambi was always in the lead, galloping down the hill. She and I shared a unique communication. Everyone told me I needed to "break her" properly, but I never wanted to tame her spirit. I loved her just the way she was, so Bambi was trained my way, with affection, respect, and patience.

I usually rode her bareback with only a lead rope around her neck. Sometimes, I just held onto her mane. She never did learn to take a bit in her mouth or wear a bridle, and that was fine with me. She always knew instinctively where I wanted to go, unless, of course, I was racing one of my sisters on her horse. Then Bambi would try to take the quickest route back to the barn. I learned to hold on for dear life.

Bambi loved me too. She would follow me everywhere, nuzzling my neck and begging me to wrap my arms around her. Bambi was "my girl," and I was hers. If only horses could live as long as people. Many years later, her death devastated me, but it was also the beginning of my long, affectionate relationships with all creatures.

Over the years, people have laughed at me because of my great fondness for animals. I have been called "the Chicken Lady" (because I raised chickens to earn money for college), "a female Dr. Doolittle" (for the menagerie I've gathered), and other names, some not so kind. I'm undeterred.

Affection is kinship with another, an emotional bond, a true fondness from the heart. I believe that many humans are programmed to give affection, but don't know how to receive it. They are afraid to open themselves, or they cynically view expressions of tenderness with suspicion, suspecting ulterior motives. For some, an undemanding animal gives us permission to both give and receive unconditional love. My animals have taught me some of my most important lessons in human relationships—compassion, love, empathy, and perseverance. Animals feel emotional bonds just as we humans do, and they are not afraid to exhibit their affections for one another and their human friends.

I have always marveled that I can come home from a completely terrible day, looking like I've been in a thunderstorm, smelling like I've been on a garbage truck, and be greeted by my dogs as if I were a queen arriving for a great occasion. Can you imagine how wonderful our relationships would be if we allowed ourselves to do this with people? To experience the simple pleasure of demonstrating our affection when loved ones arrive home by jumping up and down, barking, and dancing in circles? Celebrating their joys or participating in a good cry instead of offering "solutions" to their problems? As George Eliot said, "Animals are such agreeable friends; they ask no questions, and they pass no criticisms."

Take a lesson from all God's creatures. Show your affection for this world we live in. The more you care, the more affection you will encounter. Pass it on.

Bark, Wiggle, and Wag

The next time someone you love walks in the door, don't ask about what kind of a day they had. Just start wiggling, wagging, and jumping for joy. Bark, whinny, honk, or quack, conveying how delighted you are to see them. Let your enthusiastic affection bubble over, and watch their reactions. Sure, at first they'll think you've lost your mind. Then they'll wonder what the heck you are up to. Finally, they'll laugh at you, with you, and for you. The best part is when they get into the routine and return your affection.

Allow yourself to receive their love. (If you have difficulty with this exercise, borrow a pet for a few days and allow the animal to teach you this fun and fond exercise in affection.)

Express your affection today,
and accept affection
unconditionally in return.
Open yourself to affection
without boundaries.

The Gift of

AFFIRMATION

My sixteen-year-old brother David was killed when the tractor he was driving turned over and crushed him. More than 1500 people from across the valley and the state of California came to his funeral in an outpouring of love and respect.

One elderly couple approached our family in tears and introduced themselves. They had met David a few years earlier when he stopped at their garage sale looking for antiques. This childless couple was in poor health and ready to give up on life. David, remarkably sensitive for a fourteen-year-old, had sensed their isolation and despair. From then on, he made a point of visiting them every week walking over a mile to their home after his school activities were finished to share the events of his teenage years. They told us how David had renewed their interest in life by including them in his circle of friends. He had proven to them that they still had value in the world, and they enriched his life with wonderful stories of their past. He had never mentioned this good deed to us, but affirming others was his way of making a small contribution to the good of mankind. His affirmation enriched and extended the lives of these two people and untold others.

Do you know how to make people feel better about themselves the minute you walk in the room? By affirming them. It's incredibly simple, yet you can probably count on one hand the people you know who can do this.

The secret is to notice what is positive about others and then tell them about it. Become a cheerleader and cheer them on. Many people are so busy protecting themselves and their interests that they can't focus on anything but the negative and threatening qualities in others.

Look outside yourself. When you point out the positive in people, you inspire them to do their best. Tell others what they are doing

Cynthia Brian

right. Zero in on the good they have done that day. Even when this is difficult (or nearly impossible), make the effort. No matter how minor, bring that one good thing to their attention. People will respond in amazing ways. They too will start focusing on the positive, and you will see new light in their eyes.

The people who are important in your daily life deserve daily affirmations. They may not be in positions of power. The people who matter most to me are those who give value to the simple things in my life. Affirmation is a doorway to the heart and the soul. Let these people know that you appreciate them and care about them. Cherish them and praise them often. Affirmation is a fundamental need of all humans.

EXERCISE

Put on a Happy Face!

We underestimate how our own personal agenda affects people we know and don't know. Smiling is an incredibly effective affirmation. Even when you feel down, just making yourself smile will improve everyone's mood, including your own.

On a gray, rainy, and awful day, walk down the street and smile. It costs you nothing, makes you feel better, and can produce astonishing results in those you pass. Your unexpected smile or compliment may truly help someone on a difficult day. Put on a happy face!

Help people notice the good in themselves.
When they feel special, they will be special.

The Gift of
APPRECIATION

"A *Porsche!*" An economics professor at my son's college was astonished when one of his former students gave him a brand new sports car. The professor had always told his students that one day what they were learning in his class would help them succeed. "And when you become a millionaire," he would joke, "don't forget to buy me a Porsche."

Ten years later, one of those students came back for a visit and presented his teacher with that Porsche. The student had used what he learned to become one of the new technology millionaires. He never forgot the inspiration of his favorite professor and wanted to show his appreciation in an unexpected way.

As cheerleading captain at her high school, my daughter, Heather, volunteered her squad to cheer at the Wheelchair Olympics. The incredible athleticism of these courageous men and women thrilled her, and after a few minutes of competition, she no longer noticed they were in wheelchairs. The competitors, in turn, were touched that a group of high school students wanted to cheer for them. They showered the girls with appreciation, compliments, and lots of smiles—far more accolades than the girls had ever received from their own school teams. The squad decided to continue as official cheerleaders for as many wheelchair events as possible. *Appreciation* made the difference by making each girl feel special.

Every day when I wake up, I take a few minutes to say a prayer of appreciation for simple things, starting with being alive. Working in my garden, laughing with my children, holding hands with my husband, cleaning out my barn—all are simple things that I appreciate greatly.

We are on this planet for such a short period of time. We can curse the darkness or give thanks for the light.

Cynthia Brian

Appreciate the roosters crowing in the morning (or the rumble of traffic) and the bulbs pushing up from the winter snow (or the rain-washed sidewalk). Appreciate hot water for a bath, a stranger's smile, the broccoli for dinner. Appreciate the challenges and criticism that encourage growth and discovery. Appreciate the quiet moments that refresh. We are all gifts to the universe, and we only have this lifetime. Live in each moment. Cherish each moment. *Appreciate* each moment.

EXERCISE

Be a Gift

When you approach a group of people, what are your first sensations? Are you afraid they may not like or want to be with you? Do you think that you are not good enough? Are you assailed by other negative thoughts? Stop! *You are always enough. You are a gift.*

But how can you convey this message to all those staring faces? By regarding every one of them as a gift to you! Believe that people are waiting to make a contract with you. They want and need you in their life. Once you believe this, your body language will convey the gift of you.

Create joy in your life this minute.
Perform a random act of kindness
and appreciate the little things
the universe offers.

The Gift of

APTITUDE

Most little boys gallop around playing cowboys, superheroes, or spaceship pilots. From age three, my son, Justin, played tractor driver. From the moment Justin could walk and talk, he wanted to be a rancher and farmer like my dad. When he was very little, everyone thought this was cute but that he'd grow out of it. Wrong.

He's now nineteen and has never wavered in his interests. Every spare moment is spent helping out on my family's farm and learning the ropes. His nicknames in high school were "Cowboy" and "Trailer Boy" because he was always towing some type of farm equipment behind his jeep. Justin has a natural ability with farm machinery and a genuine love of the land.

What if you have many aptitudes? A viewer of my cable TV series wrote me, theorizing that people can accomplish great things only if they focus on a single talent and forget the rest. I disagree. Single-mindedness works for some people, but many others, including myself, are at their best when they use all their diverse talents. Aptitudes and skills are different. Aptitudes are the ability to acquire proficiency in a specific area. Aptitudes are often natural capabilities to perform a certain task. Sometimes they are inherited, sometimes they are learned. A skill is an ability you currently possess. Since most people are more likely to succeed at things that they like and that come easy to them, recognizing your aptitudes is an essential ingredient to happiness.

It is our responsibility to discover our numerous talents and use them for the good of ourselves and others. We are all great and we are all greatly needed—the plumber, the mechanic, the mom, the dad, the gardener, the farmer, the secretary, the toll taker, and the computer wizard. We can do one thing or many. The secret is to find out what you love to do and go for it. Be great at it.

We have a saying in the theater that is attributed to no one in

Cynthia Brian

particular but applies to all of us: "There are no small parts, only small actors." Be extraordinary at whatever you do.

Of course, it's okay to be ambitious. I tell clients, "Fake it 'til you make it." Sometimes the hardest person to convince of your abilities is yourself, but in order to achieve your goal, *you* must believe in it. Whatever you want to do or accomplish, start by thinking of it in the first-person present tense: "I *am* a designer (or actor or writer)." "I *am* a great parent (or teacher or doctor)." Talk as if you already are what you want to be. Talking in the future tense—"I'm *going* to be"—is fatal. Before others can believe in you, you must believe in yourself *now*.

The past is history. The future never arrives. Today is the only day you have. Be what you want to be by using the present tense.

EXERCISE

Surprise Yourself

Write "My Aptitudes" at the top of a sheet of paper. List at least ten things you are good at or that you know how to do competently. For example: "I'm good at math, communicating with the elderly, figuring out new electronic gadgets, arranging furniture, and organizing my time. I'm handy at household repairs, planting a garden, painting walls, driving a car, and writing letters." See how easy that was and how capable you really are?

Go back and put a star next to the things you really enjoy doing. Any surprises?

Do what you love!
If you love what you do, you'll never
work a day in your life!

The Gift of
ASKING

I was devastated when my dad died. At first, my sadness and grief paralyzed me. My foundation had been shaken, and it seemed as if my world had come to an end. The last words he spoke to me kept resonating in my head, but I didn't know what to do with them: "I am dying a happy man, I have lived my dreams." *I have lived my dreams...I have lived my dreams...I have lived my dreams* kept replaying in my mind.

I wasn't sure exactly what I was going to do next. But I was certain that I was embarking on a mission to encourage others to find their passion and live their dreams, too.

Through prayer, meditation, reading, and conversation, I slowly recovered from my loss and formed a plan for reaching out to others. I wanted to create a television series that would help others achieve their goals. It would be about extraordinary "ordinary people" who were doing what they loved in life. Of course, I had never produced a television series and hadn't the slightest idea where to start.

In 1995, someone handed me a fantastic book, *The Aladdin Factor* by Jack Canfield and Mark Victor Hansen, creators of the *Chicken Soup for the Soul* series. I have always believed in angels, faeries, leprechauns, and genies, so I was intrigued that Canfield and Hansen presented their lessons within a "magic lamp" formula. The key, they said, is *asking* for what you want.

This was a brand-new viewpoint that was hard to carry out at first. Most of us have been taught from childhood that it's not polite to ask for things. From this book, however, I learned how to maintain my focus, cultivate charisma, and overcome my fear of asking for help. I accepted that the best way, perhaps the only way, to obtain what you really want is to ask for it. "Ask, ask, ask, then ask again!" The authors' philosophy quickly merged with my own ideas about perseverance. I began asking in earnest to realize my goals.

Cynthia Brian

My first step was to share my dream, asking everyone I talked to if they knew how to create and produce a television series. Many barriers and detours blocked my way, sometimes making me doubt my purpose, but whenever I doubted my idea, a door would open and an opportunity would walk through.

Soon after reading the book, I chaired a major Interior Design Gala and Awards ceremony and was featured in a magazine article about enterprising women. The editor asked each of us, "What is the next important mountain you want to climb?" I answered that I was going to produce and host a television series about people doing what they love in life.

Immediately, my phone started ringing off the hook with people eager to help me climb that mountain. Within six months, I was producing, writing, and hosting a cable television series called *Starstyle—Live Your Dreams!* (visit http://www.star-style.com for local listings). Within a year, the show was reaching 20 million people and winning awards. The premise of the show is that you should follow your heart and live your dreams, not for the money, not for the glamour, but because your chosen work is what really feeds your soul. The response has been overwhelming. I have found a universe starved for inspiration and role models to emulate.

How did I achieve my dream? I asked for help. It wasn't easy. Asking for support was foreign to me, and I received numerous rejections. Some were devastating, some were blessings in disguise. Despite the discouragement of major roadblocks and the heartbreak of promises broken, I kept asking for what I needed. Asking has now become a part of my life, but I only ask for what will help me serve others. I expect people to say "yes" to my requests, and they usually do because I ask with integrity and from my heart.

One of the best skills you can ever learn is to ask for what you want. You have the ability and *responsibility* to achieve greatness. You were born to be bold and magnificent. No matter what kinds of obstacles you face in life, you can overcome them if you ask enough people to help you and if you give them a good reason to do so. Most successful people enjoy helping others become successful. It is part of their gift to the world.

I encourage you to formulate your life plan and decide what help you will need. The treasure of a well-lived life comes not from an enchanted lamp, but from asking for help with an open heart. Ask wisely and you shall receive. Knock on enough doors, and one will open.

EXERCISE

Ask and You Shall Receive

☆ *Asking for help is hard in the beginning, so start small. Sit quietly for a few minutes, and think about something you really want, need, and expect to receive at home. Maybe it's a hug, help with the dishes, less noise, or a special gift from your loved one. Write down a clear question that incorporates your wish. Make your request to someone that you know will say "yes."*

☆ *After you get a "yes" at home, decide on something to ask for in your business life. Maybe more responsibility, more cooperation, new equipment, a different schedule.*

☆ *Create a master wish list of what you really want in the different areas of your life. Then create another list of the people, organizations, schools, and so on that could help grant these wishes. Start asking for what you need and keep practicing. Most important, be grateful and appreciative when you start receiving. Saying "thanks" is as important as saying "please."*

As Mark Victor Hansen and Jack Canfield say, "Anything is possible when you dare to ask."

"Better to ask twice than to lose your way once."

—*Danish proverb*

Cynthia Brian

The Gift of
ATTITUDE

My husband and I have always wanted to be on *The Newlywed Game*. We knew we would win because no one can beat our *most embarrassing moment*.

Our wedding was an enormous affair. Being Swiss-Italian, I have lots of relatives. For something old, I had decided to wear my mom's gorgeous 1948 wedding dress—silk satin with a figure-enhancing fitted bodice, 102 tiny satin-covered buttons down the back, and a long train. Truly the gown of a princess.

It was a very hot September afternoon. To avoid passing out from the heat, I had kept underpinnings under my gown to a bare minimum. The ceremony went perfectly. Then, as we marched out of the church as husband and wife, my father-in-law stepped out of his pew. In the excitement of the moment, his foot came down squarely on the end of my train. It seemed to me that the sharp ripping sound that followed drowned out the recessional music. Everyone gasped. The back of my wedding gown had ripped off and I stood before God and 800 people on my wedding day with my nearly-bare backside in full view like the Coppertone baby.

I gathered up the torn train and tried to wrap it around me as we raced from the church. We drove off in an antique 1920 Model-T Ford that covered the twelve-mile distance to the garden reception at about five miles an hour. When we finally arrived at the ranch, I hoped to slip quietly upstairs to make repairs, but in a scene worthy of the Keystone Kops, I was pulled from the car by enthusiastic guests and thrust into a reception line, where I shook with my right hand and clutched my dress closed with my left.

After we had been congratulated by 150 or so of the 800 guests, my mother managed to extricate me and I fled upstairs. Several of the ranch women huddled around my dress, reattaching its back and train, while I sat in the corner, my arms crossed over my bare chest (the bra was sewn into the gown, of course), wearing only the sheerest pantyhose.

My dress was repaired, and we had a marvelous reception in the ranch's gardens. However, the one thing that people really remember about that day is seeing my dress torn off. Ever since, people are constantly telling me that our wedding was the most memorable one they ever attended. More laughter has been generated from that one incident than anything else in my life. At life's worst moments, we must resort to laughter. What else can we do?

There is a wondrous postscript to this story. Four years later, my sister-in-law was getting married, and we jokingly warned my father-in-law to stay far away from her gown. Well, you know how you should never warn a child not to drop something? My father-in-law became so focused on *not* stepping on her gown that he did. Wedding attendants rushed to lift him off as everyone again caught their breath. Fortunately (or unfortunately) for her, there was no repeat performance. Heather, my daughter, wants to wear my beautiful gown when she weds someday, but I'll insist she wear foundation garments, just in case history repeats itself!

Life is not only what happens to us, but also our view of and reaction to these events. My husband and I could have been devastated, but we chose to treasure our unique wedding memory. It has become the most popular story at gatherings and has given people so much laughter over the years that, looking back now, I'm delighted it happened to us.

People who can find the saving grace in a situation are usually healthier and wealthier. At the very least, they're always happier and easier to be around.

Our attitude makes the difference between experiencing something as positive or negative, good or bad. Our attitude gives us control. Attitude is a *choice*. When you are stuck in a frustrating situation like a traffic jam, you can choose to get angry and drive up your blood pressure, or you can choose to use the time for some deep breathing. You can *choose* to see an unpleasant experience as a learning opportunity. You can *choose* to see yourself losing or winning.

Cynthia Brian

Whenever I go to an acting audition, I always walk in the door with the attitude that I am perfect for the job. Sometimes that attitude is what makes the difference between getting the part and getting the gate.

Keep a "How Great I Am" Journal

☆ *Get out your notebook or journal. Whenever anyone gives you a compliment, no matter how small, write it in your journal.*

☆ *Record no negatives in this book. For example, if someone says, "You look great today...if only you got rid of that tie," write down, "I am attractive." If someone says, "Your proposal was excellent, but you had several typos," write, "I am a good writer." Any negative qualifier like "but" or "if only" is not part of this exercise, no matter how well meant or helpful. Your journal is only for good and great things.*

☆ *Each night before you go to sleep, update your journal and read through recent entries. Your dreams will be filled with promise. Before long, you will see and accept the possibilities of your greatness as your attitude becomes more positive and your list of wonderful qualities expands for pages and pages.*

Your life is the canvas.
Your attitudes are the colors you
choose to paint on it.
Make your attitude bright!

The Gift of
AWARENESS

I have thirty first cousins. I love them all, but Donny has always been my favorite. He is a few years older than I am and he is fascinated by everything life can offer. To him, the universe is a pile of gift-wrapped boxes, all waiting to be ripped open by excited fingers.

As children, Donny and I collected shells at the beach, using Donny's books to identify and label them. On camping trips, we spent endless hours digging for "rare rocks and minerals" and made collections on boards, again all clearly labeled. We pretended we were explorers and marched around the campgrounds, with Donny as the captain, gathering young campers like the Pied Piper as we sang songs and discovered new territories. Back home we shared a passion for stamp collecting. Donny and I wrote to pen pals around the world and filled our albums with exotic stamps that enticed us to visit faraway lands.

Our summer stargazing was my first introduction to the heavens. We'd lie in the cool grass on clear, moonless nights and stare at the millions of twinkling lights called stars. We'd find the North Star, the only fixed point in the heavens, and talk about the Milky Way and the Big Dipper while we navigated the night sky. We wondered whether God and the angels really lived "up there" and imagined our ancestors dancing between the galaxies. We sincerely believed in the haven of heaven and feared the fires of hell.

When Donny was given a telescope, we discovered the wonders of the constellations. There was Cassiopeia with her pointed crown in the shape of a "W"; her daughter, Andromeda, a cluster of faint stars; the Great Square of Pegasus, a guidepost of the late summer sky; and Orion, which has more bright stars than any other constellation and is easier to see in the winter months.

We were overwhelmed by the notion of infinity, by the power of

God and the universe, and by our awareness of how small and insignificant we really were in the grand scheme of life.

There is nothing like seeing the world with the eyes of a child. With this same youthful spirit, my children have joined me in watching meteor showers and the comets of our era pass through the night sky. Their awareness of the grandness of our universe and the questions they ask spark my own inquisitive nature.

My cousin Donny is still constantly alert to life. He and I have always considered ourselves explorers of the world, engaged in an adventure of discovery. Today, Donny is a renowned research scientist in Canada, working to find a cure for cancer and AIDS. Like a child, he still views the world with a keen awareness that each day offers exciting new gifts to unwrap. He has passed on this delight and curiosity to his own children. In our different ways, Donny and I try to encourage innocent wonder in everyone we meet, while we savor our own dreams and a lifetime of memories. Who knows what new awareness and dreams will come?

EXERCISE

Stargazing

How long has it been since you have really enjoyed the magnitude of the heavens? Choose a moonless night when the air is clear. Grab a blanket and get as far away from street and city lights as possible. Plop yourself down and look up.

Bring along children to share this stellar experience and enjoy the theater of the sky. You may even be rewarded with shooting stars or a comet trailing a tail of gas and dust. Like the sky and the stars, be aware that we humans are also wonders of our universe.

Every day, all day, open your eyes to
a new universe.

The Gift of
BALANCE

Bizarrely dysfunctional families are all the rage in the media just now, so it is with some hesitation that I confess I grew up in a very loving, functional family. The Abruzzinis weren't exactly like the idealized TV families of the 1950s—*Leave It to Beaver* or *Father Knows Best*—but we were pretty darn close. Balance was the secret. Everyone worked, played, and prayed together.

My parents were in love with one another and passionate about their vocations in life. They chose to have a big family. Actually, they wanted even more children, but a miscarriage and then a difficult birth with my brother David caused them to stop at the five of us.

We were a tight-knit family, spending lots of quality time together, and we had no idea that most people in America didn't do the same. My dad worked hard in the fields, stopping by the ranch house several times a day to check in. We usually had lunch together. My mom worked hard in the home as wife and mother, cooking, clean-ing, gardening, and driving us to our activities. Before we started school and later, during the summers and school breaks, we spent lots of time on the tractor with Dad, learning all about ranching and farming. We were proud that we could hook up a plow, pull barbed wire, and brand cattle. Mom shared her amazing cooking and gardening skills with us. She believed that fresh vegetables and a superb hot meal could restore both the stomach and the soul.

All of us children had daily chores and numerous animals—chickens, rabbits, sheep, horses, and cattle—to care for. We picked grapes, walnuts, and oranges in our orchards and our neighbors' orchards. Each season brought a different crop that needed to be harvested. I'm proud that my hands are still rough and calloused.

We were taught to listen to the earth and understand the seasons. I remember how we all anticipated springtime: the smell of new

Cynthia Brian

blossoms, the sight of freshly tilled earth, planting the vegetable garden, and playing baseball on the road.

Sunday was our day for worship and rest. No work of any sort was performed, except during harvest time. The rest of the year, Sundays found us together at the 9:00 A.M. or 10:30 A.M. church service, followed by our favorite breakfast at the local bowling alley. The rest of the day was spent flying kites, rolling down the hillsides in wine barrels, playing games of hide and seek, riding horseback, and going on late afternoon picnics with aunts, uncles, and cousins. Our lives were balanced, filled with love, laughter, learning, and togetherness. I can't imagine a better childhood. I am extremely blessed to have had parents who loved one another and loved us more than anything. Family was first, and I was given a great a foundation. Along with the good times, we experienced illness, tragedy, and tears, but we didn't become bitter or blaming. We focused on the positive and appreciated every moment we shared.

Since I've married and had children, I've tried to replicate the amazing family ties and balance that I enjoyed so much as a child. I have chosen to live in the country, surrounded by open space, cattle, and wildflowers. When my children were small, I worked as an actress and model, professions that gave me lots of free time, and I often took them with me. Our home was always filled with fresh flowers, the smells of homemade meals, and the squealing laughter of children.

But not everything was perfect. As the children grew, more and more time was spent driving them to activities. The family wasn't always together at mealtimes. Either my husband had to work late in his dental office, I had a meeting, or one of the kids had a game or swim meet. Life became a balancing act instead of a life in balance.

I had to acknowledge that times have changed since my childhood. There were more distractions, opportunities, and technological advances that were supposed to help us slow down, but they seemed to keep us peddling faster. What was I to do to keep our family and myself on track?

Then I reflected on what my good friend Les Hewitt of Canada, founder of The Achievers Coaching Program and coauthor of *The Power of Focus*, asks in his training: "Do you enjoy a healthy, well-balanced lifestyle? Are you doing work you love that gives you an excellent financial return while allowing you significant time to pursue your other interests?" Answering "yes" means your life is in balance. Answering "no" means it probably isn't.

When cars are out of balance, they can't operate at optimum level. People are the same. However, old habits are hard to break. It is easy to feel that the demands on your life are beyond your control. "Next week" or "next month," as soon as the current crisis or deadline is past, will be soon enough for balance. But that precious time rarely comes.

I have to make a conscious effort to relax and take time off. I truly love what I do, so it never seems like work, and I find myself occupied with my career when I should be doing other life-enhancing things—sleeping, taking a walk with my kids, or serving a spontaneous family picnic on the porch. The moment I start feeling like a hamster on a wheel, I literally stop and smell the roses. I walk around the garden to admire its beauty or get down and dig in the dirt. I sit on the porch swing with a tall glass of freshly squeezed lemonade, pet an animal, watch a sunset, and hug my kids.

We can't all have idyllic childhood memories of a balanced life, but we can choose activities that restore harmony, efficiency, love, and productivity in our current lives.

PLAN FOR A BALANCED LIFE

1. Strategize and plan your day. Every night before you go to sleep or first thing in the morning, whenever you're sharpest, set aside a few minutes to map out your most important activities for the day ahead.

2. Concentrate on what is most important. Choose which three to five activities are "must do!" then delegate or reschedule the rest. Build in a time cushion for the unexpected. (Few things are more predictable than the unpredictable.) If you work alone and must do everything yourself, concentrate on the most crucial. Get to the other items if time is available.

3. Learn something new every day. Set aside at least thirty minutes a day for reading, watching a documentary, or learning a new skill. Make it your goal to read at least one book a month, preferably each week.

4. Exercise every day. You don't have to hate it. Choose something you really enjoy doing. Moving around makes you more flexible and gets your blood pumping, bringing oxygen to your brain so you can think better. The first few days may be hard, but you'll soon crave this quick and enriching high. Don't forget, gardening is great exercise!

5. Play with your family, friends, and animals. Schedule time with the important people in your life as diligently as you schedule your business appointments, dentist, and hairstylist. Book a friend for an hour of chatting after work. Plan a special meal with your family on a weeknight. Take your kids for a walk, throw some hoops, play a game, or just talk. Make sure the time is fun for everyone.

6. Reflect and think. What's working for you and what do you need to change? I do my best thinking in the shower. Granted, I can't write anything down, but this can be a plus because I must spend my time truly thinking and enjoying the hot water. My shower time is also my solitude time. (If you are a parent, you know what I mean. Delicious.) Afterward, I make notes of anything I want to remember in an "Ideas and Thoughts" journal. This may seem like extra work, but it actually helps me use my time more efficiently. When I need a fresh outlook on something, it is usually already in my notebook.

7. Get adequate rest. Burned-out cars and appliances can be replaced. You can't. Book renewal time. If you have important activities every night of the week, figure out how to sleep late at least one morning. Schedule naps during the day to reenergize yourself. On busy weekends, reserve a time slot for snoozing.

Omitting any of these steps will throw off your equilibrium. Whenever you feel overwhelmed and out of balance, take a deep breath, go back over them, and make the adjustment.

EXERCISE

Juggling on a Tightrope

We are all jugglers of life, balancing on a tightrope. Some of us are experts, but most of us wobble once in a while. For the next week, keep track of your balancing bravado. At the end of each day, give yourself a point if you have taken time to

1. Strategize and plan your day.

2. Concentrate on what is most important.

3. Learn something new.

4. Reenergize yourself through exercise.

5. Play with your family, friends, and animals.

6. Reflect and think.

7. Get adequate rest.

Your goal is to get seven points in each category every day, earning a total of forty-nine points for the week. In which areas are you best at achieving balance? Which need more practice? Life is like a ledger that you have to keep balanced. You can only withdraw what you have put in or you will be swimming in red ink. Keep in the black!

Life is your balance sheet.
Add points for positive actions
and deductions for stress and negativity.
Are you in the red or the black?

Cynthia Brian

The Gift of

BEAUTY

No one knew how old Auntie Cleo was when she died. Probably well over a hundred, although she never admitted to being a day over fifty. Auntie Cleo, who wasn't really our aunt, had the most delightful personality and joie de vivre. Although physically unattractive by common standards, Auntie Cleo was full of personal beauty and believed that life was to be enjoyed.

Auntie Cleo was childless when her husband died of cancer, so our family adopted her, and we became her "kids." She loved cats and clothes and had tons of both. When my sisters and I were in high school, Auntie Cleo loved to promenade down the streets with us, strutting her stuff, just to see people's heads turn. She must have been at least eighty-five, but her heart was younger than ours.

She always wore the latest fashions, and since it was the 1960s, she got herself a long blonde wig, white go-go boots, a miniskirt, and a tight sweater—quite a sight on the petite Auntie Cleo. As we strolled, the cars cruising slowly behind us would approach honking, their teenaged occupants leaning out the windows, shouting and whistling. Then, as a car passed us and the boys saw her wrinkled face, the whistles would abruptly stop. Sometimes there were gasps and yelps of astonishment. Auntie Cleo loved their reactions and used them as lessons for us on the superficiality of "beauty." But because she always felt beautiful *inside,* no one could ever make her feel anything less than beautiful.

"Beauty starts inside and grows out," our parents always told us. When our souls, hearts, and minds are beautiful, that beauty will be expressed on the exterior where others can sense it. Authentic beauty, then, is our inner radiance shining outward. And when we have inner beauty, it opens our hearts, allowing us to observe the beauty all around us. Beauty is everywhere—in people and nature, in art, architecture, music, food, ideas, and the world in general.

Of course, beauty is an abstract concept and definitely in the eye of the beholder. What one person regards as beautiful may be ugly to another. One person may see a sordid slum, while another is enthralled by the color and vitality, the rhythms, intensity, struggle, and hope. One person may dismiss a pile of rocks as boring, while another is enchanted by its subtle planes and shadows that inspire tranquility or introspection.

Find beauty in all things. Every single day when we open our eyes, there is something beautiful out there. As I drive to work across San Francisco's Bay Bridge, I see the sunlight dancing and sparkling on the water. I say, "Thank you, God, for letting me see this extraordinary beauty." If it's foggy or rainy, I admire the shifting colors of water and clouds. On my return in the evening, I can look in my rearview mirror and see the sun setting over the Golden Gate Bridge or the fog rolling in, and it brings tears to my eyes. No matter how stressed I may be, noticing beauty brings me peace. The colors of a sunset, the softness of fog, or the primeval enchantment of a full moon are awesome. I can't get near them, touch them, or own them, but I can experience them. That is enough.

EXERCISE

Color My World

Whenever you feel the intense beauty around you, a wonderful way to record the experience is to draw a freeform picture of you and the world you live in. Use as many colors as possible on the largest sheet of paper available. Express yourself. Have fun. Whenever you are having a difficult day, take out your drawings and look them over.

When you notice the true beauty all
around you, you become truly
beautiful yourself.

Cynthia Brian

BEING

My "break" into show business came when I was least expecting it. I had recently returned from living and studying at the University of Bordeaux in France under the auspices of the UCLA Education Abroad program and was studying at the University of California at Berkeley, while working odd hours for an airline and as a model to support myself. As a young person smitten with the travel bug, these positions offered me great flexibility, travel benefits, and a chance to complete my studies.

One day, a famous Hollywood director called my talent agency. He wanted to audition women for the role of a European who could speak French, German, and Italian. My agency had no such actress on their roster, but they told him they had a multilingual Italian model; perhaps she could also act.

You guessed it. I was the multilingual model. Though I had never told the agency, I had done quite a bit of acting in high school theater productions. I went to the audition, not knowing what to expect, but determined just to "be" myself. They had me read in French, Italian, and Dutch (my German was limited, but my Dutch was fluent). They also asked me to do some translating. I left, unsure whether I had the job or not.

A few days later, the whirlwind began. My agent called to say that I had the part of a French flight attendant, that I was being sent on location, that I would need to join the Screen Actors Guild immediately, and that I would be working with some very high-profile actors. I was elated and terrified.

Soon I found myself on the set of *Raid on Entebbe,* the true story of how the Israelis rescued the passengers of a plane hijacked by the crazy and corrupt regime of Uganda's Idi Amin. The director was Irwin Kershner. The cast included Charles Bronson, Peter Finch,

Sylvia Sidney, Yaphet Kotto, Martin Balsam, Jack Warden, Richard Dreyfuss, Horst Buchholz, Robert Loggia, and John Saxon. Everyone was a seasoned pro, some had won Oscars, and I had never performed in front of a camera before.

In the theater, I was used to being given a script and doing a play from beginning to end. However, in the movie industry, scenes are rarely shot in sequence. Actors are often given only a few pages of the script at a time, so it is much more daunting to identify your character and get into your part. Without film training, I had to fall back on finding what I knew to be true for me. "Just be," I kept telling myself. "Don't fake, don't pretend, don't imitate. Don't act, don't do. Just breathe and *be*."

I did an inventory of what the script said about my character and realized that I could create her from my own life. She was French. I had just returned from living in France for a year. She was a flight attendant. I currently worked for an airline. Her job was to speak to passengers in their native language. I could use my multilingual skills to color the role.

Swallowing my pride, I told the director that this was my first film, and I was a bit nervous. I might need some help in blocking, lighting, camera angles, voice, and so on. He told me just to "be yourself," and he'd do the rest. I was the blank canvas, anticipating the artist's brush.

What a fabulous first experience that was for me. After the shoot, I was flown to Hollywood to do "looping," recording additional or substitute dialogue for the soundtrack. (I did the off-camera voices of airport passengers in different languages.)

Raid on Entebbe won an Emmy, and my career as an actress was launched. The film still airs in reruns, I still get residuals, and my friends love to joke about how I got started in show business with the line *"Billets, s'il vous plait"* ("Tickets please")!

Hamlet thought that "To be or not to be" was a question. It is also an answer. Being is a choice. Some of us are afraid of really being; we fear ridicule, rejection, failure, and revealing our weaknesses, so we

Cynthia Brian

try to separate living and being. Being ourselves requires emotions, impulses, moments of exalting exhilaration and sorrow, even occasional despair.

To *be*, recognize and acknowledge what you are feeling. This can involve discomfort or pain, but don't separate living and being. I could have wasted my powerful first film experience by choosing to hide behind a facade, to *act* instead of *be*. But I decided that being comes before acting, regardless of the audience. I acknowledged the obstacles and expressed my fears. This let me relax and just be. Not that technical skill is irrelevant. As soon as I returned from the shoot, I sought out acting coaches and began a rigorous program of on-camera acting training. My coaches taught me in even more depth that there is no acting in acting…just life and being.

EXERCISE

To Be or Not to Be?

Your impulses, emotions, and feelings are integral to being alive. For this exercise, go to a private place and ask yourself, "How do I feel right now?" Then tell yourself—out loud. Express everything you feel in your voice, your body, and your movements. Be what you feel, not what you think you should be. Express everything that is going on. Breathe! Then just be…or not be. The choice is yours.

Be the star you are!

The Gift of
BREATHING

It was Halloween night, and I was nine years old. My two sisters, Deb and Pat, and my brother, Fred (my youngest brother, David, wasn't born yet), were all dressed up in homemade costumes and ready for a fun night of trick or treating. Since we lived on a ranch, my parents piled us into the old station wagon and headed for the nearest town, twelve miles away.

The night was damp and chilly, and our first stop was at the rectory and convent of Holy Spirit Church, where we were warmly welcomed. I paid little heed to my irritating cough since I was dressed as my favorite nun, Sister Mary Germaine. We went on to the homes of some school chums, while my cough increased by the minute. I began wheezing, so my parents decided to call it a night and head home. We had driven about five miles out of town when I could not catch my breath. A very strange sound was coming from my throat. My brother and sisters thought I was joking, but my dad stopped the car. Mom and Dad tried to help me breathe by pounding on my chest and back.

With no oxygen, I began to panic. As I lost consciousness, I could hear them debating whether to get me home and into a warm bath or to drive back to the hospital. Fortunately for me, they chose the hospital. By the time we arrived, I had stopped breathing. The doctors put me into a large contraption, gave me injections, and somehow restored the airflow. My parents were told they had made the right decision. If they had taken me home, which was seven miles away, I wouldn't have made it.

My guardian angel had truly been watching over me and whispering in their ears. My lungs had collapsed, and a warm bath would not have revived a dead body. We later learned that I had asthma, a disease that affects 5 to 10 percent of the children in the U.S. I was always an active, athletic child, but throughout my childhood and early adult years, sudden asthma attacks struck without warning, especially in the winter months. This meant trips to the hospital, great anxiety, and the fear that this time I might die. Breathing became paramount in my life.

It is interesting how we take the act of breathing for granted. We can go without food, water, or shelter for several days, but we can't go more than a minute or two without air. Breathing is our life force. Oxygen is the silent and invisible power that permits life.

Inhaling air provides more than survival. The more deeply we breathe, the more focused, relaxed, and balanced we become. Each morning, I start my day by doing three deep, cleansing breaths. Whenever I feel stressed, I focus on my breathing.

I take my air seriously. I have great sympathy for nicotine addicts, but feel strongly that when they smoke in my vicinity, they are not just killing themselves. They are killing me. Clean air is essential for my health.

In my dad's last moments on this earth, while I held him in my arms, he struggled for breath, wheezing as I had done so many times, until he exhaled for the last time and was gone. Holding him while he died, while my own fears suffocated me, was the most difficult and yet the most blessed thing I have ever done in my life. It taught me that breathing is the ultimate spiritual experience.

EXERCISE

Practice Belly Breathing

☆ *Breathing is being. Learn to breathe properly. Lie on the floor and get really comfortable. Do not cross any part of your body; it stops the flow of energy. Put your right hand on the lower part of your stomach, just below your belly button. Inhale deeply through your nose, making the air "fill you" to below your hand. This pushes your diaphragm up, and you'll feel like you've swallowed a watermelon.*

Hold this breath for twenty seconds. (Count "chimpanzee-one, chimpanzee-two" up to twenty.) Exhale slowly through your mouth. Do this three times.

☆ Breathe like a baby. Until babies are about two-and-a-half months old, they normally breathe from their diaphragms. That's what gives them those big, extended bellies. This is the proper way to breathe. As we grow older, most of us fall into the habit of breathing very shallowly from our chests. We can't hold enough air to complete sentences and maintain stamina.

☆ When you become proficient at belly breathing (aka Watermelon or Baby Breathing), you can do it in your car or whenever stressful situations arise. (This exercise grounds and centers you, while relaxing your body, mind, and spirit.) Take a deep breath and be glad for another moment on this planet.

Exhale fear and tension.
Breathe in life.

The Gift of

CELEBRATION

He arrived in our parish from Ireland when I was thirteen. He was twenty-four and newly ordained into the priesthood. Father Patrick McGrath was a shy, thin dairy farmer from Limerick, Ireland, who felt entirely out of place in psychedelic California. That is, until he met my family.

We were outspoken, inclusive, and full of fun and mischief. And we celebrated everything. It didn't matter that we didn't belong to the race, religion, or nationality that started a festivity; we celebrated it anyway. Best of all, we were farmers—hardworking, honest, salt-of-the-earth folks with fantastic fresh food on the table and unrestrained conversation throughout a meal. We adopted him as family and have never regretted the celebrations that followed.

Father Patrick McGrath, with his heavy Irish lilt, became my very best friend, my champion, my mentor, and my celebrator for a lifetime. During my teen years, we joined together to form the first citywide youth organization in our area. We wanted teens to have a place to go, meet with other teens, have fun, and still be supervised in a nonjudgmental way.

This was no easy task. It was the late 1960s, when free love, free drugs, and antiestablishment ideologies were the norm. But Father McGrath had a way of interacting with youth. He listened. He understood. He implemented changes. He celebrated their differences. He didn't care about the Establishment's rules. He believed in celebrating life and goodness. Never judging you by the styles of the day, he looked past that and into your soul.

We established one of the first folk masses in the state, where teens played music and sang songs. We organized nondenominational ski trips, weekly ball games, and dances where new bands could play. There were also study groups, retreats, and teen hangouts. Before long, our church was the "in" spot in the county. Soon we were winning state and national awards with our motto of "Celebrate Life," and our youth members were on their way to becoming outstanding leaders in their schools and communities.

Father McGrath has celebrated on a personal level with my family from the first time we met. He knows how to commemorate an occasion and applaud even the smallest achievement. Father McGrath reveled in life itself, and he made every event by celebrating it. Through great times and horrible times, we have been together to commemorate and commiserate with open arms and open hearts.

When my dad died, Father McGrath supported us at the altar. At Justin's surprise eighteenth birthday party, Father McGrath showed up wearing his cowboy hat and regalia in honor of our horse-wrangling son. He cheered for Heather at swim meets and hailed Justin's attempts at winning in monster-truck races! Every Halloween, Father McGrath and I dress in crazy costumes and sit at the top of the driveway with a big bonfire blazing, ladling out hot cider and offering roasted marshmallows to trick-or-treaters.

Sometimes, he'll show up at the house with a basket of fresh asparagus, a lemon meringue pie, or a book he suggests that we read. Then I'll pick whatever is ripe in the garden, throw together a quick feast, and we'll all celebrate the simple accomplishments of the moment, the day, the week, or the month.

Now he is back in Ireland, working with people who have attempted suicide. He is helping people learn that life can be rough, but overcoming the bitter offers an even sweeter celebration.

When was the last time you really celebrated? We all need to be appreciated, wanted, valued, respected, and cared for. Celebrating ourselves and our lives is vital. We have all experienced sadness and tragedy, yet life is a continuous celebration. Each day that I am alive on this earth is a gift, another day for which I'm grateful, embracing every moment of it.

Once, after attending a funeral, my daughter asked me what I wanted written on my headstone. I told her I would have to think about it. She said, "This is what I would write for you, Mom: 'She celebrated each day of life, lived her dreams to the fullest, and helped other people live theirs. She loved people and animals on this earth and forever beyond in heaven.'" I'll take it!

Yesterday is history, tomorrow is a mystery, today is a gift. That's why we call it "the present." To me, the words "celebration" and "Father McGrath" are synonymous. As he often says, "Today is the only day we have." Here's wishing you a Father McGrath day. Celebrate now!

EXERCISE

Sing a Song

Singing at the top of your lungs never fails to produce a heavenly elation. Get in your car and roll up the windows or wait until no one is home. Then sing! *Who cares what your voice is like? Have fun and be part of the song. If you are at home, combine singing with dancing for the greatest workout and energy booster there is. This is guaranteed to put a smile on your face and a feeling of celebration in your body and spirit.*

Now, pass on the celebration. Get a friend or family member to sing and dance with you. Just keep singing, smiling, and celebrating each moment.

Never hesitate to celebrate,
commiserate, or commemorate—
before it is too late.

CHALLENGE

Everyone called her an old maid. She was twenty-eight years old, the youngest of twelve children in a Swiss-Italian family, and therefore the designated caregiver for her elderly parents. Her destiny was one of servitude and celibacy. Each day was like the day before, one of service in rhythm with the seasons. In summer, she would climb the steep hillsides near her village of Ticino in southern Switzerland to pick grapes, carefully storing them in the straw basket on her back. In winter, she chopped wood, tended the stoves, and cooked for her family. Her life seemed fixed.

Then one day Louise Gina's father received a letter from his friend, Eugenio, who had emigrated to America. Eugenio had helped establish a winery in the Napa Valley of California and could now afford to marry. He asked that one of his old friend's daughters come to California to be his wife. It didn't matter which one.

Louise Gina was the only unwed daughter, but she adamantly refused. She didn't want to travel to an unknown land to marry a stranger almost old enough to be her father. She remembered seeing Eugenio when she was very young, and he had seemed quite ancient to her eyes.

Her mother quietly urged her to go. "We will be fine without you. If you remain here, Louise Gina, you will become old and crippled like me from hard work. Life may be easier for you there, and you can learn to like him. This is your opportunity for a *life!*" Fortunately for me, Louise Gina accepted this challenge. She became my grandmother Nonie.

It was in the early 1900s, and the voyage in steerage around Cape Horn to California was miserable, long, and dangerous. When Louise Gina finally reached dry land, the challenges were even greater. Eugenio met her at the port of San Francisco, wrapped from

Cynthia Brian

head to toe in bandages. He had been badly burned a week earlier in an explosion at the winery. With much apprehension, Louise Gina went off with this stranger to begin her new life as a vintner's wife. Secretly, she resolved to keep a suitcase packed, in case she should ever go "home" to Switzerland.

Eugenio was hardworking and honest, but very strict, the unchallenged patron of the house. The neighbors soon called Louise Gina *la Madonna* because she was so quiet, sweet, and kind. The couple were very poor, but Louise Gina was able to prepare fabulous meals with fresh ingredients from their garden. Slowly Louise Gina and Eugenio came to share a life and their skills for survival. Within eight years, they had six children: three boys and three girls. The children wore hand-me-downs and generally went barefoot, saving their shoes for school and church. A precious family photo shows this clan of shoeless ragamuffins standing in the garden, staring solemnly at the camera.

As Louise Gina and Eugenio worked together, they grew closer, and their children learned the importance of caring and sharing. The winery became the prestigious Beaulieu Winery in Napa Valley. Their marriage thrived for forty-seven years, until Eugenio died. Still mourning the man she had grown to love, Louise Gina got out her suitcase and returned to her homeland for a visit. Her first plane ride retraced the distance in a few hours instead of the months her original journey had taken.

She and her husband had been the first in their families to go to the New World, and everyone in Switzerland was looking forward to her visit. Upon her arrival she told her Swiss family of the wonders of America. She had undertaken a great challenge and thrived. What she had thought would be frightening and miserable had turned out to be the greatest opportunity of a lifetime. After a month in her former homeland, she returned happily to her *real* home, America, much to the delight of her six children and twenty-four grandchildren.

We are often urged not to be timid, to embrace challenges. However, one of the most difficult challenges is choosing which challenges to accept and which to reject. Jumping at every opportunity can keep you changing direction so often that you never get anywhere meaningful. Becoming a "challenge junky" can be as big a trap as never sticking your neck out.

The person who relishes challenges *and* can choose wisely among them will be the happiest and most productive. The most threatening challenge can be an opportunity. Ask anyone who has survived a difficult time whether they would want to go through it again, and the answer will probably be "No, thank you!" However, they will also tell you how much they learned about themselves, their strengths and weaknesses, and how proud they are to have come through.

If my grandmother had been stopped by her fear of the unknown, her life would have been very different. But she accepted the challenge, and her family has contributed greatly to the wine industry of Napa Valley and to the fabric of America.

EXERCISE

Balloons

This is an exercise that helps actors relax and meet the challenges of upcoming auditions and jobs. When you are feeling challenged, try being a balloon. Let your feelings blow you up until you can't get any bigger. Then go ahead and pop yourself, plopping on the floor in a heap (or collapsing in a chair). Repeat this exercise three times. Next, become a balloon that is released into eternity. See yourself flying over the treetops, ever higher, higher, higher until you reach your rising star. Attach yourself to that star, and know you have the support of the universe to help you succeed.

When you feel uncomfortable or fearful,
explore the opportunity disguised as a challenge.
Without challenge there is no achievement.

Cynthia Brian

CHANGE

I have always loved my birth name: Cynthia Lee Abruzzini. Yet as a girl, I was always called Cindy, and I felt it suited me. "Cynthia" sounded so formal, so grown-up, so *stoic*. I was anything but that. "Cindy" was the real me, perky, fun, optimistic, creative, expressive, earthy, and a constant cheerleader. Life was for living and learning and experimenting. I was most definitely a Cindy.

My Italian last name brought me great pride and joy. It was different than the other names in my class. I loved that it began with the first letter of the alphabet, which meant I was always first in line and invariably sat in the front row. I was, and still am, one of those people who loves to sit up close where I can see, ask questions, and hear better, so I can learn well. My last name also had two z's in it, unlike anyone else's.

After high school, I had an opportunity to travel to Holland as a teenage ambassador. In most places in Europe, people could not pronounce my name. They called me Chinsia. After a while, I grew into this name. Back in California, I became Cynthia. But my last name remained unchanged, which felt comfortable.

However, even that security blanket was soon yanked away. After I had worked as a model for two years as Cynthia Lee Abruzzini, my agent called me into her office and said it was time to consider changing my name. I protested vehemently. She explained patiently that clients were confused. My name suggested a dark-eyed, dark-haired Italian, but when I turned up for the booking, they were looking at a blue-eyed blonde. Alternately, there were clients who liked my look, but as soon as they heard my name, made it clear that they didn't like Italians. To succeed in modeling at that time, my agent explained, I needed a neutral, nonthreatening, nonethnic, Anglo-Saxon name. Finally, we compromised, and I dropped my last name. I became Cynthia Lee.

Six months passed, and she again summoned me to her office. "Your name isn't working," she said. "Everyone thinks you're Asian! We have to find a more suitable name."

I was recently married, and my agent asked, "What's your husband's *first* name?"

"Brian," I replied.

"That's your new last name!" she cried. I walked out of that office with a new identity. I was now Cynthia Lee-Brian, eventually shortened to Cynthia Brian. And my husband, to his dismay, was sometimes called "Brian Brian."

My family and childhood friends still call me Cindy, and in my heart I will always be that fun-loving, creative little girl. However, I have grown up and grown into my adult professional and personal life as Cynthia. I never planned on changing my name. The change excited and frightened me at the same time. It meant I had to expand, take a risk, and learn new ways of working and thinking about myself. I had to grow.

You've probably used change at some time to jump-start your life. You get the blahs and decide to try something new: eating out tonight, changing your hairstyle, redecorating, buying a new outfit or car or house. In extreme cases, some people quit their job or their marriage. Self-dictated change is usually empowering and invigorating. I learned to adapt to my new name, and it has become my welcomed reality. Now I often assist my clients in choosing new names.

Unwelcome change, dictated by outside forces, is much harder. It can be unpredictable, explosive, even debilitating. To cope, start by telling yourself that "change is just another word for learning." Try to catch your breath long enough to trick yourself into seeing change as challenge. With this perspective, the benefits can out-weigh the negatives.

Sure, any change is a kind of loss. The Roman poet Lucretius wrote, "Whenever a thing changes and quits its proper limits, this change is at once the death of that which was before." But the Greek philosopher Heraclitus said, "You cannot step twice into the same river." Life is constantly moving and changing. When we can accept this, change keeps us fresh and alive.

Change is a catalyst for growth, a tool for understanding ourselves and others.

Decide to interpret unwelcome change as a fresh start, a new perspective, and an ongoing positive influence. Change, good or bad, is vital to living and loving.

EXERCISE

I Change

☆ *Get a glue stick or bottle of rubber cement, a big sheet of paper, some smaller sheets, and a pile of old magazines and newspapers. Cut out various images, sayings, and names that embody the real you, the person who is lurking inside you. Create a collage of any size with your clippings. Leave some room so you can add to it.*

☆ *Put your collage in a place where you can reflect on it several times a day. Notice how you feel about certain images, phrases, and names. Cut out the ones that particularly suit you from your first collage, and start a second collage. Keep doing this until your final collage has only one or two images and names.*

☆ *Decide what you need to change to* be *the you that is reflected in your collage. Be positive, realistic, and hopeful, embracing both change and* resistance *to change. Learn to see change as your ally. Become the new you.*

"Know your limits, then exceed them.
It is never too late to be what you
might have been."

—*George Eliot*

The Gift of

CHOICE

My career as an actor and model began a few years before my husband and I were married. While he was still in dental school, I was earning and saving money for our future together. After his graduation and our wedding, he went to work as an intern for another dentist in northern California, eventually purchasing that business. About this same time, my acting career began to soar and my local agents sent me 350 miles south to Los Angeles where I would have access to better parts, more training, and Los Angeles agents.

I loved acting, auditioning, rehearsing, and creating roles for a variety of characters for television and film! It was exciting to go to movie studios, walk the lots, meet celebrities, and audition for big-time casting directors, writers, directors, and producers. My dreams of being a professional "talent" grew a thousandfold, and my star was definitely on the horizon. It became obvious that I needed to spend more time in Hollywood if I wanted a chance to be successful. At first, I commuted to Los Angeles in the morning and flew back at night, but it soon became necessary to stay the entire week. My husband was supportive and encouraged me to follow my dream.

After a few years of this, we decided to start a family. I definitely wanted children, but I didn't want my exciting life to change. However, I realized that I might be a successful commuter wife, but I could never be a commuter mom. My husband and I had "The Conversation." I wanted to move to Los Angeles to be near the acting world. He had just established his dental practice and starting over somewhere else would seriously set back his career and our finances. We both had some serious choices to make. We could

    ☆ Continue as we were and not start a family
    ☆ Separate and follow our individual paths
    ☆ Find a compromise that would make us both happy

It became a matter of priorities. I made the choice. As much as I loved acting, I also loved my husband and was not willing to sacrifice the relationship for the chance to be a star. I wanted children and knew that the best life I could give them would be one similar to the one I knew so well, the country life with trees to climb, hills to roam, wildflowers to pick, and animals to care for.

When I thought deeply about my career, I realized that, in my heart, I already felt like I was a star. What I really loved about acting and modeling was the work itself, not the fame. So my choice was to stay in northern California, taking whatever roles were available there while being a hands-on, full-time mom.

The plan worked out well because I was soon a big fish in a little pond (San Francisco) instead of a minnow in the ocean (Hollywood). Over the years, I am constantly reminded that I made the right choice. Although all relationships have bumps and bruises, my husband and I have survived and thrived, and we have two wonderfully adjusted children who have chosen their own paths. I don't regret my choice. I have had the best of all worlds. I've never looked back and said, "I could have been..." had I chosen a different road. I am especially proud that I chose the maximum benefits for our family, and together we have created a meaningful life that has rewarded me personally many times over.

A viewer of my TV show wrote me, suggesting that the only way to live your dream fully is to exclude everything else in life. "If you want to be great," he said, "you have to give up everything else. Just eat, breathe, sleep, and focus totally. Like a new lover, give 100 percent to the endeavor." He suggested that if I wanted to be the best talk show host, I should give up everything else—don't be the lector at church, don't be the 4-H leader, don't be a mom.

I disagree.

If we give up everything for the pursuit of one goal, we're giving up life. Yes, it is important to focus on our dreams, our goals, and our desires, but our lives will always require decisions and choices.

My dream, of course, is to do it all: Create a meaningful relationship with my husband, do a great job raising my children, work to my best ability, try new things and experiences, and use the unique gifts that God has bestowed on me to help others. I'm proud that I've had one marriage, that we've weathered rough times through twenty-five years and made a commitment to each other and to life. We haven't gotten it all right. We've made plenty of mistakes and had innumerable failures. But we've learned and we've grown and we've bounced back.

You are making choices every minute of the day about what is important to you. (And if you choose not to choose, that's a choice to let others decide for you.) You can choose to live your dreams and do what you love. Once you do, some of your subsequent choices will be difficult, some painful, and some dead wrong. But they will be yours.

EXERCISE

Choose!

On a blank sheet of paper, draw three columns:

My Dreams — His/Her/Their Dreams — Choices

This exercise does not have to be life changing. It's about finding options. It can start out simply. For example, "I want a dog—she wants a cat—our choices are neither, both, or a bird."

The important thing is to make decisions, then act on them. Choose. Live with your choices. Understand that you will make mistakes. Use them as lessons to help you grow and learn to make better future choices.

Life is about choices.
Choices change lives.

Cynthia Brian

The Gift of
COMMUNICATION

Some of my best friends aren't human. I've been talking to animals since I was an infant and never knew this was unusual. Whether I was happy or stressed, I'd go have a chat, both mentally and verbally, with my chickens and sheep. They listened and seemed to understand. I sensed what they felt and perceived their needs on a very intuitive basis. Our communications seemed completely natural. What I've learned over the years is that communication does not have to be verbal. We talk not only with our voices, but with our bodies, minds, and eyes.

My communication with animals has taught me greater communication skills with humans. My children also have this gift. Both are in the 4-H Club and have always taken full responsibility of caring for their animals—ducks, chickens, geese, goats, rabbits, horses, dogs, sheep, and cats. Every place we live, we make sure we can have animals because they are a part of our lives. I think we are better human beings because of our deep connection with the animal kingdom.

Our most touching experience with interspecies communication was with Bambina. On a trip to a remote mountain cabin, Justin and Heather found a badly injured newborn fawn whose mother had died. The fawn was cold and starving, but we couldn't get it to lick milk from a bowl. But then the fawn snuggled under Heather's long blonde hair and discovered Heather's earlobe. Thinking it was her mother, she started suckling. We quickly began trickling warm milk down Heather's ear while the baby deer drank. When the fawn had regained some strength, we switched her to a bottle and gave Heather's ear a rest.

A strong bond was formed, and the deer became part of our family. We named her Bambina, a diminutive of Bambi and "little

BE THE STAR YOU ARE!   59 girl" in Italian. We planned to turn her over to an animal shelter when we returned home, but after several phone calls, we found that no one would care for her. She would be euthanized. That was the unthinkable, so we decided to raise her ourselves. Rather than being jealous, our other animals were delighted. Our cat, Halloween, who had just given birth to kittens, immediately adopted Bambina. Halloween would spend hours grooming the deer along with her kittens. Bambina's care meant round-the-clock bottle feedings for almost eighteen months, which we all shared with joy. She was such a sweet and gentle creature.

Bambina learned quickly not to eat the flowers in my garden. Instead, she'd wait patiently to nibble the cuttings, which I collected for her in a bucket.

Gradually we tried reintroducing her into the wild, taking her with us on long walks in the hills. After two years, she was old enough to explore on her own and spent most of her time with other deer friends she had made. Still, she would come back to the house regularly to check on us and visit our other animals. Whenever we went hiking, she would mysteriously appear and join us. How we loved her!

One day, the kids and I returned from the annual 4-H petting zoo that we sponsored to help city people get to know animals. As we were unloading our trailer full of animals—ducks, geese, chickens, goats, an so on—Bambina came out of the hills and into the barnyard to visit. Our dog ran out to greet her. Perhaps Bambina had learned the lessons of the wild from other deer. Or perhaps she was just startled. She spooked and started running, shrieking, and jumping as if she was being pursued by a mountain lion. We called her. Suddenly she turned, screeching, and leaped into my arms. The force knocked us both backward down a slope into a ravine where we lay stunned. We were both badly injured; I would later need surgery and Bambina was unconscious.

A storm was blowing in. Heather yanked off her jacket and sweatshirt to cover Bambina. Then she and Justin lay down next to her and held her to keep her warm as I ran to call a vet.

Unfortunately none of the vets in the area knew anything about treating a deer. Then I remembered a good friend in Wyoming who is a wildlife vet. I reached him, and he gave us excellent advice. Bambina had probably suffered a heart attack, the natural response of a deer or any prey animal when being hunted. They are so terrified of being attacked that they literally kill themselves to avoid a more painful death. In the wild, he said, this deer would surely die, but because she knew and trusted us, there was a chance she could survive.

Justin cut a large piece of wood for a stretcher. Gently, we slid her onto it and carried her down the hill to the garage where we made her a warm bed. All the time, we kept talking to her. The kids got out sleeping bags, and we bunked next to her for the long night, holding her close. She must have understood how much we loved her. Just before dawn, she opened her eyes and sat up.

Her recuperation was slow, but during this remarkable time, we communicated with our eyes. I felt I could truly understand Bambina's feelings. As crazy as it may sound, we spoke to each other telepathically.

As Bambina recovered, she made it obvious through her eyes, body language, and sounds that she wanted to live. We massaged her and built a Bambina-mobile to help her walk. Her wild deer friends would come down to visit her as she sat in our garden, but they never came close to us. For several months, her condition improved while all our animals participated in this adventure. Halloween the cat, who had mothered her as a baby, seemed to know Bambina needed help. She took up residence, again sitting on Bambina's back and grooming her. Bambina was healthy and happy.

Then one day, she fell again. This time I feared she might not survive. She seemed to understand my sadness and licked my hand to "tell" me she was all right. She ate, slept, and enjoyed the garden, but each day she was a bit weaker. I kept asking her with my voice and my thoughts if she was in pain, and she would communicate with her eyes, always licking my hand to reassure me. We brought in a specialist from a wildlife reserve who told us that it would be best to "put Bambina down," to euthanize her. Neither the children nor I could bring ourselves to do that. We didn't want Bambina to suffer, and we believed she wanted to live. We continued to tell her that we loved her, and she continued to nuzzle and reassure us.

For the weekend of Justin's birthday, we had arranged a family trip. The kids and I sat down with Bambina and explained that we would be gone for two days, but a very good friend, someone she knew and trusted, would be there to care for her. Before we left, I spoke of many things to Bambina. I asked her if she was suffering and told her what the wildlife specialist had recommended. I also told Bambina that I didn't have the heart or the courage to euthanize her because I loved her so much. I gave her permission to die in her own manner when she felt it was time, but also let her know how much we loved her and thanked her for her beautiful spirit. Bambina cuddled close to my heart. She kissed us many times, licked our hands, and, with those velvety big brown eyes "told" us to have a good trip. Her eyes seemed so sad to me, and in my heart, I feared this would be the last time we "spoke."

Two days later, as we drove up to the house, our friend was standing out front. He told us that Bambina had died in her sleep the night of Justin's birthday. We cried our eyes out, but we felt that Bambina had understood how terrible it would have been for us to have her euthanized. She had decided to spare us this extra suffering and to die on her own terms.

We have found much comfort in knowing that we communicated in a special way with a special soul. As a footnote to Bambina's story, she must have told her deer friends not to eat my precious roses. There are many deer around our house, but, since Bambina stayed with us, none come to nibble my roses.

All beings have the inborn ability to communicate with and comprehend each other. Whether you are relating to humans or other species, communication and rapport can bring consideration and the sweetness of a happy life. Communication is a connection with another being, which can be stressful, but is powerful and enriching.

Cynthia Brian

Language is our primary conveyer of thoughts and ideas, turning abstract concepts into words. However, research has shown that 50 percent of understanding communication comes from nonverbal messages. Body language speaks volumes. We communicate every minute of every day with our eyes, our tone of voice, and our bodies. Humans are capable of more than twenty thousand facial expressions. Of course, the smile is the most advantageous as it is always more pleasant to deal with a smile than a frown. Eye contact determines clear communication. Most people interpret a firm, steady gaze as a sign of sincerity. Darting, shifty eyes give the impression of being untrustworthy.

We reveal a great deal about ourselves with the way we stand, walk, shake hands, hug someone, cross our legs and arms, or sit. Sometimes our body movements contradict what our voices are saying. Have you ever said, "I'm open to your suggestions," while your arms were tightly wrapped across your chest, indicating you were not open or were perhaps frightened? We all have. Do your posture and gestures say the same things as your voice? A full 40 percent of verbal communication is registered in the tone of voice, including the inflection, pitch, speed, and rhythm. Use a loving voice while petting your dog and say, "You are a bad dog, a terrible dog"; your dog will acknowledge the sweet tone of your voice and will wiggle and snuggle with you unaware that you are voicing something negative. It is important to keep your tone of voice in sync with your meaning. In communications, actions speak louder than words. And sometimes, silence is the loudest communicator of all.

Respect and sensitivity is necessary for conversation and communication. When you want and need to communicate, lighten up and be kind to yourself. You can create harmony when you speak with your heart and mind as well as your voice.

What Is Your Body Saying?

Our bodies can be just as expressive as words, reinforcing or denying the words we use. Get familiar with how you communicate physically, using this actors' exercise. Set up a mirror and act out the following emotions. Better yet, if you have a video camera, make a tape of yourself.

As you pantomime the following emotions, decide whether your actions express what you are trying to communicate:

surprise	*fear*
pain	*beauty*
joy	*frustration*
hunger	*exhilaration*
cold	*serenity*
desperation	*exhaustion*
confusion	*love*
anger	*admiration*

Our bodies do talk. Can you "see" what your body is saying?

The three most important words
for a successful relationship
are understanding, respect,
and communication.

Cynthia Brian

The Gift of

COMMUNITY

While searching for stories for a book I was coauthoring, *Chicken Soup for the Gardener's Soul,* I was intrigued by a short newspaper article about the spirit of community that was born during an olive harvest in the hustle bustle of technological Silicon Valley, California. I phoned the newspaper to find out more and eventually connected with the Dominican Sisters of Mission San Jose and Sister Mary Charlotte who enthusiastically told me the heartwarming story. Perhaps because I have always had a feeling of community with nuns, I was totally entranced. The Dominicans were one of the orders that our family entertained for years at our annual nuns' picnic.

The Dominican convent at Mission San Jose was once famous for its olive groves, originally planted by Father Junipero Serra in the late 1700s. Since 1894, the Sisters had gathered, pressed, and bottled the oil from their olive trees, sending it to churches throughout California. But in the 1960s, as the Sisters grew older and fewer in number, the demanding job of harvesting and pressing the olives was reluctantly put aside forever. Or so they thought.

One day, a young novice, Sister Donna Maria, was refurbishing the chapel. Thirty-five years had passed since the last harvest. Suddenly, the wind blew open the door, and an olive branch fell at her feet. She interpreted this as a sign that something was about to happen involving the olive trees. And it did.

The trees were still providing fruit. The Sisters had to provide everything else. The challenges began with the olive presses. The originals were long gone. Even if they had still existed, none of the living nuns knew how to use them. The Mother House administrator, Sister Jane Rudolph, contacted several commercial olive pressers. One was contracted for the job, but had to cancel. Undiscouraged, Sister Jane called Nick Sciabica of Modesto and told him about her dilemma.

"Let's pray about it, Sister," Nick suggested. By the end of the conversation and prayer session, Nick volunteered to help the Sisters by pressing, processing, and labeling at no charge. A San Jose city councilman enlisted the services of a trucking company to haul the olives. Thirty-five parishioners volunteered to help harvest. At the turn of the century and the dawn of a new millennium, the Dominican Sisters of Mission San Jose revived their harvest.

Rain was forecast for harvest day, but the Sisters and their new friends were undaunted. They gathered for a special blessing of the trees in the olive orchard. To their surprise, they found themselves joined by hundreds of others. Word had spread about the Sisters' olive harvest. It seemed as if everyone in high-tech Silicon Valley wanted to help in the orchards that day. Vans arrived carrying children from many private and public schools. Mormon elders, Protestant leaders, disabled citizens, people young and old of all ethnic backgrounds and from many communities participated. A church choir from another town entertained the olive pickers with Christmas carols, and one man celebrated his birthday under the olive trees. Ramiro, the convent gardener, donated his day to climb the trees and cut off the branches, ripe with fruit. Giggling children gathered up the branches and carried them to a tarpaulin spread on the ground. There, the Sisters plucked the olives and placed them in buckets. Older children carried the buckets to the truck where teens dumped the olives into bins. Obviously this was not a high-tech method of harvesting, but it was the Dominican way, something beyond the harvest—a day of communion with one another.

Ten-month-old Lionel Jeremiah thought his job was to taste every leaf, and six-year-old Felice demonstrated her technique of shaking the branches to disperse the olives. Ninety-year-old Sister Mary Martin Bush worked diligently alongside wheelchair-bound Sister Walburgis Schmidbauer, who had just been released from the hospital after having her leg amputated. A two-year-old toddler dutifully picked olives, placing them carefully in her bucket, then decided it was more fun to wear the bucket on her head. "This is

Cynthia Brian

like an old-fashioned barn raising," one harvester said with delight. "I feel purposeful for the first time in years," said a volunteer in a wheelchair.

Over one hundred bottles of extra virgin olive oil were made that day. As predicted in the weather forecast, it did indeed rain on harvest day. In fact, it poured—five minutes after the job was finished. Miracles do happen!

The Sisters of Mission San Jose produced more than olive oil that day. They created a new annual tradition and a spirit of community, one that continues to reap bountiful crops of friendship, fun, and miracles.

Human beings are social creatures. Despite wanting to be alone at times, we thrive in the company of other humans. But it is more than company that humans seek. We all need to be affective, effective, and appreciated. We can experience this sense of community within our family, or we can create community with friends or people who share a common interest, dream, or goal. By establishing a community of like minds, we find a place to express our creativity and be of service. Community gives us confidence and empowers us to reach out, both as a group and as individuals.

The original idea of the Dominican Sisters was simply to do something with the fruit of the olive trees. By being open to all possibilities, they started a new tradition, reviving and expanding the old community. Every person who participated in the harvest felt he or she had made an invaluable contribution, and a fellowship of spirit was born. Now, people are joyously anticipating future harvest celebrations.

Every person is part of some community. To be served, we must first serve others. To belong, we must first accept. Take a look at the communities of your life. Are you adding to the brotherhood and sisterhood of society? Are you open to the possibilities of fellowship? Are you making a difference? Would you like to contribute? As Thomas Fuller said, "A good life is the only religion."

The Community Channel

☆ *Think of your associations with others as channels on your TV set. In your journal, make a TV listing of all of the "community channels" in your life. Start with family, friends, church, school, work, and social activities. Then get more detailed, and write what part you play in each of these communities. For example, "As part of my family unit, I am the mother to my daughter, the wife to my husband, the aunt to my nephew, and the daughter to my mom and dad."*

☆ *Now write three things you do that involve you in the camaraderie of your community.*

☆ *Finally, next to each community channel, write an adjective that best describes how you feel being a part of this group. If your adjective is not a positive one, why not? What can you do to make it positive? Or would it be better to change the channel and become part of another program?*

Climb the hill with others,
and your joy will be all the more fantastic.

Cynthia Brian

CONVICTION

It takes courage to stand alone, even when you're sure you're right. Recently I was invited to participate as a design liaison at a prominent design center. For this privilege, I had to pay an initiation fee and attend training seminars to learn about the latest and greatest products, furnishings, and electronics so I could present them intelligently to the visiting public. We representatives were then required to volunteer twelve or more hours a month to a for-profit design center for ten months. Our reward was to be our visibility to potential prequalified design clients, as well as learning from and interacting with talented designers.

After a few sessions, it became obvious that the design center was getting the best of the deal. We were being used as free floor staff, and the prequalified clients were not materializing. We were definitely disgruntled but were generally afraid to confront management. I decided to write a letter voicing the concerns of the majority and asking for a meeting to discuss issues openly.

When management received the letter, I was "fired" from this privileged enclave. I had dared to question their motives and to demand professional treatment. I had recognized the risk and was not surprised by their actions.

That afternoon, I came home and told my daughter what had happened. She replied somewhat enigmatically, "Always be a doorway, never a doormat." I asked her to explain. She said I had taught her never to let others take advantage of her, but always to leave a door open for communication. "That management probably prefers walls to doors, Mom!"

How true. How sad! I have always been a champion of the underdog. I'm not a troublemaker, but I can't stand to see creative people being taken advantage of in any arena.

By firing me, the decorator showcase management thought they had squelched opposition to their program. Their actions had just the opposite effect. Other representatives were outraged that someone asking to discuss issues had been ousted. Most quit. When they opted out, so did the showrooms, the sponsors, and eventually the revenue. The president was soon terminated. The program had to be reinvented.

My sole intention had been to communicate the needs of the representatives and the showrooms. I expressed my conviction that the system should not abuse the design representatives. My actions brought a new era of respect for designers and ended shabby and unprofessional treatment that some managers had considered a clever way of doing business. By acting on my convictions, I helped establish a better work ethic for the entire design community. I am proud I had the strength of character to do what was needed for everyone's sake, regardless of the personal consequences.

Unethical persons in power will take advantage of others whenever they are allowed to do so. We must stand up for our convictions, however unpleasant or dangerous the result may be for the benefit of all.

Most people have something they'd like to see changed, but they're reluctant to stick their necks out. At the least, they might face ridicule. At the worst, there will be reprisals. And after all their efforts, the situation might not change; it might even be worse. But standing up for our convictions, however unpleasant or dangerous the results may be, empowers us and says we won't be taken advantage of.

It's easy to dismiss your ability to make a difference. "Why make waves?" is a popular admonishment. Start by building your I-Q (integrity quotient) with this paper exercise.

No Wimps Allowed!

What injustice would you like to see corrected? Write it down:
"My conviction is _____*." List what steps you would*
take if you could overcome your hesitation and fear of acting. Then visu-
alize the positive outcome of these actions. Does it seem impossible now?
   Don't be wimpy. Be wise and powerful.

Convictions take courage.
Courage builds character.
Character reinforces convictions.

COOPERATION

If you want to experience cooperation, move to the country. Farmers, ranchers, and rural dwellers must cooperate with one another and help each other to survive. Years ago, before technology, this sense of cooperation was even more crucial.

Though we lived miles from any town and our nearest neighbor was over a mile away, we "valley people" had a true sense of fraternity. We had our own volunteer fire department where my dad served for forty-six years, many of them as fire chief. The firemen's wives would prepare sandwiches and thermoses of hot coffee, and the kids would ride along on controlled burns, feeling important as they helped contain the fires. Neighbor helped neighbor with harvesting. Farm equipment was shared when needed. We pulled one another out of ditches and helped repair damaged vehicles.

My first jobs were in the fields, picking neighbors' cherries, apricots, peaches, pears, and prunes during harvest for a few cents a box. All hands, large and small, were needed to get the crops in before rains destroyed a year's work. Although town kids greatly outnumbered valley kids in our area school, the local 4-H Club was entirely valley kids, led by valley parents. We helped each other shear sheep in summer and assisted in birthing calves and lambs in late winter. We taught one another to cook, sew, can, knit, mend fences, and drive tractors.

On our farms, every man, woman, and child contributed to the fabric of ranch life. Everyone felt important and needed. High self-esteem became a normal frame of mind and a welcome by-product of cooperative living.

At a recent high school reunion, we valley kids reminisced about being overwhelmingly chosen as school leaders. We had learned the value of hard work and cooperation, working our family fields and those of our neighbors, developing independence, perseverance, and enterprising skills, while maintaining a fellowship of farmers and ranchers. And we had gone on to lead good, happy lives with meaningful relationships, making a difference in our communities.

In times of crisis, there is nothing like the caring of country folk. Platters of food, bushels of fruits and vegetables, bottles of wine, cakes, jams, jellies, and freshly baked breads are brought to a suffering family until times get better. When my brother was trapped under an overturned tractor, the neighbors responded immediately to my dad's call for help. After my brother's death, everyone in the valley offered emotional support to our family. This cooperative environment provided nourishment essential to healing our hearts.

My sister, Debbie, and her husband, Terry, exemplify the gift of cooperation. They live in the county where we grew up. Terry is the local fire chief, but long before he was a paid firefighter, he was in the volunteer department, always helping at the scene of an accident, fire, or resuscitation. If I were ever in any trouble, I know Terry would come to my rescue immediately. His boots, hat, and fire coat are always beside the front door, ready for the next emergency. Debbie brings a pot of stew, blankets, clothing, or other necessities to anyone in the valley in need. It's a rare day that I speak to Deb when she is not cooking or baking something for a local family. Deb's heart is as big as they get.

I've learned a great deal about cooperation from the animal kingdom as well. We had a turkey share a nest with a chicken and a duck to hatch a gosling. The little goose had three adoring mothers, none of whom were of the same species. The gosling followed his three mothers everywhere, imitating their behaviors. These mothers-by-proxy nurtured their adopted little treasure until he was able to fend for himself.

Witnessing this amazing occurrence, I thought about how much better our world would be if all nations, creeds, religions, and sexes embraced their differences and cooperated. Can you imagine everyone welcoming one another into each other's lives?

Cooperation, collaboration, and teamwork are an infinite power source. They make life's successes and joys bigger and better, the sorrows and losses more bearable. To get what you want in life, you need to collaborate with others. No one is truly self-made. You can accomplish much more working together than going it alone. The power of "we" is greater than the power of "me."

The next time I'm tempted to refuse help, to go it alone, or to do my own thing instead of seeking and creating cooperation, I'll remember the lessons of the country and of the barnyard. It definitely takes an orchestra to create a symphony.

EXERCISE

A Spontaneous Orchestra

This is one of my students' favorite acting class exercises. You'll need at least three people, but it is even more fun with four to ten. Each person chooses a simple inanimate object in the room, for example, a chair, cup, pencil, or spoon. One person leads the group by singing a song. Everyone else joins in as a member of the orchestra, making music with their objects by thumping, tapping, stroking, dinging, or pinging. The purpose is to cooperate and have fun with the melody. You'll be amazed by the results. Let the band play on!

Cooperation is the source of power.
Together everyone achieves more.

Cynthia Brian

The Gift of

COURAGE

It was 1961. America was in the middle of the Cuban Missile Crisis. World War III seemed hours away, and we prayed that President Kennedy would find a way to save the nation.

My grammar school was located twenty miles from a major California military base, which we were assured would be a target for Russian bombs. The school held daily air raid drills while U.S. jets roared overhead. For months on end, we were all terrified.

The school had an evacuation plan. When war broke out, students would be loaded on school buses and driven to the small town of Chico, several hours away in northern California. Parents received a letter explaining that they would be reunited with their children after the danger had passed. My parents' immediate response was, "*No!* Our children will not ride a bus to disaster." They reasoned that the roads would be jammed and a big yellow bus would be an easy target.

From our vantage point today, this may all seem rather naïve— why, if the Russians had nuclear missiles, would they send short-range, low-flying Russian planes crisscrossing above rural California to strafe cars and buses? But it was a time of national fear, and the first casualty was logic.

My parents decided that if we were all going to die, they wanted us to be together. They notified the school that they would come for their children in case of an attack. Then my mom and dad went into action. Mom prepared a tiny sheltered hideout in a small windowless hallway with plenty of food, water, ammunition, and blankets. Dad outfitted his World War II Willy jeep like an armored tank. He camouflaged it, put a grader on the front, added special tires, and loaded it with chainsaws, wire cutters, rifles, extra gasoline, food, a tank of water for putting out fires, sleeping bags, shovels, and enough survival equipment for the four of us. His plan was to reach us by driving fifteen miles overland, going through the hills and creeks, avoiding the roads. He would cut wires, knock over fences, and destroy anything that got in the way of rescuing his three daughters.

Dad mapped out his route and walked the land to make sure it was feasible. We had rehearsals and drills. We camped out in the hallway hideout several nights to make sure we could fit. No one could stretch out, but we could all sit. We went on run-throughs with the jeep. My dad's courage was indescribable. I'm sure he was scared, but he didn't show it. He took control of a terrible situation and did the best he could to remedy our fears.

My dad's determination to risk his own life to reach us helped us believe that he would not fail to rescue us. There was nothing mediocre about him. He was a gentle giant on a mission possible. I can still hear him giving us our evacuation instructions, making sure we would run to the safety of our hiding place as we awaited his arrival. Even as I write this today, I am choked with tears.

We were the *only* kids in our school whose parents had devised a separate rescue plan. We had a secret meeting place at the school convent, and we knew with certainty that our father would take care of us. Dad was always our protector, our hero. We felt completely safe in his presence. We were convinced that we would survive the war, and sometimes we thought we would be the only family alive at the end of the battle—thanks to his bravery. Dad was our unwavering warrior.

Fortunately for the entire world, the Cuban Missile Crisis was resolved, but the courage, boldness, and love that Mom and Dad expressed for us during those terrible days are part of our hearts and souls. The words courage and Dad are inseparable in my mind. He will forever be a hero to me.

Courage comes in many shapes and sizes. It doesn't mean you're fearless, only that you have controlled your fear. Not everyone will have to face a war, but every one of us fights numerous small

Cynthia Brian

battles. Our true grit and inner strength determine how we respond. Everyday living requires risks, and risks require courage. It takes courage to stretch yourself, to go out on a limb, to stand up for something you believe in. It takes courage to say "no!" and mean it when everyone else is saying "yes." Not settling for mediocrity takes courage. A life of service and fulfillment takes courage. My good friend, Father Pat McGrath, advises, "Success is never final. Failure is rarely fatal. What counts is courage." Dad said, "No!" to the mandate that all the students ride that yellow bus. My personal model for courage will always be my father's valiant labor and his determination to save his family from disaster.

EXERCISE

"No" Is a Complete Sentence

Stand straight, rib cage up, shoulders back, good posture position. Firmly and energetically, say, "No!" Do this three times. Use your eyes, your body, your powerful being to express yourself. Try it in different voices. Know "no."

"Courage is resistance to fear, not absence of fear."
—*Mark Twain*

The Gift of
CREATIVITY

It was the wettest winter California had had in years. Flooding was widespread, and the storms seemed to last forever. With so much water, the snails and slugs were out en masse. Each night when I turned into my driveway after work, I was greeted by the sleazy sight of thousands of snails slithering across the pavement to dine in my garden.

My six-year-old daughter, Heather, was already an animal aficionado and naturalist, in tune with nature and constantly reminding me about the cycles of life and how important it was to be kind to all creatures, great and small. As an avid gardener, I was not ready to extend kindness to the armies of snails consuming my plants.

Heather spent hours each day with her chickens, ducks, and geese while they foraged for worms, beetles, and insects, scratching incessantly at the earth. I asked her how she felt about her animals eating other living things. Very matter of factly, she informed me, "That's the way God meant for his creatures to live." With the air that only a six-year-old expert can muster, she announced, "You don't see chickens born with a sack of corn, do you, Mommy? They are *supposed* to scratch for their food."

A lightbulb went on in my head. Snails are *natural,* and snails would make great chicken food!

"Heather, I think your ducks, geese, and chickens would love to eat some of the snails that cross our driveway every night. They'll give your birds extra protein and keep them healthier during this wet winter. Do you think we could go out and pick a few buckets of snails to feed them?"

She liked the idea. With all the rain, the insects were in hiding, so the chickens had been eating more commercial grains than she thought was good for them.

Cynthia Brian

Heather and I donned our rain slickers, hats, mud boots, and gloves, and, flashlights in hand, went out into the cold, wet rainy night, each carrying two five-gallon buckets. We decided to have a contest to see who could fill her buckets the fastest. With so many snails, all four buckets were filled to overflowing in just a few minutes.

The hard part was carrying these heavy buckets up the hill to the barnyard while holding flashlights, so we got ten-year-old Justin to help. By now it was really raining, and I was looking forward to getting back inside for some hot cocoa by the fire.

The fowl were asleep when we arrived, but as soon as we emptied our treasure, an eating frenzy ensued. The birds clucked, quacked, and honked. It was party time!

Heather was delighted as she watched the animals consume their escargot with gusto. Justin was more interested in playing with his goat who wanted nothing to do with the snail feast. I collected eggs and scattered fresh hay in the barn, happy that my plan was working.

All of a sudden, there was silence. The chickens had gone back to roost, and the ducks and geese were in the pond. They had had their fill and were off to bed.

"Did they eat all the snails, Heather?" I yelled from the barn.

"Mom, you better come quick," said Justin, pointing a flashlight on the ground. "We have work to do!"

All eyes went to the thousands of uneaten snails who were making a quick getaway and heading *back* to my garden.

(Gotta think fast, gotta think fast. Can't have those slimy creatures destroying my plants. But what? Get creative, Cynthia, get creative!)

Bingo—it hit me.

"Come on, kids, start dancing as fast as you can and stomp those snails so the animals will have something to eat when they wake up in the morning!"

There in the barnyard in the pouring rain, the three of us danced the Snail Stomp! We clucked, we quacked, we honked. We partied! We had a mission. We were the Snail Stompers!

The fowl woke up to another buffet, and the resultant eggs were the tastiest ever. The Snail Stomp became our nightly routine that winter, saving my garden by eventually eradicating the snails.

My kids are now teenagers, but those rainy night Snail Stomps will forever be a favorite memory. Once in awhile, when a friend wants to feed the animals, I watch Justin and Heather give each other a secret smile and say, "Sure, come on up to our barnyard, and you can feed the chickens. And we'll teach you a new dance."

Heather was right about the natural cycle of life. And I creatively solved a universal gardening problem. Some people may view our Snail Stomp as cruel. We see it as environmentally progressive; we used no dangerous pesticides or poisons, the poultry enjoyed a nutritious meal, and my garden thrived sans the ubiquitous escargots. My point is that every thought and action is an opportunity for creativity. Each of us has a well of clever and original ideas, which are gifts to support us in a successful life.

My dad was ingenious at figuring out ways to fix tractors, fences, and other farm equipment with the tools at hand. When I'm doing an interior design job and the client doesn't have the budget for what they want, I find an alternative. When we first moved into our newly constructed dream house, we had no money for furniture. My husband and I slept on a carpeted floor for a year with only blankets, no mattress. I bought the kids a tent and sleeping bags for their bedroom and put stars on the walls. They loved it and pretended they were camping under a star-studded night sky. Justin loved it *so* much that he was eighteen before he let me replace his tent with a real bed. His unique bedroom received design awards and was published in numerous books and magazines! A creative solution was inexpensive and fun.

When most people think of the word "creativity," they think of artists and artisans. But creativity encompasses anything from creative problem solving to developing new organic farming techniques to decorating a room.

To be creative, we have to be open and receptive to new ideas. Unpredictable and unforeseen obstacles become the playground of the creative mind. To create is to discover unique ways of acting and thinking. When we are creative, all our vital juices are flowing, and the result can be extraordinary. Every problem has a creative solution if we just let ourselves find it. Being creative asserts your individuality. You become your own unequaled masterpiece.

EXERCISE

The Snail Stomp

☆ *Think of a sentence, and let your body say it. Move your body without using your voice. Stomp your feet, dance, fling your arms around, but don't say anything!*

☆ *For example, how would you say "I don't know"? Would you shrug your shoulders? Put your hand under your chin? You decide, and have fun with it. Your goal is to be creative.*

☆ *Stand in front of a big mirror. Consider each of the following sentences, and use your body to express them:*

> *I love you.*   *I want that.*
> *Get away from me.*   *I'm scared.*
> *I can do this myself.*   *Oh, not again!*
> *Be quiet.*

☆ *How do your body movements convey what you are thinking? This is your creative genius at work—and play!*

Everyone is an original work of art.
Being different is your birthright.

The Gift of

CURIOSITY

Curiosity killed the cat…and nearly killed my cousin Nancy and me. It also taught us several important lessons.

Nancy and I were born six days apart and grew up like sisters. In the long summers of our childhood, we joined our relatives every Sunday at my grandparents' farm for a day of playing, barbecuing, and swimming. My Uncle Ron, a dashing young bachelor, lived in a small cottage on the property. Uncle Ron was a fascinating figure who did daring things. He rode motorcycles. He piloted boats. And he drank sodas.

We were not allowed to drink soft drinks because our parents believed they would rot our teeth. Of course, the decadent liquid became irresistible, like forbidden fruit.

One day, when Nancy and I were about six, we spotted a crate of Coca-Cola bottles on Uncle Ron's front porch. We began to salivate. Coca-Cola. Wow! The most famous soft drink in the world. What did it taste like? What did it smell like? Was it sweet or tangy or sparkling? How could we get a taste?

Pretending to go on walks to find wildflowers, Nancy and I would always end up in the grapevines near that front porch and would peer at those bottles we coveted. We debated whether to ask our liberal uncle for a sip, but decided against it. We knew full well he'd say, "If it's okay with your parents, it's okay with me." And we knew the answer to that one. Our folks would be appalled, and Coke would be out of the question.

Summer was quickly coming to a close, and now, from our vantage point among the grapevines, we could see two full crates of those tempting bottles on the porch. Finally, our curiosity overcame our consciences.

It was a very hot Sunday. We borrowed a can opener (without asking) and crept through the vineyards to our lookout near Uncle

Cynthia Brian

Ron's cottage. No one was in sight. We sprinted to the porch, grabbed two bottles, and ran. Breathless and seated under a big black walnut tree, we popped the caps, held out the bottles in front of us, and counted. "One. Two. Three!" We chugged down the contents as fast as we could until we started coughing and gasping for air.

Our throats were on fire. We couldn't breathe and both of us became violently ill. Sobbing and howling, we ran to our parents as thick black goo dripped down our chins. The grown-ups sprang up with astonishment. "Oh, my God, what have you done!" cried one. "Quick, someone call a doctor!" shouted another. Coughing and bawling, we tried to explain that we had just wanted a taste of Coca-Cola.

Uncle Ron went pale. "Did you girls take a bottle from my porch?" Through our tears and gasps, we nodded. "That wasn't Coke. That was diesel fuel!"

Fortunately we survived, and everyone learned several lessons. Some of the lessons were old faithfuls from the Ten Commandments: "Obey thy mother and father" and "Thou shalt not covet thy neighbor's goods." I learned why curiosity can prove fatal to felines and small children.

Yet curiosity is essential for living well. Einstein said, "I have no particular talent; I am merely extremely inquisitive." An inquisitive nature keeps us young, vital, and energized, constantly feeding our minds and souls. Tempered with intelligence and common sense, curiosity is a wondrous gift that can lead to many discoveries.

Asking questions is the best way to learn new things. Don't be afraid to ask because you fear appearing stupid. Most people are complimented when you ask them to share their experiences and wisdom. If you don't seek informed answers, you may jump to ludicrous conclusions and seem stupid, just what you were trying to avoid.

Be curious. But use caution. Don't jump without a net. Disaster and diesel fuel may await you. I hope to always be curious. But I'll skip the gooey black stuff and stick to a glass of red wine from our vineyards!

What's That?

Swallow your pride and let your curiosity run wild for a whole day. Every time you see or hear something that you don't understand, ask for an explanation. Write down the new things you are learning in your journal. This can be tremendously flattering to your "tutors."

Ask someone of importance in your life how they handle a problem that you are having. Consider their actions and opinions. Let each answer raise new questions. What happens to your curiosity level? Are you hooked on asking questions? Good luck, and have fun learning answers for your life.

Your life isn't based on the
answers you receive,
but on the questions you ask.

Cynthia Brian

The Gift of

DARING

Ever since the Big Bad Wolf chatted up Little Red Riding Hood, one of the more popular pickup lines has been, "I'm a talent scout for a Hollywood studio." Thus I was understandably cynical when a man came up to me on the UCLA campus during my freshman year and asked if I would like to audition for a TV series called *The Dating Game*. I had just returned from eighteen months in Europe and had never heard of the show, even though it was very popular in those days.

The premise was that a young man or woman sat on one side of a screen and asked questions of three potential dates on the other side. The audience could see all four people. The contestant would choose one of the three candidates for a Dream Date based entirely on the answers to his or her questions.

The talent scout told me that I had "the look and personality of a winner." I was sure he said that to everyone, but I confirmed that he was a real scout and decided I had nothing to lose. It might even be fun.

When I arrived for my appointment, I was surprised to find hundreds of other people, all with that "look and personality," also waiting to audition. I wasn't yet a professional actor and didn't know any better, so I figured I had as good a chance as everyone else did. Why not give it a try?

Candidates were being interviewed for both sides of the screen. First, the coordinator asked everyone to write down ten questions that they'd like to ask prospective dates on the show. Then, one by one, each candidate was videotaped in a short audition. I decided to have a really good time. I wrote down ten questions in four different languages: Dutch, German, Spanish, and Italian, but none in English. When I was being videotaped and asked about myself, I chose wild and crazy things to discuss including the eighteen months I had just spent living and traveling in Europe.

I must have made a good impression because I got a callback. And another. And another. Finally I was chosen to be the young woman asking the questions.

My entire family flew to Los Angeles to be in the studio audience. It was the first time any of them had been on an airplane, and I was told that my mother screamed, "We're crashing! We're crashing!" throughout the flight. The other passengers were not amused, but at least she got there.

Off to the taping we went. One of my grandfather's good friends, an entertainment attorney for old-time movie stars like Mae West and Clark Gable, came to cheer me on. One of my sisters lent me a beautiful flamingo-colored pantsuit that looked great on camera. My family was seated in the audience, and I was sent first to have my hair and makeup done, then to the greenroom, a soundproof room off camera where performers wait to go on.

The theme music started, my name was announced, and I made my entrance. The host asked me to say "Good day" in Italian. I was so nervous that I replied in Spanish. Since he spoke neither language, he didn't know the difference, but I wondered what people around the country would think of such a blunder.

I sat in my appointed chair, took a deep breath, and looked out at the audience for my family. All I could see was a dazzle of bright lights.

One by one, I asked questions in various languages of the three gentlemen behind the screen. The point was to confuse the three contestants and amuse the audience with the gentlemen's reactions to my questions. Their faces must have been funny to see, because the audience and crew were laughing heartily. My final question was in Dutch. I asked, "If we were on top of a mountain, and I asked you to jump to prove your love for me, would you do it?" To my astonishment, Contestant #1 blurted out, "No, I won't jump! I won't jump! Save me!"

When it was time for me to choose the winner, I chose him. I assumed he spoke Dutch. (I found out later that he heard the Dutch word for "jump," *liepen,* and improvised.) He turned out to be David Jolliffe, the popular star of a TV comedy series, *Room 222.* His nickname was Carrot Top because he had a huge red Afro-style hairdo. My family, and especially the entertainment lawyer, were shocked and upset that I had picked "that hippie" as my date. As if I could see him!

For our Dream Date, we won a trip to Mesquite, Texas, to see Larry Mahan, a famous bronco and bull rider perform in the National Rodeo. David was the perfect companion, fun and entertaining. We rode in parades and were lauded as movie stars; we met Larry Mahan and even went to a party with the Dallas Cowboys. It was a lot of fun, and David and I became good friends. He created quite a stir later when he visited my dorm and played his guitar.

Being daring can reap wonderful rewards. We can choose to live each day fully and let our dreams soar, or we can stay in a cocoon, safe and warm, never daring to emerge as a butterfly. It takes courage to dream big, to risk being laughed at, to be wild and crazy. We all have the ability to be daring. Trust your instincts.

I didn't know it then, but my appearance on *The Dating Game* marked the beginning of my acting career. Risking humiliation and daring to be different shaped my destiny. I had so much fun being on camera that I yearned to do it again. I realized that I was willing to risk making mistakes, saying the wrong words, and being blinded by bright lights just for the experience of being on stage.

The Dating Game is now in reruns. David and I lost touch when I moved to France, but I've seen his photo in trade journals and union newspapers over the years. Here's to you, David Jolliffe, for your willingness to walk on the wild side with me. Did you wonder what I asked you in Dutch? Now you know.

Becoming an Eagle

☆ *Here's another favorite acting class exercise to expand and energize you. Stand straight, with your feet slightly separated. Close your eyes, and take a deep belly breath. Imagine yourself as a glorious eaglet leaving the nest for the first time. Look around the canyon at the beautiful lake below. You can see 360 degrees. It's a perfect sunny day, and the sky is blue and crystal clear.*

☆ *Slowly lift your arms and imagine them becoming wings. Prepare to take the leap. Look again at the horizon, and begin to gently flap your wings, feeling the power you possess. Dare to risk falling, certain you can't fail.*

☆ *Lift off, and soar toward the heavens. You can fly. When you have experienced your newfound skill, glide back to your nest. Take another deep breath, exhale, and open your eyes. You are now an eagle!*

Push the limits, risk ridicule,
stretch, dare to dare.

Cynthia Brian

DEDICATION

We were called the Three Musketeers, later changed to the Three MsKeteers! Eileen, Janet, and I met during our first few days of freshman year at UCLA. Eileen and I met in an elevator when I helped her lift her heavy suitcases. We both met Janet in French class. As fate would have it, we all lived in the same dormitory, Hedrick Hall, and soon discovered we shared mutual loves for family, learning, ice cream, French, and skiing. It wasn't long before we were inseparable and planning our futures together.

Once we learned of the junior year study-abroad program under the auspices of the Education Abroad Program, we dedicated ourselves to going to France together. Only a handful of UCLA students would be selected. For two years, we immersed ourselves in French, helping each other study. After the applications were reviewed and exams taken, we had personal interviews with the judges. The big day came when the winners were announced. Eileen, Janet, and I were on our way to France.

Janet and I had already shared an apartment during our sophomore year, so Eileen and I decided to rent rooms in the same building in Bordeaux while Janet chose to live with a French family. The three of us planned great adventures together in our quest to absorb art, literature, architecture, music, history, theater, and everything French.

On a trip to the medieval fortress at Carcasonne, I began experiencing excruciating abdominal cramping and awoke one morning in a pool of blood. I was rushed to the hospital at Pau where emergency surgery was performed for a ruptured ovarian cyst. In this tiny Pyrennes town in the 1970s, medical care was not up to the same standards we enjoyed in the U.S. No nurses were provided for postoperative care. Friends or family were expected to care for the patients' needs.

Eileen and Janet alternated spending the night in the hospital with me, acting as my nurse. Had it not been for the committed care of my two comrades, I might not have lived to remain part of the Three MsKeteers. They fed me, bathed me, changed bedpans, administered pain medication, read to me, and entertained me. I've been told that I was delirious with pain for two days and that I spoke in every language except English during that time. On the table next to my bed were two jars. One held the remnants of the ruptured cyst, the other my appendix with a note: "Appendectomy *complimentaire!*" The physicians had given me a free appendectomy while they were operating.

After recuperating for six weeks, we went on to have a year of unbelievable adventures, studying and traveling throughout Europe, the Middle East, and parts of Africa. We had jubilant times and frightening experiences, but we never forgot our educational goals.

When we get together now, one of our husbands will shout out, "Story fifty-four" or any number, and we'll all laugh hysterically. We had so many funny experiences and so many stories from those days that we began numbering them. Of course, we quickly forgot what the numbers meant, but they were great fun to retell. Our husbands think the three of us are very funny together and are amazed that we survived our crazy adventures.

During hard times and good times, we have been there for each other, thirty years of sharing joys and burdens. We have been blessed with an inviolable friendship, which will continue to our deaths. We are also dedicated to making a positive difference in the world. We have learned to focus on what we want, contemplate our goals, and be mentors to others.

Being dedicated is being devoted. Dedication implies consistent concentration and focus on another person or activity. We were devoted to one another in our college years. We were devoted to our goal of going to France as a team. There will always be unseen forces that affect our paths, but if we are dedicated to the positive progress of our lives, we will be winners.

For me, dedication is akin to religion. William Penn said, "Religion is nothing else but love to God and Man." I translate this as, "Love thy God, and love thy neighbor." Help yourself while assisting others to be and do their best. Dedicate yourself to excellence and improvement in everything you do. Surround yourself with positively motivated people, and watch your life flourish.

EXERCISE

Magic Wand

What two people in your life are you are most dedicated to? Write their names on a piece of paper. How have you contributed to their success, their well-being, and their growth—spiritually, physically, mentally, and emotionally? Write this down.

If you had a magic wand and could make their dreams come true, what would you like to see happen for these two people? How would this change or improve their lives? How would your own life be enhanced? Do you feel the power of dedication?

Dedicate yourself to making a difference,
not just making a living.

The Gift of
DELIGHT

In my dreams, I fly. I flap my arms, and up, up, up I go, sweeping over fields and towns and countries and oceans, smelling the fresh air and experiencing the wonders of the clouds. Perhaps I have never grown up, a bit like Peter Pan. I take great delight in experiencing new things, new foods, new people, new places. I'm forever challenging my acting students to take measured risks, to spread their wings and fly.

As children, my siblings and I climbed to the top of our barn with an umbrella and "parachuted" off into the haystacks, Mary Poppins style. We crashed and were buried deep in the hay, howling with utter delight. We wore capes like Superman and rode brooms like the Wicked Witch. Of course, we never actually flew, but that didn't stop us from trying. Other times we pretended we were the Lone Ranger and Tonto, summoning our horses with a whistle, and trying to land on their backs after "flying" from the limb of a tree. Mostly, we hit the ground, where a bewildered horse nuzzled our dazed brows.

The day I turned twenty-one, I went skydiving. The other dive students were hesitant to jump, but I couldn't wait. What an experience to be soaring through the sky! I even tried flapping my arms like wings. I felt weightless and powerful. Skydiving was pure delight.

One day, soon after I was married, I was feeding my domestic geese when the gander flapped his wings and suddenly took off. He was as astonished as I was that he could fly. He started honking at the top of his lungs, and his mate honked back, probably telling him to be careful or to get back down to earth. I was frantic with worry. In a panic, I phoned my husband at work. His staff was in spasms of laughter that I, a country girl, would think that he, a city boy, would know what to do about a flyaway gander.

I ran back out outside and into the woods. Both the goose and I were chasing the overhead gander when he came crashing down into poison oak. As we ran to his side, the gander wobbled to his feet. A bit dizzy from the fall, he fluffed his feathers and reassured his mate. Then he began honking excitedly and flapping his wings. Just like us kids, he wanted to go again!

Delight is sensation of pure bliss and elation we experience when something gives us great pleasure or joy. Being delighted is being close to nirvana, totally satisfying in a sweet and innocent way. The sheer delight of trying something new is worth the risk of failure or disappointment.

My gander was never able to fly again, but that didn't stop him from trying on a daily basis. He was obviously having a grand time preparing for flight and delighting in the process. I've never flown when I flapped my arms but in my imagination, I delight in wondrous flights of fancy. My acting students enjoy the exercises I have created about flying, and, together, we conquer our fears by "flying" to success.

People can survive without many things, but delight in being alive is essential. Find something, no matter how irrational or impossible (as long as it is legal and morally sound) that gives you great delight. If you can't experience it now in real life, experience it in your dreams.

You can feel real ecstasy through the gift of delight. Be open and receptive to the unexpected adventures that await you daily. They are there for you!

Fly Like a Bird

Don't you wish you could fly? You can, if only in your mind's eye. Stand upright and take three deep cleansing breaths, breathing with your belly. Bend over at the waist. Extend your arms. Shut your eyes and see yourself as a beautiful fledgling at the edge of the Grand Canyon, with the other side a mile away. You want to soar. When you are ready, step off the edge, flap your wings, and fly! *You can make it to the other side.*

We never know whether we'll be successful at something until we try. Sometimes even eagles need a push. Take a chance. Feel the exhilaration of doing something new, something scary. Dare to experience delight.

Spread your wings and fly!

Cynthia Brian

The Gift of
DESTINY

Many people believe that our destiny is predetermined. I believe that our destiny is a choice, not a chance.

I was ready for a publishing contract. I had written several chapters of this book, and each week on my radio program I would read a chapter matching the gift to that day's theme. This was an excellent way to get feedback from listeners on what touched their hearts and enriched their spirits. People told me they loved the concept, and many asked to purchase the manuscript. It was obvious that a successful and life-changing endeavor was underway.

During the summer of 1999, I had signed on with a new literary agent, a wonderful man named Ed who felt a heart connection with my book. That's who I was looking for, someone who recognized that such a book could enhance other people's lives. He loved the manuscript and felt that it would be a best-seller. My "grammar-mère" and chief cheerleader, Eleanor, had encouraged me from the start to work only with agents and publishers who felt as much passion for my work as I did. Eleanor had worked with many authors on many books and kept telling me this book was different—it was full of heart and stars!

In late summer, Ed sent the manuscript to several prominent publishers. Three showed interest, and we anticipated formal offers any day. However, unless the topic is sensational or timely, publishers can move very slowly.

In November, my daughter, Heather, and I took a trip to Key West, Florida, for a mother-daughter vacation. On the last night, we did something touristy and went to a Haunted Mansion séance. No one knew who we were. Only five others were in attendance, and we all giggled at the thought of taking any of this seriously. At one point, the young man conducting the session spoke directly to me.

"The spirits tell me that you are a writer. They want you to know that you will find the right publisher in February." I laughed it off as a lucky guess.

At Christmas, I was doing a live radio interview with the author of a book about angels. Suddenly she stopped. "Cynthia," she said, "I have a message for you from your angels. You will find the right publisher for your book in February." I was taken aback, but this was going out live, so I thanked her and continued the interview.

A few weeks later, Paul, a volunteer for our nonprofit positive-programming media library, Be the Star You Are!, read my astrological chart as a holiday gift. My celestial chart, he said, pointed to my getting a publishing contract around February.

Three similar predictions were too many to overlook. I called my agent and told him what the spirits, angels, and stars were saying about February. "Perhaps you should get ready," I said. Ed didn't act surprised. He commented that we're all the architects of our futures, so why not design our own time frame?

In mid-January, my longtime girlfriend Marcia invited me to a women's networking meeting, a group of entrepreneurial women in high positions who gather to support each other. Marcia knew I was constantly looking for sponsors for my TV and radio programs, as well as benefactors for my nonprofit organization. Each attendee spoke for several minutes, describing what they wanted. I mentioned that I was writing a wonderful book and searching for my dream publisher. After the meeting, a lovely young woman, Nicole, wrote a name and phone number on a business card and handed it to me. "Call this woman," she said. "She is the Vice President of a publishing house, and I think she may be interested in looking at your manuscript."

I leave nothing to chance. Early the next morning, I called and left a message on the Vice President's answering machine. Then I called Ed and asked him to follow up as my agent, sending her a copy of my formal proposal with sample chapters.

Within a week, she called me back. "If the rest of the manuscript is as good as your proposal," she said, "we should meet." I sent more chapters, she liked them, and we set up a meeting for February 10. When the ever-astute Heather heard the date, she exclaimed, "This is the right publisher, Mom. It's February!"

My new publisher and I noticed a certain element of destiny in our connection. She wanted to acquire my book for an imprint called "Heart & Star." As soon as Ed and I heard the name, we knew we had found a good home for my book. The contract was arranged, and we began to hold regular editorial meetings.

Had more than chance had brought us together? She and I discovered that we were both the eldest daughters from Italian families, and both of our fathers were farmers. The similarities didn't stop there. Both of our fathers had died on December 8, a special feast day in honor of Mary, the mother of Jesus. They had also both died of liver cancer after a lifetime of perfect health.

The coincidences went on. When we were in junior high school on opposite sides of the country, we had both taken the unusual name of Germaine for confirmation, me for my favorite nun, Sister Mary Germaine, and she for the little-known French saint, Germaine, who was also Sister Mary Germaine's namesake.

It was clear to both of us that this book was our shared destiny, that it was divinely guided, and that perhaps our fathers in heaven had brought their two oldest daughters together to create something special. We decided to let our hearts and the stars guide us in this venture. We had been given the gift of mutual destiny, of good fortune, and of love because we were bold enough to explore the possibilities before us. Now it was up to us to pilot this starship in the right direction. We don't know the ending of this story. We are on a joyous ride and have developed a loving bond, something I am told is rare between publishers and their authors. Our destinies are definitely intertwined, and it is up to us to put this karma to good use.

So what is destiny? It is fate, fortune, karma, kismet, luck, lot, and providence. How do we find our destiny? I believe that we are all on this earth for a purpose. When we find our life's purpose, we find our destiny. We create our future by opening the doors in front of us. Of course, we still have to do plenty of hard work to garner good fortune. We must listen, look, learn, laugh, respond, follow up, and be proactive.

I could have easily passed off the séance prediction as a lucky guess, the author's prophecy as a coincidence, or the astrological chart as generic. I could have skipped the women's meeting, not made the follow-up phone call, or not informed my agent of all that had been foretold. I could have redirected my destiny elsewhere. But I listened. I kept myself open and followed my instinct and my inner voice. Believing in destiny is not enough. You must act to create your fate.

People come into our lives for a reason. Sometimes they stay, sometimes they are with us only a short while to teach us a lesson or help us on our way. All of us can use the gift of destiny. Our destiny is an unending sequence of choices. We have the free will to make decisions. Follow your heart, listen to your spirit, and live your destiny.

───────────── **EXERCISE** ─────────────

Fate and Fortune

☆ *What do you want to achieve more than anything else in the world? Write it down. Why do you want to achieve it? What will your life look like once you have achieved it? How will you feel? Who can help make this dream come true for you? How will you reach them?*

☆ *Answer these questions. Then gather some old magazines and cut out pictures and words that attract you, that typify your dreams. Don't worry about making sense. Just cut a big pile.*

☆ *Get a large piece of cardboard, at least 11 x 14 inches, and make a collage. Paste on whatever pleases you and gives you a sense of hope and fulfillment. Use the back of the cardboard, too, if you like.*

Cynthia Brian

When you've finished, punch a hole in the top, attach a ribbon, and hang your masterpiece somewhere special where you can see it daily. My collage hangs in my office where my clients and visitors see it also. Don't be surprised when many of the images you have created show up in your life. There's no magic or voodoo involved. You are just reminding yourself of the things you want and need, making yourself more aware of opportunities around you.

 As times and circumstances change in your life, repeat this exercise, and make a new collage. Be open to all the possibilities of destiny.

The only way to predict
your future is to create it.
Choose your destiny.

The Gift of

DETERMINATION

My paternal grandfather, Fred Abruzzini, was the son of Italian immigrants who emigrated to Canada at the turn of the century. With only an eighth grade education, Grandpa Fred set off for California to work for his uncle, Benjamino Cribari, who had a small winery. Grandpa Fred was determined to succeed, but his timing couldn't have been worse.

It was 1920, and Prohibition, the "noble experiment," had just become law. All alcoholic beverages were forbidden, and the wineries were in big trouble. Wineries were only allowed to produce a minute quantity of wine for sacramental and medicinal purposes. Wine grapes, the results of decades of specialized cultivation, were being sold for grape-flavoring syrup, grape juice, and an alcohol-free imitation wine. Then came the 1929 stock market crash that kicked off the Great Depression. Most wineries had already gone bankrupt. The ones still surviving remained open on a tentative basis.

Grandpa Fred built a reputation for honesty and efficiency at the Cribari Winery. When the federal tax agents found suspicious irregularities in wine production reports at the larger and more prestigious Beringer Brothers Winery, they suggested to Bertha Beringer that she might hire someone with a solid record for wine inspections. Someone like Fred Abruzzini from the Cribari Winery.

At Bertha's invitation, Grandpa drove north to St. Helena to look over the situation. When he saw the great vats and underground storage vaults, Grandpa said, "Now *this* is a place to make wine!" But he wasn't sure whether he should leave the security of his job with Cribari. He had worked for his uncle for twelve years and was destined to become a shareholder.

Finally, he accepted the challenge. In exchange for free rein and a percentage of the profits, he became general manager, wine master, and chief promoter at Beringer Brothers. Of course, there were no profits in those days. But Grandpa Fred was determined to turn the business around.

He straightened out the wine records and organized the books. Then he used his Cribari connections to buy more grape juice for altar wine sales to provide essential cash flow. Next, he turned to the winery's long-neglected prune trees, restoring them to vigor and planting more in the vineyard's fallow land. He used the prunes in a big marketing push. Salesmen presented beautifully packaged prunes when they visited churches to sell altar wines. Beringer wine sales skyrocketed.

By 1932, there was talk that Prohibition might end if Franklin Delano Roosevelt became president. Grandpa Fred gambled on a Democratic win and began crushing more grapes to make port. His bet paid off. Roosevelt was elected in November 1932, and Prohibition ended in December 1933. Grandpa was ready with a big ad: "At last, after fourteen years of suspended animation, Beringer's famous cellars...have become a madhouse."

It took great determination to rebuild an industry that had been shut down for fourteen years. Speakeasies had made alcoholic beverages synonymous with sin. The image of fine dining and glamour had to be restored. Grandpa Fred came up with a determined promotion idea. At that time, few people had heard of Napa Valley, California. None of the wineries that are famous today— Beringer, Beaulieu, Martini, Inglenook, Christian Brothers, and Charles Krug—were doing very well. In May 1934, Grandpa Fred opened the Beringer caves to public tours, creating California's wine tourist industry. That September, during the first revival of the annual Vintage Festival since 1919, he brought five thousand visitors into his cellars for a tour and a chance to buy Beringer wines.

Still, Grandpa knew he needed even more publicity. He sent beautiful gift packages of Beringer wine, walnuts, and prunes to dignitaries and movie stars, along with a note saying: "Come up to the beautiful Napa Valley, and we'll treat you like a star."

Cowboy star Tom Mix brought his traveling show to be part of the entertainment. Heavyweight champion Max Baer and *Gone with the Wind's* hero, Clark Gable, visited and became Grandpa Fred's close friends. Grandpa lured famous visitors and gave them lots of publicity, making sure their photos were taken in front of an enormous Beringer wine barrel. It wasn't long before public figures, movie stars, politicians, or sports celebrities visiting San Francisco made it a point to travel north to Beringer Brothers.

Grandpa Fred didn't stop with celebrities. In 1939, the World's Fair was held on Treasure Island in San Francisco Bay. He drew up a map of Napa Valley. "All roads lead to Beringer!" it said at the top. Grandpa Fred, my Grandma Juanita, and their three sons (my dad, Alfred, and my uncles Jack and Ron) traveled to Treasure Island and handed out maps to fair goers. To make visiting the winery easy, Grandpa Fred provided free buses for anyone who wanted to make the side trip.

To greet all these new guests, Grandpa Fred renovated a building called the Rhine House into a reception hall and tasting room. He surrounded it with picnic tables and built huge, outdoor barbecue pits, still standing today. Visitors could enjoy free barbecue and steak dinners while overlooking the vineyards and hazy purple mountains in the distance. By 1940, over twenty-five thousand people were visiting the Beringer Winery each year. Corporations and social clubs began scheduling their picnics and meetings in St. Helena. Visitors went home and told their friends about the incredible hospitality at Beringer Brothers Winery.

Today, winery tours are a staple of tourism and wine sales in California, and indeed around the country and the world. Grandpa Fred Abruzzini, called the "Father of the Napa Valley" (noted in several historical books on the region), is revered as an innovator and marketer extraordinaire. When he retired after twenty-four years with Beringer, all the major Napa-Sonoma wineries were conducting tours and wine tastings, basking in being part of one of the most beautiful wine-producing regions of the world. Napa Valley was literally put on the map by a determined young man with an eighth grade education!

How did Grandpa Fred succeed, with his limited education, in turning a downtrodden winery into an incredible success? Simple. He was absolutely committed to being the best in his field. He was resolute in his plan and tenacious in his efforts. He was willing to stand behind his decisions, to take risks, and to be innovative. When he failed, he started over. All these characteristics define the word "determination."

Some people equate determination with a hard-nosed approach to life. Grandpa Fred, despite his spunk, was a simple, soft-spoken man, described as "earthy" and "real." Everyone adored him, from the humblest farmworker to the most exalted celebrity. He had the ability to make others feel good about themselves. His ten grand-children all share his amazing gift of determination. We are honored to call Fred Abruzzini "Grandpa."

EXERCISE

Rise and Shine

Are you determined to rise? Right now, are you in the top 10 percent of your field? Probably not. What can you do to propel yourself up to the next level? And the level after that? Do you study the careers of others who have been successful doing what you want to do? What risks should you consider? How can you be both relentless and ethical in your efforts? How can you maintain your stamina and determination? Determine your field of excellence, and then persist with determination. Let your true being shine brightly.

Sometimes people do
extraordinary things
because they have no other
choice. The rest of us use
determination.

My mom and dad met in high school in St. Helena, California. She was the head cheerleader. He was the captain of the football team. Both their families were vintners.

At the time, they were good friends, but Dad had a girlfriend and Mom danced the nights away with lots of different beaus. Dad graduated from high school and enlisted in the army, to become a paratrooper during World War II. Mom graduated and went to work at the Grapevine Inn, earning a reputation as the best waitress in Napa Valley. The war ended, Dad returned from the Aleutian Islands, and they ran into each other again. The chemistry clicked, and they became a pair. Mom was the baby of six children and, although Dad was the eldest in his family, he was scared to death to ask Pa, my Swiss-Italian maternal grandfather, for her hand in marriage.

Finally Dad mustered up the courage one day when Pa was working in his vegetable garden. Dad needn't have worried. Pa listened to Dad's nervous request for a marriage blessing and responded with something like, "Good, she's *your* problem now." A love story began.

Mom and Dad moved to the ranch where they would live their entire married life. Farming was difficult work, but they labored side by side to make ends meet. They started by growing apricots, peaches, pears, and walnuts, and slowly switched to grapes, cattle, and kids. Mom cooked, cleaned, gardened, and had babies. Dad plowed, planted, enjoyed Mom's cooking and beautiful gardens, and doted on his children.

We were all supposed to be boys. Farmers needed boys to help in the fields. But the first three babies were girls, all prenamed Gary Allen, but renamed Cynthia, Deborah, and Patricia. Unfazed, Mom and Dad announced that we girls could do anything that boys could. We believed them. We drove tractors, cultivated fields, sprayed, and picked fruit.

Then one wondrous February day, a boy was born. We named him Alfred after my dad. Several years later, we received another gift, our beloved David. Mom and Dad never *did* get a Gary Allen, but they were happy with their brood of five rambunctious kids. None of us went to preschool or kindergarten, both unavailable where we grew up, so, until we started grammar school, our family shared every meal. Mom and Dad shared three meals every day all their lives.

During our childhood they never left us overnight, and we had only occasional baby-sitters. They were devoted both to each other and to their children. It wasn't until their twenty-fifth anniversary that Mom and Dad took a trip alone.

I remember how my dad would be at the hardware store in town and call home to talk to his "girlfriend." Mom and Dad were a loving couple, a united front, a devoted union. My father thought my mother was the most gorgeous gal around. What she was wearing or whether her hair was fixed up or whether she gained or lost a few pounds never mattered. He idolized her.

My mom used to tell us how lucky we were to have such a handsome father. In Mom's eyes, as well as ours, Dad was king. He was strong and talented. He could fix anything, drive anything, and had a calm, sure way about him. When you were in Dad's presence, you felt absolutely safe.

My parents had worked out their places in life, and they helped each other and us be the best people possible. They were constantly doing special things for each other, holding hands, and laughing a lot. They made many plans for the days when they would travel together after all the children were raised and the farm handed over to one of us. They set an example of true adoration and devotion.

My mother's beautiful ranch gardens were the setting for the joyous weddings of four of us children. They were also the site for sixteen-year-old David's funeral, when devotion and love sustained all of us.

Then my dad developed a rare cancer. My mom was forced to watch the man she loved be devoured by a terrible killer that destroyed their hopes and dreams for a bright retirement together. Just before he died, my dad told my mother, "True love never dies." When he was gone, she clung to him, crying out in agony: "My hero! My hero! He is the greatest man who ever lived."

True love never dies, though sometimes it requires hard work. Through joy and pain, conflict and challenges, love and devotion are the glue that holds us together throughout our lives and beyond. The power of love is nothing less than life's most mystical force. No subject is discussed, pondered, debated, and misunderstood with such frequency and intensity. When we experience and share devotion, we alter our own lives and the lives of our descendants for all time.

EXERCISE

Devotion

☆ *Get a piece of paper, grab your partner, and do this devotion exercise together. If you don't have a partner, you get to play both roles!*

☆ *Write down five things your partner does that make you really happy. Then list five things you do that you think make your partner really happy. Now switch papers.*

☆ *Are you on the same wavelength? Discuss any differences. Then do at least three things on your partner's list as soon as possible. You will feel more loving and more loved.*

True love never dies.

Cynthia Brian

The Gift of
DIFFERENCES

Over a romantic dinner on our twenty-fifth wedding anniversary, I asked my husband, Brian, why he thought our marriage had lasted a quarter of a century. Without blinking, he responded, "Because we're different people."

We met at the funeral of a mutual friend, Richard, who died in a hang gliding accident. Shortly after the funeral, I traveled to Africa (one of the wonderful benefits of working for the airlines). When I returned, Brian invited me to a barbecue, but I didn't want to go because I had not seen my family in several weeks. Still, he persisted.

On our first official date, Brian was more than an hour late. His battered old truck had run out of gas, he said, and he had lost his keys. This should have been a warning signal (I am a very organized person), but I was young and naive and thought he was charming. However, when I learned that he was in dental school, I was somewhat unnerved. I had a terrible fear of dentists, because all of my twenty baby teeth had been pulled out as a child. Little did I know that Brian was equally put off by animals, while I already had a menagerie of critters. But we also found commonalities. We were both daring athletes and our first purchase together was a river raft for white-water rafting. Our subsequent gifts to one another included a coffee grinder, a crepe pan, books, and water skis, so we knew our futures were linked. We decided to get married as soon as he graduated from dental school.

At the altar, we hung two banners. One read, "You Are the Sunshine of My Life." The other said, "Together We Are Three: You, Me, and We!" These two maxims plus Father McGrath's motto of "Care, Share, and Be Fair," became mantras for our marriage. Now, as we look back over our years together, we realize that our shared core values have been our strength, but it's been the *differences* that put the zest in our relationship.

☆ Brian is a city slicker. I'm a farmer's daughter.

☆ He originally hoped I'd work in his dental office, but I was terrible at it and more of a menace than a help. He fired me…thank God.

☆ He thought he had married a sophisticated model, but, as the saying goes, "You can take the girl out of the country, but you can't take the country out of the girl." I'm much more comfortable in my barn-cleaning clothes than couturier fashions.

☆ Brian likes city noise. He can have the TV and stereo playing at the same time. I prefer silence or the sounds of birds, cows, crickets, and waterfalls.

☆ He is late for most occasions. I prefer to be on time.

☆ I'm extremely organized, know where everything is, and keep my car's gas tank full. Brian has papers and junk on every imaginable surface and rarely can find things like keys, wallet, sunglasses, or date book, and yes, his gas gauge is perpetually on empty.

☆ He takes an hour to get ready. I can shower and dress in under ten minutes. (Of course, sometimes it shows.)

☆ When I come home from work or an event, I immediately hang my clothes neatly in the closet or send them to the laundry. His clothes stay wherever they land. Ironically, he loves his clothes pressed perfectly, while I don't mind a few wrinkles.

☆ Brian loves to shop. Unlike many women, I was born without the shopping gene and hate it more than anything in the world.

☆ I'm an avid gardener. Brian doesn't know a flower from a weed.

☆ Brian is a fun-loving party animal in social situations. I don't mind skipping parties, as I adore solitude and am perfectly content on a porch swing watching the sunset.

☆ I'm decisive, opinionated, and unconcerned with what others think of me. Brian weighs every situation, is the peacemaker, and strives to please others.

Cynthia Brian

☆ Brian is mild mannered and soft spoken on the job. I am outrageous, loud, and assertive in my business life.
☆ He fixes teeth. I repair broken irrigation pipes and outdoor lighting, paint the walls, and smile for the camera.
☆ I'm an artist, whimsical and creative. He's a doctor, analytical and scientific.
☆ He's a pessimist; I'm an eternal optimist. If you were to ask him, he'd say he was a realist and I am an idealist. Optimist or idealist, my glass is always half full.
☆ We balance one another! Life is not dull.

You can see that we are very different creatures. After all these years, we still frustrate one another, but when we argue, we recognize that neither of us is right. We just have different ways of operating. We are truly like Venus and Mars, with me as Mars. And we are great together!

We recognize that we are both good, decent people. We both believe in honesty, integrity, love, diligence, children, earning a living, and all the various gifts in this book. We love to travel and have adventures, engage in athletic activities, eat great food, drink fine wine and strong coffee, read inspiring books, sit by the beach, go to movies and plays, and spend time with our children and special friends. We have learned how to avoid each other's hot buttons, and we work to support each other. On our wedding day, my Aunt Helen gave us well-known advice that has saved our relationship many times: "Whatever happens during the day, never go to bed angry." For a couple with plenty of differences, this has been excellent counsel. Practicing it can be difficult, and it doesn't always work, but it helps when we try.

We have learned to divvy up the details of daily life. Brian has accepted that the children and I love animals and adopt every stray creature. I have accepted his tardiness and absentmindedness. Because I hate to shop and he's happier when I look nice, he buys all my clothes, and I'm more than delighted to wear the fashions he brings home. He has great taste in clothing! He even does the grocery shopping, so I do the cooking. He has taken on the responsibility of being our "social director," making weekly dates with friends and one another, while I am the "travel specialist," planning and coordinating our major family outings and trips. Because he hates the minutiae of home ownership, I manage the household, pay the bills, and keep our lives organized and running smoothly. In other words, our differences have helped us have an interesting life together. We focus on our strengths, diminish our weaknesses, and complement one another. We are never bored.

Sometimes the biggest differences between you and others in your business or personal relationships can be great assets. Bringing different talents to the table can create powerful combinations.

Like myself, opposites attract because of their different energies. In his excellent book, *The 100 Absolutely Unbreakable Laws of Business Success,* Brian Tracy talks about the "Law of Attraction." Each of us is a living magnet, he says, and we attract the people, situations, and circumstances into our lives that are "in harmony with our dominant thoughts." In other words, "Whatever you want wants you."

Everything you attract into your life is a result of who you are. If you want to change your life, start by changing your thoughts, your visions, your strategies, or your comfort level. Recognize that just because you don't agree with a situation, person, or circumstance doesn't mean that you can't get along. Our differences add color, texture, and expression to the patterns of our lives. Can you imagine how monotonous this world would be if we all thought the same thoughts, wore the same clothing, and lived the same lives? Think about it. If we were all identical, the world would only need one person. Being different is our birthright. It is our differences that make life interesting and worth living.

After twenty-five years of marriage and a plethora of differences, I know that my husband and I are here on earth to teach each other about compassion, understanding, acceptance, and a multitude of other skills. We remember to care, share, and be fair, and to understand that we are two individuals creating a unique and sacred relationship. We are still the sunshine of one another's life, although we recognize the shadows. We look forward to the next twenty-five years of our differences.

In the happiest partnerships and communities, each individual maintains autonomy, yet is committed to being part of a team. This is rarely easy. It takes work and awareness and growth. But it is worth the effort. When you celebrate both your similarities and your differences, you celebrate life.

EXERCISE

We Are Not the Same

Take an inventory of your core values and preferences. Write down the habits of others that create the most harmony for you and the idiosyncrasies that drive you crazy. What are you willing to adjust to and live with? What will you not tolerate? If you have a partner, ask him or her to do the same thing. Compare and discuss your differences.

Together we are three: you, me, and we.

The Gift of
DIRECTION

The walls of my childhood bedroom were wallpapered with scenes of a magic land far, far away. I remember every detail of that world. There were windmills and carpets of tulips everywhere. Barking dogs chased frolicking children on a yellow background. The boys had pageboy bobs and the girls had long golden braids tied with blue ribbons. Everyone wore yellow wooden clogs. The boys boasted blue bloomers and short white or green jackets over striped shirts. The girls wore pink-and-white frocks with white aprons and white Dutch caps.

In one scene, a little girl was happily carrying two pails of water from a yoke over her shoulders and a duck waddled behind. In a corner, two jongens (boys) sailed their homemade boat in a pond while a windmill whirled in the background. My favorite scene was a boy yanking mightily on a giant rose-colored tulip as a young meisje (girl) tugged at his waist.

In my imagination, I lived in this sunny world. How I longed to visit this enchanting foreign land with its happy children, tulips, windmills, dikes, ducks, dogs, and wooden shoes. As I spent hours dreaming of my journey, I didn't realize that I was charting the direction of my life.

During my senior year in high school, I fulfilled my resolve to travel and experience other cultures. I applied for and was chosen as a teenage ambassador to Germany. For months I diligently studied German, but just five days before I was to leave, my assignment was changed. You guessed it! I was going to Holland, the land of my dreams and childhood wallpaper.

During eighteen months in Holland, I learned to speak fluent Dutch, picked many tulips, bought a pair of wooden clogs, and had my photo taken wearing authentic Dutch garb in real Dutch villages that looked exactly like my wallpaper. I felt as if I had come home.

Before writing this chapter, I climbed into my attic and dug out a frayed old roll of that wallpaper. As I gently traced the faded figures, I suddenly understood why I have saved it all my life. It was my road map for the direction I took, for a life filled with travel to exotic lands where I experienced new cultures, peoples, and languages. My journey began in my bedroom as a little girl many decades ago.

Every great achievement starts with a dream or a vision. Once you decide what you want to do, you can find a way to do it and the road to get there. Over the years, I've found that a passage from Lewis Carroll's *Alice's Adventures in Wonderland* has been enormously helpful, both to me and my students, in finding the right direction. Alice is lost and stops to ask directions from the Cheshire Cat.

"Would you tell me, please, which way I ought to go from here?"

"That depends a great deal on where you want to get to," said the Cat.

"I don't much care where —" said Alice.

"Then it doesn't matter which way you go," said the Cat.

"—so long as I get somewhere," Alice added as an explanation.

"Oh, you're sure to do that," said the Cat, "if you only walk long enough."

Whatever you truly expect, you deserve it and will usually get it. Confucius said, "A journey of a thousand miles begins with a single step." The difference between those who attain their dreams and those who fail is that first step. Aim toward your goal and step forward.

As you stride along, you will pass up a lot of people who are milling around aimlessly. Most people have no idea what they want or where they are going, so it is no wonder they wander. Of course, when they get nowhere, they complain that the world has given them a bad lot in life. Once they place blame outside themselves, they are doomed to shuffling in circles forever.

Take responsibility. Design your own life, and choose the direction that will put you on the road to achievement. Ask yourself, What? Who? When? Where? Why? and How? often. What do you want?

Who can help you? When do you want it? Where do you go to get it? Why is it necessary? How are you going to achieve it? My formula is to dream big dreams, write a plan and create a map, acquire the needed skills, go into action by taking the first step, and then do something every day to keep in motion. Finally, believe in yourself.

Obey your internal compass. Find the right path, and stay on it, no matter how bumpy it gets. Take occasional side trips when you need a change of scenery; the adventures will take you up hills, through rivers, across deserts, and underground. When you hit dead ends and roadblocks, make a detour. Keep going. Whether you seem to be moving quickly or slowly, keep going. Eventually you'll arrive at your destination, and the journey will have been worth the ride.

EXERCISE

Which Way Are You Going?

Get out your journal and write five questions:

☆ *What do I want to accomplish?*
☆ *Who do I want to be with me?*
☆ *Where do I want to end up?*
☆ *When do I want this to happen?*
☆ *How am I going to make it happen?*

Then write the answers to the questions. When you have no destination, then any road will do. But if you fix your direction and stick to your plan, failure is out of the question.

"We must either find a way, or make one."

—*Hannibal (who crossed the uncrossable Alps)*

The Gift of
DREAMS

I'm a dreamer. Always was, always will be. Dreaming is my magic carpet to happiness and success.

When I was a little girl, I dreamed that one day I would be a famous ball bouncer. My parents always told me that I had the ability to be anything I wanted to be, so I should reach for the stars.

Until we got a television, my favorite stars were county fair and circus performers. I'd seen many dazzling acts, but none specialized in bouncing balls. I figured I had hit on a brand-new idea for a star circus act. Every day I practiced bouncing balls—big balls, little balls, multiple balls. I especially remember being alone in our playroom with all the doors closed, talking to my "audience" while performing the spectacular feat of bouncing my tiny handball off the walls. I was the star, Cynthia, the Great Ball Bouncer!

This was the first hint of my dream of being in the entertainment profession. Then I saw the Disney movie, *The Parent Trap,* starring the British child idol, Hayley Mills. My dream changed, or perhaps expanded—I would become an actress. I begged for singing, dancing, and baton-twirling lessons. My sisters and I began performing at county fairs, Farm Bureau meetings, and school productions. I came alive when I was on stage.

One day, a talent scout for Disney was in the audience at a fair where we were doing a leapfrog dance routine. He came backstage and asked my parents to let us appear in an upcoming film, *Pollyanna,* starring Hayley Mills. My excitement was beyond belief. My dreams were coming true.

But my parents said, "No daughter of ours is going to be a Hollywood actress." They feared the limelight would corrupt an innocent mind. I remember being devastated that my parents felt that way about my dream. However, they were my parents and must know best. By then, I had started attending Catholic school and was completely entranced by the mystery and intelligence of the Holy Faith Sisters. So I decided that becoming a nun would be just as good as being an actress. An impressionable child, a new dream was born. Little did I know that being a nun involved strict vows.

By the time I turned eight, I had a beautiful reproduction of a Holy Faith habit, had mastered (in my mind) the Irish lilt, and often dressed up as a nun. The Sisters indulged me and even let me wear the habit to school a few days a year. I was sure all the other students thought I was a real nun.

I continued to perform in as many local activities as possible while studying and obtaining the best education available, still believing that the Sisterhood was my calling. After high school, I went to Ireland, to the convent where Sister Mary Germaine, my first-grade teacher, resided. I hadn't seen her since I was a little girl of seven, but the bond was still strong. We met in a small room and I told her of my plans to become a nun. After thoughtfully listening, she gently suggested that I spend more time thinking about God's calling for me, and thought God would be better served if I used my creative talents in a different vocation. At first I was crushed. Then I realized she was right. With my outspoken personality, I would have great difficulty keeping a vow of silence. And what about the vows of poverty, obedience, and chastity? Thank goodness Sister Germaine knew me better than I knew myself. She offered me her homemade black habit shawl as a memento of our friendship, which I still treasure.

So I became an actress instead of a nun. Real dreams don't die easily. I decided to follow my heart and go full steam ahead into the entertainment business. Sister Germaine became my biggest supporter and fan.

Dreams are the catalyst for our hearts' fulfillment. When we follow our hearts, magic unfolds. As the songs say, if you don't have a dream, how can you make one come true?

Although I was raised by the greatest parents on earth who supported all of us in pursuing our extracurricular activities, they did not encourage my dream of being an actor. They didn't have enough information to help me. And Hollywood was a frightening prospect to them. They suggested I ask Grandpa Abruzzini if he knew anyone who could help me, since he had befriended many Hollywood luminaries in the 1930s and 1940s at his winery. Unfortunately for me, it was now the 1970s. Too many decades had passed, and most of his contacts had died or were in no position to offer assistance. I was on my own.

My family followed my career with enthusiasm and pride, but I had to struggle to find the way to my "star." I made many mistakes along the way, from paying a lot of money for the wrong type of publicity photos and enrolling in unnecessary classes, to hiring unethical agents and wanting jobs so badly that I compromised my safety. Rejection was difficult in those early days as I tried to find people in the business to trust. Finally I understood that my instincts and values were my greatest guides. I trusted myself.

When I consult with the parents of talented children today, the first question I ask the mom or dad is, "What does your child want?" If the child wants to be an actor, I help, coach, and mentor. But if it is the parents who harbor a dream for their child, I advise against acting as a career. I believe with all my heart that whatever we dream, we can and will do if we want it enough. The best thing we can give our children is the gift of supporting their dreams.

There is no Prince Charming or Xena, Warrior Princess, coming to our rescue. We have to dream our own dreams and find our own way. My son, Justin, has wanted to follow in the footsteps of his grandfather, my dad, and become a farmer ever since he understood what a farmer was. He was ridiculed by fellow students who had no idea what they themselves wanted in life, but he never lost sight of his own dream. Today Justin is a top student in an agricultural college and is running a farm. He pursued his dream and created a life he loves. My daughter, Heather, has followed my footsteps somewhat and adores acting and animals. She has been in front of the camera since she was three days old and has raised and nurtured hundreds of critters, combining her two loves by doing a TV and radio segment with me called "Animal Cuts." I don't doubt that she'll win an Emmy or an Oscar some day. Whatever happens, I will be there to support

Justin's and Heather's dreams, even if those dreams should change. After all, my original dream was to be a ball bouncer!

Fantasy alone isn't enough to achieve your dreams. But it can energize you to acquire the skills and knowledge you need to make it all come true. This may take years, though, so be sure you know what you want. Then find a mentor or coach, someone who will support your efforts. Get rid of the naysayers in your life. Most of all, trust yourself and believe in your dream (or dreams!). Your dream may change or need refining. That's okay. Just keep dreaming. We don't know what we will achieve in life, but dreams are the place to start.

EXERCISE

Dare to Dream!

☆ *If you don't already know what your dream is, the best way to find out is to write down what you love in life. What are you really, really, really good at? What do you love to do? If you knew you couldn't fail, what would you try to do? List everything you can think of. If you didn't get paid a penny, what would you do or be just for the fun of it? What would make your heart sing, the hours pass, your heart swell with excitement and joy?*

☆ *This, dear friends, is your dream. Happiness is doing what you love and loving what you do.*

☆ *When you have identified your dream, write it down in the first person—present tense. Post copies everywhere. Tell everyone you know about it. Think about it all the time. Your dream is beginning.*

The bigger your dream,
the bigger your future will be.
Dream big!

Cynthia Brian

The Gift of

ENTHUSIASM

I am CEO (Chief Enthusiasm Officer) of my organizations and companies. It is difficult for me to contain my enthusiasm. I love life and enjoy it to the fullest. I think of failure as fertilizer, and fertilizer helps things grow. I delight in the process of personal growth and discoveries.

When I was in my early twenties, I planned a trip to Ireland to visit my pen pal, Nora. My friend, Father Patrick McGrath, who led the local youth program with me, asked me to visit his family in Limerick. He spoke so often of his parents and brothers and of their big farm that I was eager to meet everyone.

In Limerick, the McGrath family greeted me warmly. While we were having tea, Mrs. McGrath said, "Pat has told us you're bubbly like champagne. Now that we've met you, we understand how the two of you have accomplished so much with the local teenagers. You are like a ray of sunshine." I was honored and thanked her for the lovely compliment.

Father Patrick's brothers, Tom and Anthony, excused themselves to do the evening milking. I offered to help.

"If you don't mind getting dirty," Anthony said with his Irish lilt. "We can use all the extra hands available."

"Dirt?" I laughed. "I grew up covered in dirt. We called it 'clean dirt' on our farm. That's why I'm so healthy!" They handed me a pair of old rubber boots, and off we went to the barns. On our ranch in California we raised cattle, not dairy cows, but some neighbors had a few milking cows. I had helped them out a few times, but milking was not my strongest skill.

Tom gave me a few quick pointers on their cows. I sat down enthusiastically on the stool and grabbed a bucket. I put it under a cow, nestled up to her belly, and started milking. We were having a grand time, working side by side and talking about Father Pat as a child and his move to America. As we finished milking one cow, we'd move on to the next. I felt right at home.

I was so busy enjoying the process that I didn't notice when a stray cow backed up to me. She lifted her tail and defecated on my head, accompanying the act with a booming "Moo!" I was so startled that I jumped up screaming. The men stood frozen, not knowing what to do. Then I started laughing. That broke the ice, and we all laughed. I couldn't believe it. I had flown halfway around the world to visit my best friend's family, and his cow had just pooped on my head!

Tom and Anthony shooed the offensive cow away and led me back to the farmhouse. Excrement was dripping from my long, blonde curls, and the smell was—well, you can imagine. Mrs. McGrath took one look and cried, "Ah, boys, Bessie didn't take a fancy to a new girl in the barn, did she!" She began cleaning me up with a rag.

"Can I take a quick shower?" I asked. The brothers had invited me to a dance that evening.

"Ah, no, darling, we have no showers," she replied.

"May I have a bath, then, please?"

"Ah, no, it's not bathing day. We'll just warm up the tea kettle, and you'll be as grand as before."

Tom, Anthony, and I went to the dance and had an absolutely, outrageously wild, fun time. The fertilizer in my hair made me an instant success with all my new country friends. I could have chosen to be angry, frustrated, or depressed, or to go back to America to take my shower, but instead I chose to accept, be lively, and laugh!

The next day, I was right back milking, but I kept an eye on ol' Bessie. (Ultimately, she accepted me.) My cheerful reaction to this incident and my enthusiasm for more adventures on the farm endeared me to the McGrath family forever. I was adopted as one of the clan. Of course, you've never seen anyone anticipate "bathing day" more than this enthusiastic California girl who loved clean dirt!

The word "enthusiasm" comes from the Greek *en theos,* which means "God within" or "in God." When you are filled with enthusiasm, you radiate buoyancy, liveliness, and a sunny warmth. Enthusiasm helps you bounce back from and keep going after trying circumstances. Everyone has "God within," but some people suppress this bright star burning inside them. Aeschylus, the great Greek dramatist, proclaimed, "When a man is willing and eager, God joins in." Other people join in, too.

Let your own enthusiasm bubble over. Give yourself permission to risk being wild, crazy, playful, and fun loving. Laugh, be goofy, make mistakes, and fall down. All great accomplishments were made possible because someone was enthusiastic.

EXERCISE

I Am the Greatest!

You can do this exercise alone, but it is better with a small group. For a group, everyone joins hands and sends a positive squeeze around the group. If you're alone, clasp your hands overhead in a victory gesture. Then take a deep breath, throw your arms in the air, pound your chest, and yell, "I am the greatest!" *Do it three times, and really mean it. Feel the empowerment. From now on, after you finish each chapter, pound your chest and shout, "I am the* greatest!"

Ask yourself: What makes me feel enthusiastic? What puts a bounce in my step? What puts a smile on my face? Write down the first answers that come to your mind. Enthusiasm is your God-given gift.

Pop the cork, and let yourself bubble like champagne.
Become your own Chief Enthusiasm Officer!

The Gift of
EXERCISE

In grammar school, they called me a tomboy. I was usually the only girl chosen to play in the boys' ball games. In high school, I was labeled a jock and was named the second-best athlete in my class. (Carlene Lynch was number one!) In college, I advanced to scuba diving, surfing, skydiving, white-water rafting, and world-class skiing. Whether climbing trees or throwing a shot put, I preferred being outdoors and moving. Except for golf, there were few sports I didn't love. Needless to say, so much exercise kept my body in fantastic shape, my mind alert, and my spirit spunky.

As an adult, I've slowed down. I still occasionally enjoy playing on a coed softball team, snow skiing, water skiing, swimming, walking, snorkeling, and riding horses, but I tend to get most of my exercise in the garden. My husband thinks I should go to a gym, but gardening works my brain and muscles while feeding my soul. For me, no gym can come close.

Not long ago, I was getting a massage at a spa. The masseur kneading my sore back blurted out, "You sure are muscular! Are you a body builder?"

"No," I replied, "I'm a gardener."

At the turn of the century, our country was still an agrarian society. People got their exercise by working the fields. Today we are a technological society that relies on gyms to keep in shape. People sit all day. Then they exercise to extremes and end up with muscle strains, sprains, and every type of ache and pain.

When I must spend long hours writing, I develop what I call "computer butt." The lower extremities widen and it seems harder to get up and go outside. Here's a grim truth. Unless exercising is fun and makes you feel good, you're not going to do it for long, no matter how much you scold yourself. Yet your body, mind, and

Cynthia Brian

spirit all beg for regular exercise. Naturally, I have some tips on how to get all three kinds!

EXERCISE YOUR BODY

Our brains need oxygen to function. The best way to move oxygen is to set your heart pumping. But it's no fun if you have to tell yourself, "I must exercise."

Do you know what my exercise program is? No program! I play with my dogs, goats, and geese. I ride my horse and bale the hay, run with my kids, go on hikes in the hills, work in my garden, clean out barns, haul wood, take a swim, or vigorously clean my house. This is exercise. I walk up stairs instead of taking the escalator or elevator. I prune my trees and indulge in a wide variety of sports that I love.

My husband and I have been on the same coed softball team, "Nothing in Common," for over twelve years. Running those bases and being an outfielder keeps me hopping.

I've had my share of sports-related injuries. I had surgery on a knee when I fell down a crevice while rescuing a deer, and I shattered the bones in my right thumb in a skiing accident. But the benefits of exercise far outweigh the risks. My body belongs to me, and it is my responsibility to keep it in peak condition if I expect it to function the way I want it to.

Find something physical and pleasurable to do each day. You don't have to go to a gym or have a personal trainer to be in shape. Walking is terrific exercise. If power walking seems intimidating, take pleasure walks. Swim, bicycle, go horseback riding, vacuum! Give yourself permission to be fit in your own way.

EXERCISE YOUR MIND

Our greatest assets are our minds and imaginations. However, minds, like bodies, can't stay healthy on junk food. They need to be challenged and exercised on a daily basis.

Read books, magazines, and newspapers. Take classes. Study a foreign language. Get involved in a club. Advance your knowledge of technology. Sharpen your visualization skills. See films and plays. Go to museums and sports events. Discuss current issues with friends. Get off the couch and become part of the world. My goal is to learn something new every day, even if it is just a new word. (Keep a dictionary close at hand. It's fun to expand your vocabulary.)

And since you're exercising your mind more, give it plenty of soothing, restful sleep. Most adults need eight hours a day for their brain to function normally. In our society, the busier we become, the more we relegate sleep to the end of our priority list. Show your mind the same care you would an expensive new car. Cars can't run on empty, and neither can your mind. Rejuvenate yourself by regularly letting your mind rest and be at peace.

EXERCISE YOUR SPIRIT

Your body and mind are vessels for your spirit. Though we recognize the presence or absence of spirit, philosophers struggle to define it. Here is my attempt: "Spirit is our soul, the deep essence of who we are, the tone of our personality, the emanation of our basic substance." (You probably have some ideas of your own.)

If something is so hard to describe, how can we exercise it? We exercise our spirit by knowing who we are and what we need to replenish ourselves so we can be resilient, resourceful, and spunky.

I have always been a very gregarious, outgoing person. My life is busy and full of exciting people, places, and things. Others rarely understand that underneath my congenial personality is a very private, quiet soul. I need lots of time alone to exercise my spirit. I've found that a very effective way to do this is to be with nature. I prefer the sounds of birds and falling water and rustling leaves to any music made by man. My spirit sparkles when I am lying on a sandy beach, relishing the warm sunshine and pounding waves, or when I'm staring into a starry sky. Quiet is my guru. My meditations are best accomplished while I am weeding my garden, planting new vines, or collecting eggs from my chickens. This is when I am most able to feel a part of the universe and close to God. If I can't be in such places, I take a few moments to visualize them.

Cynthia Brian

Your spirit may respond to totally different stimuli—images of activity, speed, or energy, mighty symphonies, swirling colors, intense conversation. Exercise your spirit in a way that makes sense for you. You may need music or a church or people to talk with.

Having typed this page, I am now shutting down my computer and retreating to the garden to implement these suggestions and rejuvenate my body, mind, and spirit.

EXERCISE

Wild Thing

☆ *There is nothing better for the soul than shaking your body and dancing around like a wild person. Turn on your favorite music and dance to the beat. Let every part of your body move to the music. Become the music. Let loose. Be free. Rock out!*

☆ *Go outside and climb a hill. Run up and down some stairs until you run out of breath. Take your dog (or a borrowed pet) on a nature hike. You can both sniff the fresh smells as you romp through the woods or splash in the surf.*

☆ *Throw a ball and then you run and fetch it. Play soccer with a child. Fly a kite on a windy day. Jump in a lake, swim to shore, and shake your booty. Go out to your yard and attack that patch (or acre) of weeds that you've been meaning to clear. Then do a few cartwheels on your lawn or in the park. Who cares if you are not an athlete? You are having fun!*

☆ *Fall down in the snow and make snow angels. Indulge in a steam bath. Stick out your tongue. Blow bubbles and make funny faces. Be a wild thing!*

You have only one body, mind, and spirit in this lifetime. Treat them like the temples they are!

The Gift of
FAIRNESS

For the first seventeen years of my life, the twelve-mile road from our ranch to the nearest town never had a stop sign. Then one day when I was driving home from school, a stop sign suddenly sprang out of nowhere.

I didn't see it in time and rolled right through it. Of course, there was a cop right there. He pulled me over and nailed me. As he wrote the ticket, I kept repeating, "This isn't fair! There was never a stop sign there before!"

"Tell it to the judge," the officer said.

So I went to court. My sisters and I were very good drivers. We'd been driving farm vehicles on the ranch since we were seven. I prided myself on my ability, and I was out for fairness. I went into court prepared and presented my views passionately.

The judge listened patiently. Then he said something I've never forgotten and which has kept me in check many times over the years. He said, "I totally see your viewpoint, and I understand that you feel this ticket is unfair. Change is never easy. But what if you drove over the same bridge every day, and one day the bridge was open? Would you notice and stop your car in time? Or would you decide that opening the bridge wasn't fair and allow yourself to drown in the river? Don't take anything for granted. Life is not always fair. It just *is.*"

He suspended the ticket, and I never forgot his lesson.

My determination to find fairness in every situation was unfair. Life doesn't work like that. One of my TV viewers wrote, "The world is inherently unfair. We are not limitless and all-powerful. If we were, we wouldn't need God."

The inevitable incidents of unfairness shouldn't keep you from striving and thriving, always doing your best. Just leave room for error and Murphy's Law. Accept that the concept of fairness couldn't exist without unfairness in contrast, just as day couldn't exist without night. Something that is fair for one person may be unfair to another.

Treat others as you would like to be treated. Leave cynicism and pessimism to others. Love and build with your heart, being fair and realistic in all you do. You will be a richer person for generating such goodness.

EXERCISE

Do unto Others...

☆ *Set aside one day. From the moment you get up in the morning until you go to bed that night, treat others exactly the way that you would like to be treated.*

☆ *At bedtime, make notes of the difficulties you encountered. Was it hard? Or easy? Did you avoid the white lies that commonly smooth our paths? Or did you find yourself using them because, in a similar situation, you would have wanted support instead of criticism?*

☆ *Wait a day while you ponder the positive and negative aspects of your experience. Then share your experiences with a good friend or family member, and ask for their feedback.*

☆ *Could you spend another day following the Golden Rule? A week? The rest of your life?*

"Care. Share. Be fair."

—*Father Patrick McGrath*

The Gift of
FAITH

Ordinary colds and flus never touched me as a child, but when I contracted normal childhood diseases like measles, chicken pox, or mumps, I became deathly ill. After a mild bout of mumps on my right side when I was eleven, I was inflicted with a more serious case on my left. One morning my mom tried to wake me. I couldn't be roused. My temperature had soared, and the only sounds I made were moans. Our family doctor ran spinal taps and feared meningitis.

Unconscious, I was rushed to a children's hospital where more tests were run. The diagnosis was encephalitis, a disease causing swelling in the brain. I could not move a muscle, I could not talk, I could not open my eyes, but I could hear, and I heard the doctors' dire prediction. My prognosis was not promising. Of four similar cases in the U.S. that year, all the children had died. If I somehow survived, my parents should be prepared for severe brain damage and the probability that I would never walk, talk, or feed myself again. My fevers were too high, and my bodily responses were minimal.

My parents' grief was enormous, but they had faith. I was surrounded by love. Not for one instant did I lose faith that I would make a full and complete recovery. I felt my time to die had not come yet because I still had great things to accomplish.

Although I slipped in and out of consciousness, my faith and will to live manifested itself through positive visualizations. I visualized the sun shining and the birds singing. I saw myself riding bareback through the hills on my horse, Bambi, and rolling down the hills in barrels with my sisters, chased by barking dogs. I saw myself directing and acting in more plays and performing at county fairs. I felt the presence of my guardian angel and the protection of many angels supervising my struggle.

One day, after several weeks in the hospital, my eyes opened, and I whispered, "Have faith. I will live." It was a long recuperation, but

I made a full recovery. God spared me that time.

My faith in God, my faith in myself, my faith in my body's ability to heal itself, and my faith in my future contributions to the world kept me alive. Today I shut my eyes and can literally see, hear, feel, and smell everything in that hospital room. I was saved by faith, hope, and love. Fear can be a powerful motivator, but to live in fear is to live a slow death. It is better to live in faith.

☆ Faith can protect you from darkness and help you climb out of any hole.
☆ Faith helps you survive by giving you a companion—God.
☆ Faith gives you belief in yourself and the inner strength to survive.
☆ Faith blocks pain when you are under attack.
☆ Faith empowers, encourages, and leads to transcendent ecstasy.

We can exist without faith, but we can't live without it. I have enormous faith—in God, in myself, in the goodness and godliness of others.

We can accomplish great things when we have faith in something greater than ourselves. How often have you been told that you won't be able to accomplish something? If you have faith in the project and yourself, in your talents and ability to stick it out—*voilà!* You succeed. The size of your success is determined by the size of your belief.

EXERCISE

Creative Faith

☆ *Decide on something you want to create in your life. You may want to start with something that's easy for you to believe in, such as improved health.*

☆ *Set a clear goal of what you want to achieve. Using the present tense (as if your goal already has manifested), create a mental picture of your improved health. It is helpful to physically draw your image. Focus on this image several times a day so that your improved health becomes an integrated part of your life. Think about your goal in a positive light, see yourself receiving the energy needed to be healthy, and have faith that you can achieve this goal.*

 Continue to use this faith process until your goal becomes reality or until you adjust your goal to new circumstances.

You can dream, and you can plan,
but faith is the crucial catalyst
that creates the reality.

Cynthia Brian

The Gift of

FEEDBACK

The birth of my son, Justin, was difficult. Thirty-three hours of labor ending in a posterior delivery took a toll on the muscles in my back. When I became pregnant with Heather, my doctor prescribed weekly physical therapy with a woman named Barbara. Before long, Barbara and I realized we had more in common than a patient-therapist relationship. As our friendship deepened, we found it easy to express our joys, fears, and doubts without judgment.

We listened and offered each other feedback without finding fault or belittling one another. Opening up was challenging in the beginning. We all carry scars from the ridicule of others, but Barbara's analyses were different. She didn't blame or try to change me. She didn't even say, "This is what you should do." She offered comments only when asked. We both benefited so much that we made a pact to be each other's support system.

When my daughter was due, Barbara asked if she could be present during the birth to help in case of any difficulty. I was elated and welcomed her wisdom and expertise into the private sanctuary of birth. She massaged my back, helped my husband relax, and gave encouragement during labor, then witnessed the miracle of Heather arriving into this world. At that moment, Barbara and I knew we would be bonded forever.

During the next few years, we added feedback on business and success to our conversations about relationships and life longings. When she went back to school to become a family therapist, I said I was sure she'd be a huge success. She, in turn, praised my aptitude with interior design and supported my studies as I prepared for my certification exam. We still meet every two weeks and share the challenges of our lives. Our one rule is "No faultfinding, ever!"

Everything we share is completely confidential. We brainstorm, we write goals, we laugh, we cry. Nothing is outside the realm of our conversations. We've assisted one another through difficult business negotiations; shared resources, books, and tapes; and co-navigated one another's ships through tumultuous waters. Barbara and I have taken control of our lives and increased our self-confidence, self-acceptance, and communication skills by choosing to share in the gift of feedback.

Nourishing feedback from a trustworthy person is invaluable. Negative criticism, also known as faultfinding, ridicule, teasing, scorn, or condemnation, sends shivers down my back. Words affect our lives, and negative words, even when offered in a positive manner, can hurt our self-image. Whether cruel, mean-spirited words are said carelessly, maliciously, ignorantly, or innocently, they do damage. The foundation of positive feedback is the open expression of your fears, doubts, and insecurities without consequent rejection or ridicule. Through the process of feedback, you can see yourself reflected in the eyes of someone who believes in you. My family, friends, colleagues, clients, and listeners have given me much valuable input over the years, but I feel especially blessed and richer for Barbara's uncritical and supportive feedback.

EXERCISE

Getting Feedback

Is there at least one person in your life you can trust to give you honest feedback? Identify this person and suggest that the two of you become each other's support team. Ask to meet or talk on a regular basis. Set the rules: No faultfinding, ever. Only listen, encourage, and offer feedback when asked for it. It is a priceless gift.

In electronics, "feedback" is returning energy to the source. It's the same thing in life.

Cynthia Brian

The Gift of
FORGIVENESS

"But, *moth-er!*" Those of you who are parents have heard this many times. Before you give in to your teenager's request, are you sufficiently prepared to forgive the consequences?

While I was writing this book, I often tried out material on my weekly radio programs. This was a great way to fine-tune my stories and get reactions from listeners. One week Dr. Gerald Jampolsky, author of *Forgiveness, the Greatest Healer of All,* was scheduled to appear, and I hadn't yet written a chapter on the gift of forgiveness. As the date approached, I hoped a story would come to me, but none did. During our interview, I read a poem instead. Soon after, the chapter wrote itself.

My Christmas present to my husband that year was a weekend away for fun, sun, rest, relaxation, and romance during February when northern California weather is at its dreariest. My gift included airline tickets nonstop to Palm Springs, a rented convertible, a bottle of champagne, and two nights at a glorious French Chateau on Lake La Quinta. I made arrangements for our daughter to spend the weekend with friends, which upset her terribly. Heather felt we should trust her to stay at home alone. She had always been a very responsible young lady, and we should have confidence in her. We explained that there had been several local incidents where teens threw raucous parties while their parents were out of town. We didn't want Heather to find herself in an unpleasant situation she couldn't handle, despite her best intentions. Of course, she thought this was ridiculous.

Talks remained heated for a week. As she and I walked the lamb together at night, we discussed trust and responsibility. Mostly I just listened to her pleas. She told me what a very busy weekend she was planning while we were gone. She would need numerous changes of clothes for her various activities, plus she had to be home three times a day to feed the animals. "Why can't I just stay in my own home?" she implored. "You are locking me out of my life! I'll have to pack my entire closet." Her reasoning seemed sound, and I was truly considering her request. Happily for us, my intuition prevailed.

On that long-anticipated Friday in February, my husband and I locked the house and left for what we knew would be a magical weekend. Both of us were really ready for a rejuvenating retreat.

But our pleasure turned to anxiety when Heather phoned early the next morning. Between sobs, she explained that she was okay. However, an unauthorized party had taken place in our yard the previous night. About two hundred teenagers had arrived uninvited and started a bonfire. There was damage to the pond, the flower beds, the light fixtures, and the lawn. We were in shock and didn't know how to react. We tried to get all the facts, but quickly realized that there are always three sides to every story: yours, mine, and the truth.

The *good* news was that no one had been hurt and the animals were all fine. The bad news was that our private space had been invaded, and we had no idea what awaited us at home. We were angry with our daughter for revealing that we were away and furious with the disrespect of the local teenagers.

When we'd done everything we could do, Holly Harris, proprietor of Two Angels Inn, compassionately took me into the mansion's meditation room and led me in some relaxing yoga breathing and exercises. Because I believe that there is a reaction for every action, I kept wondering what the lesson in this frustrating event was supposed to be. I was too disappointed and angry to imagine anything positive.

But as we were leaving for the airport, Holly and her husband, Hap, suggested that perhaps this was going to be an exercise in forgiveness.

Forgiveness is extraordinarily difficult when you are hurt and angry, but I realized that they were right. I needed to forgive. However, I also needed to be a responsible parent. Back home, I telephoned as many parents as possible to inform them of the unauthorized, unchaperoned teen gathering that their child had attended. I met with the school principal and police to discuss arranging chaperoned teen parties in the future.

Heather took full responsibility for allowing the party to occur. She was genuinely remorseful and accepted the consequences of her actions, patiently enduring our restrictions while she paid off the damages. Because of this incident, the ramifications that followed, and the gift of forgiveness, our relationship has become stronger and more open.

Sometimes things happen that shock us, disturb us, anger us, and disappoint us. When our stomachs are in knots, it is a signal that forgiveness may be in order—not for the sake of the perpetrator, but for *us!* Forgiving doesn't mean that a heinous act is condoned. Many people I've talked to who have survived atrocities have said that only when they were able to forgive others were they able to get on with their own lives.

Time spent blaming and complaining is totally wasted. We are the winners, not the losers, when we forgive and let go because then we can also forgive ourselves. In this case, I was angry at myself for being naive, and I was disappointed in the behavior of the teens. But after I had taken all the steps I could to prevent a repetition of the event, it was time to heal the pain and move forward. Forgiveness is the greatest healer of all.

President Lincoln once pardoned a young man scheduled to be shot for desertion during the American Civil War. The young man, Roswell McIntyre, had been drafted into the cavalry and sent into battle with little training. He panicked and deserted. The generals wanted him executed, while the boy's mother pleaded for forgiveness. After thinking and praying on the matter, President Lincoln wrote, "I have observed that it never does a boy much good to shoot him."

In the Library of Congress, you can see the original document in Lincoln's own handwriting: "This letter will certify that Roswell McIntyre is to be readmitted into the New York Cavalry. When he serves out his required enlistment, he will be freed of any charges of desertion." Nearby is a placard: "This letter was taken from the body of Roswell McIntyre, who died at the battle of Little Five Forks,

Virginia." The boy was forgiven and got a second chance to fight bravely. He gave his life in that war.

Is it difficult for you to forgive? To let the past be past? It sure is for me. One of the loveliest customs I have read about occurs in the Babemba tribe of South Africa. When a person of the village has done something terribly wrong, he is taken to the center of the village. All the villagers form a circle around the guilty person and, one by one, tell him how much he is loved and remind him of all the good he has done in his life. His positive attributes, strengths, and kindness are recited at length. Finally, a joyous celebration takes place, and the outcast is forgiven and welcomed back into the tribe. *Wow!* The power of forgiveness restores peace to the family unit and the village.

We can't change the past, but we can create a joyous future through forgiveness.

EXERCISE

Burning Up

As hard as it can be to say "I'm sorry," it is harder still to forgive others for real or perceived hurts. Make a list of all the people you have hurt. At the bottom write, "I am truly sorry for any pain or suffering I have caused you. Please forgive me." (You may choose to share this message with some of them.)

Then make a list of everyone who has hurt you. Write at the bottom, "I forgive you." (This may be the most difficult thing you've ever done!) Finally, burn the second list. Release all your negativity as the flames erase your words. Let go, and get on with your life.

Forgive, forget, and forge ahead.

Cynthia Brian

The Gift of
FRIENDSHIP

When I was nine, my fourth grade teacher, Sister Mary McCarten, announced that a student in Ireland was looking for an American pen pal. I had no idea what a pen pal was, so I did not raise my hand. After class, Sister whispered to me that she thought I was the perfect match for this young Irish girl. "She's the eldest in her family, very bright and outgoing, and loves to have fun. I know you both very well, and I feel sure you will become fast friends."

Nora's letter arrived from Dublin about two weeks later—beautiful cursive handwriting formed with a fountain pen on fine, pale blue parchment paper. Fascinating foreign stamps decorated the envelope. Her words flowed off the page into my heart.

Everything in her existence was lovely. Her mum was Mary Daly and her dad was Brian Daly. "Nurse" looked after the lot. She was also nine and went to a convent school taught by the Holy Faith nuns, just as I did in California. I was fascinated by the idea that this Irish girl, so like me, lived in a strange land and probably spoke with a strange voice.

I wrote back, and soon the letters were flying across the ocean at amazing speed. Every day, when our postman, Mr. Ichikawa, came to the end of our lane, I was waiting to see if a letter had arrived from Ireland. As soon as I received a letter, I'd spend hours writing back, giving Nora all the news of California and life on the farm— my 4-H activities, taking care of chickens, driving tractors, picnics in the hills, and dressing up like Holy Faith nuns. We were becoming best friends. None of the nuns seemed surprised when, nine years later, Nora and I planned our first live get-together.

I had been chosen to be a teen ambassador to Holland, and Nora was being sent to work in Belgium. We decided to meet at the Antwerp train station. I was so nervous. What if I didn't recognize her? What if we couldn't find anything to talk about? What if, after all these years of writing, we really didn't like each other? Our eyes met across the tracks. Like in the movies, I ran toward her yelling *"Nora!"* in my loud, farm girl voice as she sang *"Cindy!"* in her beautiful Irish lilt.

Our meeting only endeared us more to one another. We were absolutely the best of friends, with many adventures awaiting us. I flew to Ireland to meet her parents and eight brothers and sisters, becoming an honorary Daly family member. We traveled the Irish countryside, went dancing, explored museums, and spent hours in girl talk. I actually introduced her to her future fiancé, Fergus, at a party. A few years later, the wedding date was set, and I was to be her maid of honor. As I was sitting in the Los Angeles airport awaiting my flight to Ireland, I was paged to take an emergency call. It was her mother, Mum Mary. Fergus had just been killed in a plane crash. Devastated, I continued my journey so I could stand beside my best friend at her fiancé's funeral instead of her wedding.

With this tragedy, our friendship deepened. Letters flowed across the eight thousand miles, and we visited every time I was in Europe. The years passed. She met another wonderful man, Per, married him, and became Nora Nordan, moving to Norway. I married that same year. We both had children, and we continued to share our joys and sorrows over the miles and years. Whenever possible, we got together, and sometimes talked on the phone.

More than three decades have passed. We still consider ourselves sisters and best friends. We have both saved all our letters and cards over the years and dream about creating a movie based on our friendship. Through good, bad, hard, and sad times, we have been there absolutely 100 percent for each other. I am still dazzled by her intelligence, compassion, beauty, and great humor. She still finds me the wild, crazy, enthusiastic energizer I always have been. Now we are e-mail pals, but still write proper paper letters from time to time. The world changes, technology advances, and we remain best friends. I am a proud honorary Irish woman because of my friendship with Nora Catherine Daly Nordan. Thank you, pen pal!

Nora taught me the value of having and being a true friend. Friendship should not be measured in quantity, but in quality. We may have many wonderful and caring acquaintances, but only a few true friends. I know in the depths of my spirit that, no matter what happened to me or my family, Nora would be there for me in every way possible. And she knows she can count on me for anything.

Real friendship is not about competition. It offers mutual respect, admiration, trust, joy, kindness, and support. A friend does not judge, but will tell the truth when necessary, even if it's painful. A true friend loves you unconditionally, despite all your flaws, but is never a "yes" person.

Stop for a moment and think about the people in your life. Do you have true friends, people you trust, people you can count on through thick and thin, no matter what circumstances and distances separate you? Do you have people in your life who love you just the way you are while supporting you in your growth, changes, and advancements?

To keep and deepen your friendships, be a true and honest friend. You can't buy friendship. You have to earn it. When you have a real friend, you have the greatest gift in the world.

EXERCISE

Friends Forever

Here are a few things you can do to be a friend forever:

☆ *Listen with your heart. Really hear what your friend says and know how to read between the lines.*

☆ *When a friend is having a bad day, do something special to show you care. Write a note, send flowers, bake cookies, offer a back rub.*

☆ *Take time to be a good friend—time is the most precious and difficult thing to give.*

☆ Say "no" when you mean no and "yes" when you mean yes. Don't be wishy-washy.

☆ Offer advice only when your friend can benefit from it.

☆ Say "please," "thank you," and "I treasure you" often.

☆ Be there when you are needed most.

☆ Show up the rest of the time too.

☆ Never take advantage of a situation.

☆ Give true friendship priority in your life.

Oprah Winfrey says, "Lots of people want to ride in the limo with you, but what you want is someone who will take the bus with you when the limo breaks down." Are you there for your friends when they need you?

One true friend will make life worth living. Find a friend today.

Earn a friend by being a friend.

Cynthia Brian

The Gift of
FUN

Do you remember the Beach Boys' song from the 1960s: "She'll have fun, fun, fun, till her daddy takes the T-Bird away!" Since we never had a T-Bird, I decided at an early age just to have fun, fun, fun until the end of my days. If you ask people what they do for fun, many will mention attending sporting events, concerts, or movies, or going to a wild party. Perhaps they love eating out, dancing, riding horses, or playing tennis. These are all great answers. Fun is whatever you want it to be. For me, fun was being pregnant. Even though I had suffered through thirty-three hours of labor with my first child, Justin, my nine months of pregnancy had been great fun. The thought of repeating the birthing ordeal was not enticing, but the sheer delight of being pregnant helped me overcome my worst fears when facing a second delivery.

The truth is, I loved being pregnant! I had never felt more alive, vibrant, and creative. I looked forward to every moment, to see how my body was changing, and to feel the minute movements of the child growing within me. Of course, in the days when I was having children, modeling and pregnancy didn't go together. This was before pregnant stars beamed from every magazine cover, pregnant fashion models strutted on the runway, and TV shows rewrote their scripts to incorporate a pregnancy in the plot.

Fortunately for me, I didn't "show" immediately. Because I was in excellent health, I continued taking amusing modeling and acting assignments. When I was several months pregnant with my second child, Heather, I was hired to play three famous movie stars: Marilyn Monroe, Rita Hayworth, and Hedy Lamarr. The client had booked three similar models (plus me), then provided elegant matching gowns, wigs, and makeup artists so we'd look like quadruplets of each of these fabled celebrities.

I wasn't sure how to keep my secret from my modeling colleagues, but I feigned modesty and squeezed into my costumes behind closed doors. The shoot was a fantastic success, the photos were gorgeous, and no one guessed I was pregnant.

The next day, I literally couldn't get into my jeans. The baby had repositioned herself, and now I looked very pregnant. When I turned in my voucher from the modeling job to get paid, my agent kept looking back and forth between the glamour photos of a few days before and my current figure. "What happened to you?" she asked incredulously.

For the next four months, I engaged in energetic nest building. I made curtains, bed coverings, and baby clothes. I wallpapered the baby's room. I did fun things with Justin, going to the park, swinging on the tire, building forts and sandcastles, and having picnics in the poppy-covered hills. We took mother-child classes and water aerobics together. Justin helped me plant the vegetable garden and teach our dog, Nefertiti, new tricks. My husband took long walks with me in the evening, while Justin rode his Big Wheels alongside. This was a time of pure, simple pleasures, fun to the very best degree.

A few hours after Heather was born, I received a telephone call at the hospital from one of the other three models in the quadruplet shoot. A television series we had done in Europe ten months before was premiering in five minutes. "Turn on your TV," she said excitedly. "You are about to debut!" Brian, my husband, found the right channel. Sure enough, there I was, a bright, thin model, extolling the sights of the Mediterranean.

A nurse walked in and asked how I was doing. "Oh, I'm great," I replied. "I'm watching myself on TV."

She glanced at the woman on the television screen, gave me a knowing look, and patted my knee sympathetically. Obviously, she figured I was delusional. "Don't worry, honey. You'll be yourself again in the morning."

Talk about letting go of ridicule!

After she left, Brian and I laughed hysterically. This story has

Cynthia Brian

become a classic in our circle of friends. Whenever anyone mentions fun, my pregnancy adventures are retold with great delight and enjoyment.

Fun is essential for excellent physical, mental, and emotional health. Finding amusement in simple activities like hobbies, sports, work, or daily duties enhances our immune systems and brightens our spirits.

Fun is letting go of the fear of ridicule. Fun is just being in the moment and enjoying everything around you. My students always brighten when I announce the rules in my classroom: "You must smile, you must have fun, and you must be wild and crazy!" Everyone knows how to play, but, as adults, we often forget the abandon of our childhood recreations. Fun and frolic make us alive. Fun is the brain's way of reframing the seriousness of a situation. Fun is our path to being authentic and real.

Have you ever been at a solemn or dignified event, and something triggered a sense of pleasure or joy? How we interpret the moment determines our experience of the world. The most creative and happy people are those who can find some pleasure in every situation. Build fun into your business and your everyday life. It's not just something to do "after work." Let fun infuse everything you do.

Gold Stars

It's time for some fun! Remember how your teacher gave you gold stars when you achieved a goal? Get a box of stars at a stationery store. I want you to stick a star on your calendar every day that you enjoy the simple pleasures of life.

The opportunities for fun are limitless. Read a comic book, climb a tree, play croquet, dress up in a costume, kick a beanbag around, wear a funny hat. Be a star: Take a video of yourself singing, dancing, or being silly. Frolic in sprinklers, play hide and seek, be a child for an hour. Rita Mae Brown says, "I finally figured out the only reason to be alive is to enjoy life." It's okay if you have a day or two without a star, but make fun a part of your daily routine. Then count all your gold stars!

Enjoy the small things in life every day.
One day, you may realize that they were the big things.

Cynthia Brian

The Gift of
GENEROSITY

A newspaper article that caught my eye in the early 1990s led to an extraordinary experience. It described an idealistic mother and daughter who were disturbed by the lack of meaningful films for and about women. (At the time, statistics compiled by the SAG/AFTRA unions indicated that 75 percent of all acting jobs went to men.) These two women decided to mortgage their homes and join assets to start a repertory film production company that would provide strong roles for actresses and ongoing work for both cast and crew. They were looking for additional funding to launch their company.

Their infectious passion and enthusiasm made me reach for my checkbook. Their generosity of spirit set these women apart from the usual Hollywood crowd of money mongers that I knew all too well. I had long been a promoter of female writers and producers and of films depicting women as heroes and role models. Until women take a larger part in writing, producing, and financing films, substantial roles will continue to be limited for women.

That year had been a great acting year for me, and, being a major supporter of people who follow their hearts and live their dreams, I sent the biggest check I could afford, along with a note saying, "I want to be the first person who congratulates you on your leap of faith. I believe in you, and I am putting my money where my mouth is."

Keep in mind, I did not know these women. I sent the money based on a gut instinct that they were trustworthy and deserving. My accountant assured me this was a stupid thing to do, but I didn't care.

About five years later, their company completed its first film. I received an unexpected check repaying me with interest, along with a thank-you note for being the first to believe and invest in their dream. My generosity, they said, had made a difference (I admit a very small one compared to the average film budget) in creating a new reality.

That's not the end of the story. During the next decade, I went on to produce television and radio shows championing my belief that people should follow their hearts, live their dreams, and enjoy a better tomorrow. I also founded a nonprofit corporation called Be the Star You Are!—a media library dedicated to collecting, promoting, and providing positive, uplifting, and life-enhancing books, audiotapes and videotapes, art, and music to groups in need of hope and inspiration. Public service announcements for this charity asked for contributions. A few weeks later, we received a check from one of the women film producers with a note: "Dear Cynthia, I want you to know I believe in you and your endeavors! Here's to a happy, fulfilling year to you, your family, and Be the Star You Are!"

You see! When we act from our hearts, miracles can unfold, sometimes even ten years later! How many times have you heard, "What goes around comes around"?

My literary agent once lost his wallet on a train. When he got home, he realized it was gone and went back to the train station to retrace his steps. He was more concerned about the considerable inconvenience and expense of replacing his driving license, credit cards, and door locks than losing the money. There was no sign of the wallet.

He trudged home, frustrated and depressed. The phone rang. A woman told him she had found his wallet and wanted to return it. With relief and surprise, he left his family to guard their home (just in case it was a scam) and drove to the woman's home. She handed him his wallet. Nothing was missing. He tried to give her a reward, but she refused. He asked if he could take her and her husband to dinner. Again, she refused. "You can repay me by helping someone else when you have a chance to."

Two days later, my agent was eating lunch in a busy downtown park. Amid the hurrying feet, he noticed a lady's wallet on the ground. He was able to trace the very despondent owner and repay the generosity that had been shown to him.

Generosity freely given is rarely forgotten. The film producers did not forget the gift I gave them. When they saw a way to reciprocate, they did. But generosity doesn't require direct repayment to the giver. My agent had felt so blessed by the return of his wallet that he was extra alert, looking for an opportunity to help someone else. He found it.

To receive joy, we must first give it away. When you are generous with your love, wealth, time, and heart, you will discover that you are being generous to yourself. Yes, "what goes around comes around." Sometimes tenfold. Sometimes in ways we don't know.

EXERCISE

Generous Soul

When was the last time you gave spontaneously to something or someone you believed in? Close your eyes and ask yourself, "Who needs me, and how can I be of help?" What is needed most? Money, time, a hug, a good listener, a shoulder to cry on?

Once you have decided who needs your help, take action. Perhaps a neighbor has been ill and could use a helping hand. If you have a favorite charity, volunteer your time or make a donation. If there is a relationship that you would like to rekindle, pick up the phone, order flowers, or send a gracious note. If you haven't hugged or kissed a loved one recently, don't let another minute go by without expressing your love. The glow of doing a good deed will keep your star shining brightly.

It is more blessed to give than to receive.
(Acts 20:35)
The generous soul shall be made fat.
(Proverbs 10:25)

The Gift of
GIVING

Dogs were always a big part of growing up on the farm. My dad loved dogs, and most of the dogs were his, except for Skippy and Bullet. They were definitely my dogs.

My dad and his dog Raider were inseparable. Raider helped navigate the jeep and followed Dad as he plowed the vineyards on the tractor. Raider was the last dog to roam the hills and vineyards with Dad. After many faithful years, Raider died. Soon after, following a powerful battle with cancer, Dad also died. The date was December 8.

Our entire family was in mourning for my dad, but my immediate concern was for my mother. She and my father had been married almost forty-five years. They had been together since high school, and now Mom was completely alone on a big ranch, miles from anywhere, and her protectors, Dad and Raider, were gone.

I decided that a new puppy would be perfect for Mom, both for companionship and protection. I heard about a woman who was trying to find homes for some chow chow puppies. Ironically, they had been born on Dad's birthday in November, and I felt one would be the perfect Christmas gift for Mom.

On Christmas Eve, I met a gorgeous little female fur ball and instantly fell in love with her. She looked exactly like a cinnamon-colored teddy bear and was about the same size, but with a fiercely wagging tail. (Dogs can express more with their tails in seconds than most people can express with their tongues in hours!) I was really excited. Then a thought hit me. Maybe I should let Mom know about her gift in advance so she could prepare for this beautiful creature. So on Christmas Eve, I rang Mom and told her that we had a gorgeous gift for her—a new puppy. Instead of the joy and excitement I expected, Mom was furious. "How dare you try to replace your father with a dog! I don't need a dog to clean up after.

Don't you dare bring me a dog. How could you be so cruel?"

I was flabbergasted. Of course I knew how terribly sad Mom was. I was grief stricken too. I had truly thought I was helping, but my gift was absolutely wrong.

What would I do now? Here was this wondrous puppy licking my face, and it had no home. It was Christmas Eve, and I couldn't and wouldn't send her back. So I made a parental decision. Our family dog, Nefertiti, had died two years earlier at the age of sixteen. We hadn't looked for a new dog because we weren't quite over losing her. But the decision was easy. My kids, Justin and Heather, had been completely distraught over the death of my dad, their Papa. I felt that having a new life to care for might help to mend their broken hearts.

As a child, I had always wanted to wake up Christmas morning and find a puppy under the tree. My childhood dream was about to become a reality for my own children. Just before dawn, I brought in a sleeping puppy from her special hiding place in the shed. I wrapped her small cage in gauzy fabric and gently put her under the Christmas tree. Then I woke up the kids and excitedly announced that I had just heard reindeer on the roof. "We had better go to see if Santa has come!"

Quickly, we put on our bathrobes and padded downstairs. Sure enough, Santa had eaten the cookies, drunk the milk, and taken the carrots for his reindeer. Left behind was a bouncing package, tied with a big red ribbon and a tag that said, "Open Me First!"

The kids tore into the box, and out jumped the greatest Christmas gift ever!

"It's a bear!" shrieked Heather.

"No, it's a bear dog," said Justin as the puppy jumped and squirmed and licked and barked. Heather suggested naming her "Jingle Bear," and everyone agreed. Now we had a new dog, and the light of love that had been dimmed by death began to shine again.

We opened all our gifts, gave thanks for such a wonderful Christmas, and loaded the car to go to the ranch for our traditional

Christmas dinner with the rest of our clan. Then I realized that we shouldn't leave Jingle Bear alone. With much trepidation, I telephoned Mom for permission to bring her. Mom surprised me. "Sure, go ahead and bring her," she said pleasantly. "Your sisters are bringing their dogs too."

When we got to the ranch, Jingle Bear rocketed out of the car and made a mad dash toward Mom. "Oh my puppy, my puppy," she cried, holding her in her arms. I looked at Mom in horror.

"No, Mom," I tried to explain, "that's Justin's and Heather's puppy. Santa brought her this morning to help the kids get through this sad time in their lives." I took my mom in the next room to talk. "I didn't realize she'd be so cute," Mom said. "I'm sorry I told you I didn't want a dog. I really want her now. Please let me have her."

What was I going to do? What a mess!

I immediately called the owner of Jingle Bear's mother to find out whether I could rescue another puppy. All the cinnamon chows were spoken for, she said, but there was one black female left. "I'll take her!" I said. I was saved from the agony of choosing between my children and my mother.

So that's how Mom got a dog and we all got a second Christmas Bear. Mom named her black puppy "Bear," and she's been a wonderful gift of love, companionship, and protection. She guards the ranch like any good bear would, and won't let anyone out of their car or truck unless Mom gives her the command. Bear recognizes the sounds of all the kids' and grandkids' vehicles, and welcomes them with a wagging her tail. Jingle Bear is equally devoted to our children and guarding our household. The Bears didn't replace Dad. Nothing ever could. But they restored joy on a sad Christmas, helping to heal the holes in our hearts. That's the great thing about dogs. They give such comfort because they never ask why we're sad. They just warm our hearts and bring us joy.

How many times have you been told that it's better to give than receive? Giving is a virtue that was deeply instilled in us as children. My family never went anywhere without bringing a gift of fruit, vegetables, fresh eggs, or wine to our hosts. Regular donations were made to our church and various charities. Offering friendship and help to others in need was an important part of our upbringing.

However, I learned—or relearned—one important lesson that Christmas. Live animals are a terrible gift unless they are wanted by the receiver. I *should* have known this already. Most of the animals in our menagerie that we have rescued were once gifts to someone who didn't want them or couldn't care for them.

Our Christmas Bears give us unconditional love, protection, and companionship, and we generously receive their love and reciprocate by providing food, great homes, land to roam on, and lots of hugs. At Easter, Justin rescued another pup who's named Wolf. But that's another story.

EXERCISE

Giving and Receiving

Take a moment to remember your feelings when you gave a wonderful present to someone or made a donation to a favorite charity. (You may want to record your feelings in your journal.)

Don't forget that another aspect of generosity is learning to receive graciously and gratefully. How do you feel when you receive a gift? How do you react? The next time a friend or loved one asks what you'd like as a gift, don't respond, "Oh, nothing." Allow others to feel good about themselves by giving to you. Learn to accept appreciatively and to enjoy the spirit of the gift. Sometimes the way you receive can be the greatest gift of generosity.

We make a living by what we get.
We make a life by what we give.

The Gift of

GRACE

Growing up, I often heard people talk about grace, but I didn't know exactly what it meant. Our family always said grace at mealtimes. My sisters and I were called graceful dancers, and my mom was always referred to as a gracious hostess; however, it wasn't until I swam with dolphins that I truly understood the meaning of grace.

One Thanksgiving, my teenage daughter, Heather, and I took a mother-daughter trip to Key West, Florida, and booked a trip with a delightful lady named Captain Sheri on her Wild about Dolphins expedition in the Gulf of Mexico. In the weeks before we arrived, few boats had had any luck contacting dolphins because of hurricanes and storms. But as we left the marina in Sheri's unnamed craft, we were jubilant with anticipation.

A famous artist, Carlos Aleman, had covered the sides of her boat with beautiful paintings of dolphins, but, despite many suggestions, Captain Sheri was still at a loss for a name. Immediately, my mind began working. "Angels of the Sea!" I cried. Many authors I had read or interviewed had considered dolphins to have angelic qualities.

A variety of music from opera to rock was played to attract the bottlenose dolphins. Sheri explained that they enjoy certain sounds and respond favorably to music. I called out to these "angels," hoping they would appear near our boat. After several hours of music and searching, all we had encountered were flying fish, a shark, two frigate birds, and a turtle.

We were getting a bit discouraged. Then Sheri played a recording that instantly sent tingles up my spine—the calls of dolphins and whales followed by the most spectacular rendition of "Amazing Grace" that I had ever heard. Within seconds, Heather shouted, "Look! Here they are!" First one, then two, then three beautiful, magical, bottlenose dolphins surfaced and danced at our stern.

Somehow, we all knew that Heather, with her sixth sense for the animal kingdom, would be the first to see the dolphins.

Their movements were elegant, and even the most cynical among us was touched. Words bubbled from the deepest part of my soul. "Sheri," I whispered, "I *know* the name the dolphins want for your boat. It's 'Amazing Grace.'"

Tears came to her eyes. "My dog died last month," she told me, "and we bought this CD for his final good-bye. As we were spreading his ashes in the ocean, one of the pregnant dolphins gave birth, and we named the little dolphin Tasha after my dog. I just realized, that's Tasha and her mother who are playing with us now, along with Tasha's baby-sitter." (Sheri explained that each dolphin mother and baby were usually accompanied by another female who acted as baby-sitter and godmother.)

Because there were three dolphins, Captain Sheri invited three of us—Heather, myself, and a German tourist—to swim with them.

The dolphins' grace was indescribable; their spirit was pure and free. That day was a new high for Heather and me. We felt that we were among angels. For the first time in my life, I fully understood the dictionary definition of grace: "divine love and protection bestowed freely upon mankind; sanctity, holiness, a gift and virtue from God, to be honored, to find favor with, good will, prayer, play, and forgiveness."

We were blessed that day as we frolicked in the sea. I learned from the dolphins that we are all capable of experiencing amazing grace. Angels are always around us, helping us soar if we just take the time to notice them.

Soon after, Captain Sheri wrote me that she had decided to name her boat *Amazing Grace*.

Every day offers us a new beginning. The gifts of grace can be found in the details of ordinary life when we open our eyes and welcome beauty into our hearts. Enjoy the innocence of a child's giggle, the purring of a cat, the sounds of the wind through the park. Watch birds bathing in a fountain or smell the fragrance of a hot cinnamon bun. There is a sacredness and sanctity in nature that beckons us to stop, listen, and contemplate. Grace is remembering that we are sacred beings and that the entire universe is connected and deserving of respect and honor.

EXERCISE

Amazing Grace

Take a day off! Go someplace with moving water—a beach, lake, or stream. If you're in a desert, use your imagination. Write down five things that make you truly happy and five things that have really upset you recently.

Now picture complete peace. Welcome any inner guidance that comes to you. Let the waves or the rapids or the desert winds take away your pain and refresh you. Imagine you are the perfect being you were born to be, and feel yourself filling with grace...amazing!

Every day brings opportunities for grace—
if you are open to them.

The Gift of
GRATITUDE

It was the day before Thanksgiving, and a big, fat turkey was strutting around our barnyard, gobbling up the feed we threw to her. "Isn't Gracias lucky she lives with us?" my daughter, Heather, commented. "Otherwise, she'd be someone's Thanksgiving dinner." Gracias was our beautiful Bronze turkey that we had raised from a baby. She adored us.

"All our animals are lucky," replied my son, Justin. "They came to us, and we gave them a good home. Our animals are to play with, not to eat."

When the entire menagerie was fed, we all climbed in the car and drove to the supermarket to buy the food for our Thanksgiving dinner. Our family has a tradition of sharing the shopping and cooking for our feast so everyone feels they have contributed to the ceremony. We decorate our home with cornstalks, different-colored pumpkins, gourds, and Indian corn from our garden and the kids' drawings of turkeys and pilgrims. Thanksgiving is a time of giving thanks for all our blessings, our education, our jobs, our health, our home, and our family.

At the supermarket, we bought a twenty-five-pound turkey and the other ingredients we'd need for our meal. All the way home, Heather and Justin were singing, joyfully looking forward to this very special family time. But when we pulled into our driveway, we realized something was terribly wrong. The dogs were barking crazily, people were yelling, and we could hear shrieks from the barnyard at the top of the hill.

We leaped from the car and ran as fast as we could up the hill. What we saw stopped us in our tracks. The torn bodies of our animals were scattered everywhere. Some were still writhing and moaning.

Our neighbor's vicious dog stood in their midst. He had obviously escaped his cage and dug under our fences. Near his blood-spattered feet lay several chickens and our favorite mother duck. He stared at us sullenly, Gracias writhing in his mouth. We pried his teeth apart, but we were too late. Within minutes, she died in the arms of the children. We all began to sob and wail, our hearts broken by this tragedy.

Then anger set in. We wanted to kill this malicious monster who had murdered so many of our pets. But that would make us murderers too. We carefully pulled ourselves together. The neighbors, who were as sad as we were, arrived to retrieve their killer dog, promising never to let him escape again. We set to burying the dead.

I wondered whether this mayhem had been a sign from God that Gracias was meant to be a Thanksgiving turkey. We put our store-bought turkey in the freezer. As we began the sad task of plucking, cleaning, and preparing Gracias for the table, we said a few prayers and gave thanks for the joy that she had brought into our lives.

Although it began so disastrously, we will always remember that Thanksgiving as one of the most special days we have spent together as a family. We learned the value of life and how quickly it can be taken away. We learned to appreciate each other and all living creatures. We felt grateful for our ability, even in the face of sadness, to forgive the neighbors' dog for doing what came naturally to him.

The next day, we went to work making our pens and barnyard safer and sturdier. We dug trenches two feet deep and filled them with cement as a footing for a chain-link fence, topped by an electric barricade. It was several years before we were brave enough to raise another turkey. Because of the lessons we learned and the actions we took on that Thanksgiving so many years ago, our new turkey will live out his years as a barnyard pet.

Be grateful for what you have. When we are grateful, we are rewarded with a sense of honor and personal strength. Say "thank you" for every gift you receive, positive or negative. Life may be giving you a lesson in appreciation. Learn to be grateful for everything. Gratitude exalts the heart.

Say "Thank You"

During the next hour, say a sincere "thank you" to everyone who does anything nice for you, your family, your friends, or the world. Write one thank-you note and mail it.

The more gratitude you show in life,
the more you will have to be grateful for.

The Gift of

GROWTH

"Kids don't come with a manual," I told my apprehensive teenage daughter. Heather and I were driving home from a modeling assignment, and she had just confided her concern about taking on parenthood when she becomes an adult. "What if I make a mistake, and my kids don't turn out to be good kids?" she asked.

"We just do the best job we can with the tools we have," I said. "As parents, we need to listen, to grow with our children, and to be there for them." I told her how fortunate I had been to have wonderful role models in my parents and how I was trying to be a positive role model for her and her brother.

Taking a deep breath, I asked her what she had learned so far from my example as a mom. Several blocks went by in silence. Finally she said, "I've learned that a woman can be a working mom, have a fun career, be a good parent and wife, and make a difference in the world." Wow!

Heather's worry about the future led to a wonderful discussion about personal growth—spiritual, emotional, mental, and financial. Heather is not alone in wondering how we can be good parents, providing stability for our children and teaching by example, not by commands. How, instead of pointing out their mistakes and failures, can we convince our children that a happy life is full of trial and error, constantly offering new choices and new opportunities?

My garden has taught me that people are much like plants. If I am not constantly vigilant, the weeds take over. They sprout up everywhere, choking out the flowers. But when I pay attention and weed my garden, the flowers reach for the sun and grow into magnificent beauties.

Life is like that. Unless we make a conscious effort to eradicate the negative stuff, it can take over and strangle our personalities. But

Cynthia Brian

when we strive to grow, stretch, and reach for the sun, we face a lot of hard work to keep the weeds out.

So how do we grow strong? How do we take charge of the garden of our life and survive droughts and weeds? The best way is to take a small first step. A saying I repeat to myself often is: "By the yard, it's hard; by the inch, it's a cinch!" I've learned that if I want to go the mile in style, I have to start small, growing and changing a little at a time. Of course, sometimes I stumble. But I have another favorite saying: "Failure is fertilizer!" If we can learn from our mistakes and setbacks, then they really weren't failures, just compost for our life.

For me, growing has always included studying books and audiotapes on personal growth and then trying some of the ideas I've learned from them. I read the autobiographies of successful people to see how they reached their goals. (Why reinvent the wheel when someone else has already mounted it on the wheelbarrow?) Many studies correlate success with the number of books a person reads. Read a positive, life-enhancing book often, and try out the strategies; you will soon see a significant change in your life.

Growth is transforming, like a flower opening to the sunshine. I always feel closest to my Creator while I am in the garden. When I am stuck and need fresh concepts, the garden nourishes my parched mind and soul.

One of the easiest ways to grow your knowledge or skills is to take a class. Figure out where you are lacking and what would enhance your life, then enroll in a workshop. It could be financial planning, cooking, organizing closets, vocal techniques, or growing bonsai. The first small step to growth is wanting to learn. Everyone either grows or stagnates. Which do you choose?

A Formula for Growth

☆ *Over the years, I have discovered a formula for growth that I use in my acting classes. First, get in touch with your dark side. Then name the feeling, own the feeling, analyze the feeling, and transform the feeling. In other words, "Name it, claim it, frame it, and tame it."*

☆ *Suppose my dark side is simmering with anger. I'd start by identifying what is wrong: "Boy, am I mad!" (Name it.) Then I'd make a statement describing the problem: "This is who I am at this moment, an angry person." (Claim it.) I don't assign responsibility for my dark side to anyone else by saying, "Oh, he makes me so mad" or, "Look what she made me do!"*

☆ *Next, I explore where this anger is coming from. (Frame it). Maybe my anger has an identifiable cause—I've been hurt or mistreated by someone or witnessed an injustice. Or maybe my anger is self-produced by frustration or stress. Once I determine this (frame it), I can transform my energy into something that will work for me. (Tame it.) Energy is neither inherently negative nor positive. It just is. I have a choice. I can keep my anger, letting it distort my life and actions, or I can change it and use that energy to resolve the problems that inspired it.*

☆ *Be sure you identify your dark feeling correctly. What is causing your anger? Another person has been promoted over you, and you really resent it. Isn't this jealousy rather than anger? Rename your dark side. Claim your loss instead of focusing on the actions of others. Explore (frame) what has triggered the jealousy, which is actually a loss of self-esteem.*

☆ *Consider your own strengths, gifts, and talents and how they will serve you in the future. Transform the dark and dangerous emotion of jealousy into renewed self-esteem. Turn your energy from regrets for the past into expectations for the future.*

☆ *You can help others work through this process. If someone tells you, "I'm afraid," they're describing a dark emotion. Never dismiss them by saying, "You shouldn't feel like that." Obviously they do feel like that. Instead, ask them to tell you more about their feelings. They have named their dark emotion. Help them claim it, frame it, and tame it. They'll grow, and you will too.*

"Should" and "could" do little good.
When you teach by showing, you nurture growing.

The Gift of

HAPPINESS

It had been a really horrible winter. Rainy, cold, gray, and depressing. We were outdoor kids and had spent too many days indoors. We were *very* unhappy, and we were sure it was all our parents' fault.

So the first rainless day in March, Debbie, Patty, and I decided to run away from home. We told Mom and Dad about our plans to go find sunshine and happiness. With a chuckle, they asked if we needed help packing. "No," we responded, "we're old enough to pack our wagon ourselves." We were three, four, and five years old respectively, living on a big ranch far from the madding crowd. We had no idea where we were going, but we just knew we had go away to be happy. Our grandparents had bought us a big red wagon with removable wooden sides for Christmas, and we were eager to try it out.

The packing began. We included all of life's essentials: our dolls, toy cash register, dinosaurs, pogo sticks, jump ropes, play phone, puzzles, picture books, miniature tool set, stuffed animals, hula hoops, Monopoly money, rock collections, roller skates, a plastic shovel, and our battered shared tricycle, which was tied to the back of the wagon. It took hours to get ready. We had many important decisions to make and couldn't agree on the necessities for our trip. Items like food, water, clothing, and blankets never crossed our minds.

Finally, we were ready. Excitedly, we kissed our parents good-bye and told them we were off to wonderland. They acted as if running away was a common occurrence and wished us a safe and happy journey. Mom handed us a sack of sandwiches she had packed, and Dad suggested we take along our dog Bullet (named after Roy Rogers and Dale Evans's dog) to protect us and play with us. (Of course, they kept a distant eye on us the whole time.) With our cowboy hats on our heads, our holsters on our hips, and our stick horses as our mode of travel, we started off, singing "Happy Trails to You" as we pulled our heavy load. The tricycle caboose wouldn't cooperate, so Patty decided to sit on it and steer while Debbie pushed the wagon and I pulled. The dirt road was bumpy and the potholes were deep and full of muddy water from the rains, but we plugged along, *cheerfully.*

Then suddenly we saw heaven ahead. Mustard—tall yellow spires blanketing the fields—beckoned us to come play. Breaking into a run, we dashed toward this beacon of springtime. The mustard plants were taller than any of us. We could stand and not be seen by each other a few feet away. "This is it!" we exclaimed.

"Let's set up house!" As we unpacked our valuables, we stomped around in the mustard making rooms for each of us and putting everything in a special place. "This is the kitchen, this is the porch, this is the living room, this is the bedroom, this is the garage." We lay down in the mustard and rolled around, inhaling the pungent fragrance of this intoxicating plant.

How lucky we were to find such a paradise! Our dolls and stuffed animals loved it too. Bullet found squirrels to chase and barked with enthusiasm. The sounds of rushing water filled the air and we wandered over to the creek. There we found miners' lettuce, dandelions, wild strawberries, and watercress growing. Pretending we were pioneers, we made a salad using our dolls' utensils and settled in for our first meal together. We thought it was absolutely delicious! Our shoes came off, and we waded into the water but it was too cold to think of swimming or catching polliwogs. We quickly decided that throwing rocks would be more fun. Lots of wildflowers—shooting stars, lupines, and poppies—adorned the banks, and we picked big bouquets for our new home in the mustard fields.

The rest of the day was spent playing hide-and-seek in the mustard, arranging and rearranging our treasures, and hunting for new rocks. Time sped by, and before long it was dark. The moon came up, and the night sounds sent shivers down our backs. None of us dared show fear. After all, we were *happy!* The coyotes howled, the owls hooted, and Bullet barked at night-foraging rabbits. At first we had retreated to our separate mustard bedrooms, but soon the three of us curled up together and counted the stars while Bullet was posted as sentry. We decided that this was the happiest day of our lives, but we wondered if Mom and Dad missed us.

None of us were awake when Dad came to get his girls. We woke up in our own beds in the morning, the smell of Mom's cooking wafting from the kitchen. At breakfast we all agreed we had indeed found the Promised Land far, far away, and we shared stories of our thrilling adventure with our parents who listened with rapt attention. We didn't realize that our enchanted faraway world was only a mile down the road, on our own property. We had never left the ranch.

There truly is no place like home.

That day I learned that happiness is an inside job. Happiness occurs within our hearts. It is not external. No one can make us happy, but cruelty and insensitivity can make us very unhappy. We can all help each other avoid unhappiness by eliminating hateful words, cruel deeds, and abusive looks.

However, anyone who assumes that other people and things can "make" them happy will forever be disappointed. We are responsible for our own happiness or sadness.

One key to happiness is having dreams. Sometimes we need to do something different to reawaken the happiness that already dwells in our souls. My sisters and I dreamed of finding a land of sunshine. By setting out on our journey, we were making a dream come true, though there was no more sunshine down the road than where we had started. Our parents, in their wisdom, allowed us to go. They knew no one could give us happiness. We had to find it within ourselves.

Why do so many people think that happiness is outside themselves? The average child encounters 431 negative messages every day: "Don't do that!" "You're too young for that!" "I've told you a thousand times not to do that!" "Give me that; you'll hurt yourself!" It's hard to find inner exuberance when you're bombarded by negativity. Our mom and dad helped us find our own happiness by encouraging our search.

Though you can't make anyone else happy, you *can* help them find happiness within themselves. Give your friends and loved ones

Cynthia Brian

permission to make their own mistakes. Smile to a stranger and affirm that happiness exists. I love George Eliot's saying, "Wear a smile and have friends, or wear a scowl and have wrinkles." Smiling is infectious, so pass the smile bug around.

Happiness and sadness are intertwined. Too much sun can create a desert. Too much rain brings floods. A balance is essential for growth. Abraham Lincoln said, "Most people are as happy as they make up their mind to be."

What makes you happy? A sunset, beautiful music, the smell of flowers or dinner cooking, a baby's laugh—all can lift our hearts and remind us how wonderful life can be. So can the *memory* of these things. You control the images you choose to focus on. No one else does. Abundance and joy come from within, not from other people.

EXERCISE

Catching the Happiness Bug

Happiness is infectious. Once you've eliminated the things that make you feel unhappy, you'll discover how easily you can be happy.

1. How much do you enjoy the following caring activities each day?

Relaxation _____
Meditation _____
Exercise _____
Nutrition _____
Fun! _____

Use the following grading scale:

A = Awesome
B = Beautiful
C = Coming along
D = Dragging

2. Write down a list of the stressors in your life. For example, "I feel burned out at work; my spouse doesn't understand me; I don't have enough time for myself; I'm constantly interrupted; I have no appetite (or excessive appetite); I am frequently angry; impatient with the kids."

3. *Now that you recognize your stressors, what can you do to improve your score in the five caring daily activities? What would give you more pleasure and happiness while releasing stress? If you keep tabs on what gets you down, you'll be able to concentrate on what brings you up. You can catch the happiness bug!*

Before I get out of bed in the morning, I take about three minutes to talk to God. I give thanks for everything I have in life, especially my health, and ask for help to live my life to my greatest potential and to serve others. During the day, although I am always stretched for time, I make an effort to grab a couple of pieces of fruit and to drink plenty of water.

When stress begins to build, I take a few deep breaths. If possible, I get outside in the fresh air and listen to nature for a few minutes. Most of all, I smile. This helps others smile, which reflects back to me and makes me smile more. It is amazing how doing just a few small things for yourself every day can "grow" happiness. Try it. As my friend and mentor Father Patrick McGrath taught me:

> *Help each other to be happy.*
> *Never mind if help be small.*
> *Giving a little is far better*
> *Than giving none at all.*

No matter how wonderful or wretched
things are, you decide if you're happy.
Happiness is an inside job.

Cynthia Brian

The Gift of

HARMONY

My husband and I are avid travelers. We were thrilled to be going to the Galapagos Islands, which inspired naturalist Charles Darwin. Nature is a fundamental element in my life and contributes much to my values as a human being. To be among such rare, beautiful, and strange creatures of land and sea was a dream come true.

Brian and I are both scuba divers and had brought our own equipment because we were told there were no rentals on our boat or on the islands.

One day we were snorkeling in what is called the Toilet Bowl, a huge volcanic crater where the waves rush in to fill the bowl and then recede, dropping the water level about twenty feet. It's a favorite swimming hole for playful fur seals who surf the wake as the water rushes in and out of the crater, inviting human visitors to cavort with them.

We were the only ones who had brought underwater equipment, so some of our fellow travelers asked to use our masks and snorkels to view the rich sea life. Unfortunately, my snorkel was soon whisked from the borrower's mouth by the rushing water and lost in the black volcanic material.

I was dismayed because we had several other islands to visit and no way to replace my snorkel. For about an hour, everyone looked for it, diving between the frolicking seals. The fur seals seemed to be enjoying our game. Dusk approached, and it was time to go back to the boat. As everyone left, my husband and I did one last search. No luck. Despondent over our loss, we got out of the water, dressed, and were walking away when we heard several fur seals calling to us. Ar-uhk! Ar-uhk! Ar-uhk! We turned around, and there was my snorkel in the mouth of a seal.

One seal was tossing the snorkel back and forth with her seal friends as they called to us. It was as if they were saying, "Come back! Come back! Do you have to leave? We were having so much fun. But don't go without your snorkel."

We were flabbergasted. We walked over to the seals. The one with the snorkel gently put it in our hands and looked at us with those incredibly beautiful large brown eyes as if she was thanking us for an enjoyable afternoon. Then she dove under the water and disappeared.

Brian and I looked at each other and understood that we had just experienced a magical moment that crossed all boundaries.

This experience will always be in our hearts. We were profoundly grateful that the Galapagos Islands exist in a time and space where harmony for all living things is still the norm rather than the exception. We felt a deep connection with the world—humans, animals, plants, the sun, the sky, the universe.

All living matter is united in spirit. It is essential that we do our part to maintain our planet for future generations. What we do today will impact tomorrow. We have a beautiful world, and it is our responsibility to keep it pure, safe, and sacred. Our universe as we know it can only survive when we live in harmony with the world around us. Humans are the only species that can control the survival of our earth, mountains, rivers, oceans, plants, animals, fish, air, and sky. We have the power. We have the choice.

If we take the time to notice and respond, we can experience this harmony.

The Moan

This is one of my favorite class exercises for dissipating stress and creating harmony. Do the belly breathing exercise (described under Breathing, page 44), but on the exhale, extend whatever sound your breath is making. Let the sound come from deep inside and moan it out. Breathe in "the air of unity" and exhale "the struggles and strain of everyday life." (Do it three times.)

Wow, this feels good!

Notice yourself in others and others in you.
We are all one.

The Gift of

HEALING

It was midnight on a Monday night, and my sixteen-year-old brother, David, and I were still on the phone arguing whether he was going to catch the 6:00 A.M. flight to Los Angeles with me so he could visit the set of a film I was working on.

I was tired and wanted to know whether I needed to drive two hours to pick him up. "David, are you coming or *not?*" I snapped. "I don't have all night to discuss this." Immediately, I was sorry for my sharp tone. If it wasn't for my kid brother, I wouldn't have been working on the film. David had always believed in me and wanted me to be a star. When he was just eleven, he had secretly sent my photos to directors, getting me my first TV commercial. Some day, David assured me, he was going to manage my career.

"I'll come *next* week, Cyn," David said. "I have one more field to plow."

When David didn't come in for lunch the next day, Mom sent Dad with the jeep to get him. As Dad started toward the upper vineyards, he saw a rising column of dust. When he got closer, his heart began to pound. Through the dust, he could just make out the wheels of the Ford tractor spinning crazily in the air. He hit the gas and screeched to a stop next to the tangle of overturned tractor and disk tiller. David was pinned beneath, lying gray and still.

Dad tried desperately to heave the tractor upright, but all his strength couldn't move it. Calling to David to "hang on," he raced back to the house and phoned for neighbors and the local volunteer fire department. My sister, Debbie, was one of the first to arrive. As she struggled to free David, she noted, in one of those odd images that fix in our minds in times of crisis, that David had taken off his tee shirt because of the heat and still held it clutched tightly in his hand.

My pager went off during my lunch break on the movie set. No family member had ever paged me while I was working in Los Angeles, so I knew this was serious. My husband answered my return call and very calmly told me there had been an accident. "Come home on the next plane." He felt it was better not to tell me what had happened, but emphasized the urgency. I shouldn't wait for an inexpensive standby ticket as I usually did. Take the first plane.

In a daze, I arrived at the airport and was told all flights were booked. I remember standing there, hysterically begging everyone and anyone to sell me their ticket. Some kind soul did, though I can no longer remember who or how.

Though I've flown huge distances around the world, the hour between Los Angeles and San Francisco was the longest flight of my life. I was sure my beloved paternal grandfather, a man I adored and worshipped, must be badly hurt or dying. The idea that my youngest brother might be threatened never occurred to me.

I do remember landing and running through the airport, totally in a fog, to my husband's arms and a waiting car. Brian's face was pale, but still he wouldn't tell me anything. "Please, Brian!" I started to sob. Finally, he pulled to the side of the road.

"There's been an accident on the ranch," he said slowly. "A tractor flipped over."

"Oh, my God!" I screamed. "It's Dad! Is he all right?"

Brian said Dad was fine. And, yes, Fred was fine. We seemed to be having a numbing and ridiculous game of Twenty Questions, as if Brian were deliberately tormenting me. I realized later that he just couldn't bring himself to say the terrible words.

Then he, too, started to cry. "It's David," he said. I was begging him to stop, to take it back, but already there was a knife piercing my heart. "He's dead, honey. They couldn't save him. He was killed instantly. He didn't suffer."

The hour-and-a-half drive to the ranch was a complete blur. Somehow Brian kept the car on the road as I shouted and wept. Not David! Not our baby, our shining star! Why not me? Why not the rapists, the drug dealers, the thugs and murderers prowling the streets? Why David, who was so young, so sweet, such a dazzling promise of a new tomorrow?

Then it hit me. My last words to David had been curt, almost angry...and I could never take them back.

Our entire family was shaken to its foundation. It was our first real encounter with absolute grief. None of us had any experience in recovering from such abject loss, but we did the best we could to stay alive and hold each other up.

People in mourning do curious things. We comforted ourselves by wearing things that David had worn. We enshrined his bedroom exactly the way he had left it the morning he died. The book he was reading still lay open on his desk. His notebook sat with the pen marking the original page. His curios, artwork, and clothes all remained in the exact position of that dreadful day.

It took us all ten years to get past the bad memories. Eventually I learned to put my pain on paper, which relieved my physical symptoms. Finally, we could let go. We remodeled the room. David, Fred, and Dad had been digging a lake on our ranch. We finished it and named it Lake David. We set up David Abruzzini scholarships and memorials. But even after twenty years we are still healing. The pain is never gone completely, but we can talk and laugh about David more easily now. We never forget.

Death is final. I want David to be with God, but that doesn't make my family feel any better. We can't hug him or kiss him or argue with him anymore. I don't know for sure if there is a heaven. I believe on faith that I'll see David again. I talk to him every day in prayer, and he is one of my special angels. Still, the loss of his earthly humanness here and now, his death, leaves a hole in my heart.

Like all actors, I had learned how to cry on cue, but I had never really felt the emotions behind the tears until David died. Since then, I have only to recall the moment I heard the news, and my body trembles, sadness overwhelms me, and I can't stop the tears.

What have we learned from our experience? That grief is a normal and natural reaction to a loss and change. To heal, we had to deal with everything said and unsaid. We'll never get to see what David would have become, to see him grow up, go to college, get married, have children. We mourn both David and what he would have become. We also learned that when others are hurting, all we can do is be there and show we care. People need love, compassion, and personal presence when they undergo a death, a severe illness, or any loss. Grieving people appreciate the flowers and food, but what they need most are the stories. We loved hearing all the stories about David's life from others. Stories help heal the heart.

Since David's death, our family has had to deal with many more deaths, tragedies, and losses. It was as if the floodgates were opened by that one immense shock, and the rivers of sadness steadily flow by. We have chosen to recover but healing is hard. There is no short-term relief. Time helps, talking helps, writing helps, being together helps. The knowledge that it is *okay* to cry, to laugh, to fall apart, and to say stupid things are all a part of the healing process.

I feel deeply sorrowful when friends suffer the death of a loved one. But each loss is different, and healing is different for each person. What may work for me may not work for you. All well-intended responses are right for that moment. Do whatever it takes to move forward—take the time you need, ask for support, get into therapy, go back to work, be alone, or gather with friends. Talk, cry, laugh, be silent…whatever helps you heal is what you need to do. Don't apologize to others for the darkness in your heart. You are suffering and your pain is real. The longer we live, the more sadness and heartbreak we will face. Although you may never be the same again, you will heal and life will go on.

It takes great courage to say good-bye. We can say good-bye to the pain, but we will never say good-bye to our loved ones. We will only say farewell, until we meet again. We all have one more field to plow.

Down and Out

There will be times when you are feeling down, depressed, overwhelmed, unloved, even useless, worthless, and hopeless. Everyone experiences this. If your pain is severe and unending, seek professional help. But if it's just a terrible case of the blues, here's an exercise that may help.

Accept your feelings. Go with them. Find a private place and really wallow in your negative emotions. Experience them as part of who you are. Set a timer and take five minutes to feel enormously sorry for yourself. Sulk, wail, sob, beat your chest. Think of every unfair thing that has ever happened to you in your entire life. Go all the way back to your earliest memories if necessary. When the timer dings, blow your nose and start fresh.

We all have one more field to plow.

Cynthia Brian

The Gift of

HEALTH

Everyone agrees that health is better than wealth. So why do most people abuse their bodies and take wellness for granted until they've lost it?

My dad was a mountain of a man. He was as strong as an ox, could lift his five young children at one time, and could swim upstream while pulling a parade of rafts full of frolicking children. Working on the ranch provided lots of natural exercise: plowing fields, chopping wood, fixing tractors and trailers, building barns, digging reservoirs, and running irrigation pipes. He ate three healthful meals a day, surrounded by love from my mom and their five children. He breathed clean air and led a relatively stress-free life. I don't remember him ever being sick in his life, no colds, flus, or headaches. Then one day, at age sixty-three, he threw up blood and fainted. We rushed him to the hospital where a gigantic tumor was found in his stomach. He had a very rare cancer.

How was this possible? While we were fighting for my dad's life, we talked about what factors besides heredity might have contributed to his cancer.

One possibility was cigarettes. Dad had begun smoking when he was in the army. In those days no one knew the dangers of cigarette smoke. Smoking was encouraged, and cigarettes were even given out free to soldiers. Dad smoked until the 1960s when new medical information became available. He quit cold, but it may not have been soon enough.

Another possibility was farm chemicals. In his early years of farming, Dad had used weed killers now known to be carcinogens. Then in the 1960s, a glut of grapes brought low prices, and our family almost lost the ranch to creditors. Dad experienced great stress trying to keep up with expenses while feeding a family of seven. The tragic losses of his father, killed by a falling tree, and of his son, killed by a falling tractor, took their toll. The drought years of 1985–1992 brought more stress because Dad didn't know how much longer his vineyards could hold out with such little water. His life's work hung in the balance.

No one can say what caused the cancer. Dad and his doctors felt that if he had never smoked or been exposed to carcinogens or if he had been able to communicate his emotions more clearly, this cancer might not have occurred. But he had been healthy his entire life and was grateful for that.

Dad didn't want to die, but he had lived his dreams and felt fulfilled. He died a happy man, but he died too young. We miss him deeply. His death made me look closely at how I live. I want to be as healthy as possible for as long as I can.

Diets and health fads had never been part of my vocabulary. Growing up on the farm, we were very healthy youngsters. We ate the tasty, nourishing food we grew. We worked daily in the fields, which kept our bodies finely tuned, and we laughed, played, prayed, talked, shouted, and hugged, which kept our hearts and minds fit. In those days, I had never even heard of dieting or exercising. Living a healthful lifestyle came naturally.

Then I went away to college. No longer did I have fields or gardens to raid when preparing my dinner nor farmwork to keep my muscles toned, and, of course, no family support around me. I worked two jobs to pay my tuition while carrying a full course load at the university.

At first I was fine. I managed a health food store and was quickly spotted for a television commercial promoting vitamins. The character I played was supposed to be "so healthy" because she took all those vitamins. In truth, I had never had a vitamin pill or supplement in my life, only my mom's great cooking of organic, homegrown produce.

As time went by, my healthful eating habits deteriorated. I had so little money for food that I made poor choices and purchased items that were not necessarily good for me. Lots of sugary and fatty things interspersed with fast foods became the norm. (A few years later, I paid for my poor college eating habits with severe hypoglycemia.) As I gained weight, I experimented with diets. The more I dieted, the more I gained and the worse I looked and felt.

Then one day, a lightbulb went on in my head. I remembered how I had had an enormous appetite on the farm and that I had never gained weight or been sick. We ate when we were hungry, we didn't binge, and we didn't go on any crazy fad diets. We ate healthful foods including lots of fruit and vegetables, grains, and juices with nutritional value. I decided that the secret was not to deprive myself. I cut out the junk food and started eating healthful meals again. Once I did this, I felt better, had more energy, and interestingly enough, it actually cost me less money! Of course, I still crave and indulge in dark chocolate from time to time. But I have realized the importance of eating a balanced diet combined with exercise to maintain optimum health.

The leading causes of death in America are heart disease, cancer, AIDS, and alcoholism, followed by accidents, pulmonary disease, influenza, diabetes, and suicide. Poor diets, alcohol, drugs, and cigarettes are the main sources of abuse. Over and over, Americans choose profit over clean air and water, adequate exercise, reduced stress, sufficient sleep, nourishing foods, and personal relationships.

If someone put you in a high-stress fun house room, deprived you of sleep and human contact, kept you from moving about, and fed you only high-fat, high-salt fast foods, maybe even piping in noxious fumes, you'd feel mightily abused. Yet, many Americans choose this life voluntarily!

It is possible to be happy without health. But why wreck your health intentionally? Watch your diet, eat more fruits and vegetables, exercise regularly, sleep and rest plenty, reduce stress, shun fast foods, laugh a lot, and love more. A Spanish proverb says, "A man too busy to take care of his health is like a mechanic too busy to take care of his tools." Your body is all you've got. No replacements, no refunds. Take care of it.

Are You Healthy?

Ask yourself these questions: Are you in good shape? Do you exercise? Are you overweight or underweight? Do you smoke? Do you use drugs? Do you abuse alcohol? Is your cholesterol over 180? Is your blood pressure high? Do you have healthy relationships with others?

If you're not happy with some of your answers, there's only one person in the world who can do anything about it. The natural reaction is to make drastic changes, but resist that impulse. Take it one small step at a time. What can you start today that will have positive effects on the rest of your life?

☆ *Start with a physical from your doctor or health practitioner.*

☆ *Each day, walk a few more steps until you build slowly from a block to a mile.*

☆ *Eat two fruits you enjoy every day. Drink an extra glass of water. Once a week, choose a salad over an order of french fries.*

☆ *Every day for the next week, do one nice thing for someone you know and for someone you don't know.*

At the end of a month, take a long look at yourself in the mirror. What do you see? Are you feeling better about yourself?

Continue on your one-step-at-a-time journey to healthy living. Add positive habits little by little. Nothing happens overnight. Health is a lifelong commitment. Being healthy has a profound effect on your happiness and quality of life. It's worth the effort.

Health is wealth. Are you rich? If not, why not?

The Gift of
HONESTY

My son, Justin, had just had his second birthday, and we were gently encouraging his relationship with the bathroom plumbing. I had read the how-to books and was trying all the suggestions. Although I've never met an adult still in diapers, most mothers reach a time when they wonder, "Will this child ever be toilet trained?"

My godchild and niece, Melissa, was about to celebrate her First Holy Communion with one hundred other eight-year-old children. The entire family was in attendance at the crowded church to celebrate with Melissa. Justin sat quietly on my lap. During a silent moment in the service, he looked up at the altar with the traditional statue of Jesus outstretched on the cross and wearing only a loincloth, and he happily shouted, "Look, Mommy, Jesus wears a diaper just like me!"

The entire church broke into laughter as I scrunched down in my seat, trying to become invisible. The priest, who was laughing as well, announced into the microphone, "Blessed are the little children," to which Justin responded, "Listen, Mommy, God is talking to me!"

Honesty is inherent in children. They usually say exactly what they are thinking and feeling. We probably don't want to carry such total honesty over into grown-up social situations ("That was a dreadful dinner, Aunt Martha"), but a childlike honesty is an enormous gift in most adult situations, both to ourselves and those around us. My brother, sisters, and I were taught as children that our word was our contract. I can't remember my dad ever actually signing a piece of paper. If he said he'd do something, he'd shake hands on it, and that was that. He was completely honest in all his undertakings.

My sister Debbie is another example of honesty personified. What's in her heart is on her tongue. Sometimes she may be outspoken, but she is loved by everyone who knows her. You always know exactly where you stand with Debbie and trust her completely. She has worked in the tasting room of a winery for most of her adult life, and her customers rely on her veracity when they make their purchases. Over the years, several people, not knowing she and I are sisters, have told me that I must be sure to visit that particular winery when Debbie was working.

When you have a reputation for honesty, people trust you. However, as judges instruct juries, any evidence of even a single falsehood, and the jury may disregard everything the witness says. One dishonest word or act, and trust is destroyed forever. Without trust, relationships sour, and your reputation is gone forever.

Justin's professors and employers tell me that one of his biggest assets is his honesty. Perhaps it started that day in church.

EXERCISE

"Tell Me About Yourself"

☆ *This is the number one request at job interviews and acting auditions. It is probably the most common opener in the world. Unfortunately, most of us respond with a question: "What do you want to know?" Then we say what we think the listener wants to hear. Maybe it's true. Maybe not. (Job résumés have become one of the leading examples of creative fiction, surpassing even pickup lines in bars.)*

☆ *You can be both honest and exciting at the same time. Get a tape recorder. Think about the following question carefully. Who are you and what do you do that would inspire, interest, and motivate others to want to know more about you? You probably could provide a laundry list of awards, jobs, and accomplishments. Don't. Instead, choose three areas that you are passionate about and jot them down.*

Cynthia Brian

☆ *Now record your answer to the question into a tape recorder, describing your three passions with intensity and clarity. Don't ramble. Be succinct.*

☆ *Play back the tape. Listen for inflection, excitement, and determination. Do you like you? Do you like what you are saying? If not, start again. Repeat until you feel totally comfortable with your answer, confident that the next time someone asks you about yourself, you will engage them with your truthfulness, spontaneity, and love of life. Use this exercise to find honesty within yourself and with others.*

"Being honest is easier than being a liar.
An honest man is the noblest work of God."

—*Alexander Pope*

The Gift of

HOPE

My smile has always been one of my best assets. I was an outgoing, happy child filled with laughter, joy, and mischief. That is, until my secondary teeth started to come in. One by one, my permanent adult teeth started to fill my mouth, but my twenty baby teeth showed no inclination to leave.

My smile was starting to look like a shark's, filled with rows and rows of teeth. I started covering my mouth with my hand when I talked. My parents took me to our family dentist who, one by one, pulled all my baby teeth.

Most children are delighted to lose a tooth and put it under their pillow for the tooth fairy. My baby teeth, all twenty of them, were surgically removed. I must have set some type of dental record. Understandably, I came to fear dental visits. Just the smells when I walked in the door made me woozy. The only way my parents could get me there was with the promise that, if I wasn't too sick afterward, we'd stop at Taylor's Homemade Hamburger Stand on the way home. Usually, I was too sick.

Even after all my primary teeth had been removed, the damage of having so many teeth crammed into such a small space had left its mark. My adult teeth were crooked, stacked like mismatched dominoes. So my hand remained firmly over my mouth.

An orthodontist agreed that I needed costly braces, more than my family could afford. But my parents realized that the ridicule I was enduring for my crooked teeth would eventually affect my self-esteem. My mother had endured the same thing growing up. She remembered her pain and embarrassment as a teenager, and how hard she had worked to save enough money to fix her own crooked teeth before she and Dad were married. She didn't want me to go through the same thing.

Cynthia Brian

Mom and Dad had a powwow and resolved to get me braces, no matter what sacrifices the family would have to make. (They had made similar decisions for my sisters and brothers and as the need arose over the years.) When they announced I would get braces, we all celebrated. A great load lifted off my shoulders. I wanted my smile back. My dream was that one day I would go to high school with straight teeth, and I vowed I would always offer a bright smile to everyone.

For months, I wore braces. The day before my eighth grade graduation, the braces came off, so I did start high school with straight teeth. I kept my vow to smile at everyone. In fact, I won the school's "Best Smile" award. My family referred to it as "the $800 smile."

Whenever I was sad, disheartened, or having a bad day, my dad would say to me, "Come on, honey, show me your $800 smile!" That always made me laugh. Even today, when I am feeling low, I'll say it to myself. It gives me hope for a happy tomorrow.

And, surprise, I married a dentist—a great one, I might add, who has a close-up of my smile on his business cards. I no longer fear dentists. I am grateful that they can offer us so much hope, health, and happiness.

One of the most amazing things about hope is that people with the most right to be hopeless—like those with painful terminal diseases—are often full of hope. They no longer anticipate a positive outcome for themselves, but they keep their spirits high with their hopes for *others*. But even with such incredible role models, our own miseries invariably take center stage. All of us have felt hopelessness at one time or another. Usually because of a loss or potential loss, but even little things can trigger a despair—incessant rain, a leaky faucet, a pimple on an important day, or the azalea that didn't bloom.

Nature and my garden have taught me that life is a cycle of growth and hope. The rebirth of spring follows the storms of winter, and the harvest of fall follows the sweet warmth of the summer. To everything there is a season.

Professionals can help restore our hope. There are psychiatrists, of course, but there are also plumbers for that leaky faucet, dermatologists for acne, and nursery experts for your plants. (You'll have to talk to God about the rain.) Turn to the qualified masters when your health, welfare, or personal satisfaction are in trouble. There's no need to suffer when help is all around you. And lack of funds is no excuse. Just ask my parents.

It's funny what twists and turns life sends us. The little girl with a mouthful of extra teeth and a wish for a beautiful smile grew up to be paid to smile on TV and in magazines. That's hope in action.

EXERCISE

Create a Hope Chest

My mom gave me her hope chest when I got married. It is still filled with hopes and dreams that I pull out whenever I need them.

☆ *Start a mental hope chest of your own, stockpiling positive self-images and solutions. Remember that losing hope, even briefly, is like a hole in a dike. Unchecked, you could drown in a cycle of hopeless-helpless-worthless. Stop the flood by filling yourself with hope.*

☆ *Think of a recent event that tipped you over the edge and made you feel hopeless. For example, "My car has a dead battery, so I can't get to work. My boss is a jerk who wants to fire me, and there is no one I can call to help me. I'm friendless and jobless, a pathetic loser who can never get anything right. Everything is against me." One incident has triggered a landslide of emotions.*

☆ *How can you make your "hopeless" situation better? Are you missing opportunities by focusing on your setbacks? How can you reinterpret what happened?*

Cynthia Brian

☆ *Suggest three ways you could have responded to the dead battery situation. Let your imagination fly. Chronicle even outrageous and far-fetched ideas. Sometimes they offer the best solutions for hope.*

Here are three sample scenarios:

☆ *Scenario 1: "I can take a taxi. It will cost extra, but I'll get to work, and everyone will be happy."*

☆ *Scenario 2: "I can call the local service station or my automobile club to charge my battery. Or I can rent a car. I'll let work know I'll be a little late, but I'll be there."*

☆ *Scenario 3: "I'll quit my job! I'm miserable and have been hoping for an opportunity to resign. This is it!"*

Sometimes taking action can stop the cycle and reconnect you to hope. Look to your mental hope chest for answers.

"Hoping means seeing that the outcome you want is possible, then working for it."

—*Dr. Bernie S. Siegel*

The Gift of
HOSANNAS

What's my definition of a hosanna? Hosannas are anything that make you feel special—the skills and resources you enjoy using and glory in sharing, not necessarily for profit. Hosannas are the fuel for "being the star" of your own life. Hosannas are your unique gifts that connect you with the world.

My mother, Alice, is the best cook in the world. Her kitchen is her sanctuary. Of course, if you asked her, she'd say *her* mom was the best cook in the world. That may be so, but my mother learned to cook from my Nonie (my maternal grandmother), so they both win the award.

Cooking, gardening, and children have always been my mom's three passions. She molded all three into miracles. For as long as I can remember, my mother has grown all her own vegetables and herbs to create her delicious dishes. Everything in the kitchen was made from scratch: rich, meaty, garlicky spaghetti sauces, raviolis, gnocchis, risotto alla Milanese, and creamy polentas.

We swore that "Alice's Restaurant" was better than any other eatery. When she rolled pastas wrong, she made *malfattis,* Italian for "mistakes." They were our favorites! Nothing went to waste, only to our eager stomachs.

Our house was always filled with the delicious smells of Mom's kitchen. Her Swiss hotcakes for breakfast were indescribable, and her roasted rosemary lamb with mint and garlic was scrumptious. Garlic went with everything. When you're Italian, garlic is like an apple—at least a clove a day! Even her tomato and basil salads with olive oil and vinegar were divine. We always fought over who got to *pouchi-pouchi* (dip the bread in the vinaigrette at the bottom of the bowl). Through our childhood and teenage years, our friends made every excuse to be at our house at mealtime. It didn't matter how many people showed up for dinner, seven or seventy, Mom always had plenty to go around and could whip up a feast in no time at all. One of Mom's indisputable hosannas in life was her cooking.

I remember when frozen TV dinners were the rage. We begged to try them. To placate us, Mom would prepare a fresh dinner and serve it on a tin plate!

She was happy when you were eating second and third helpings, and enraptured when you expressed contentment. She felt responsibility as the nurturer, cook, and feeder of her tribe. If someone protested that he or she wasn't hungry, Mom would immediately offer to cook them something else more to their liking. *"Mangia, mangia,"* was her mantra. Along with spices, herbs, and seasonings, Mom added a special ingredient that only a mother can add—love.

Mom's garden is also a hosanna. Nobody can grow bougainvillea like she can. The bright fuchsia flowers cover an entire side of her two-story farmhouse. Her green thumb is unequaled, and her acre of gardens is always overflowing with magnificent, blossoming specimens. It's been photographed for several magazines. Everyone she knows, from the doctor to the priest to the mailman, receives regular boxes of bounty from her vegetable garden. In our childhood, our teachers always had fresh bouquets of the most fragrant blossoms from her flower beds. Mom's garden gives her incredible pleasure.

Of course, her children were her heart. Mothering was her calling. Not overmothering, just loving unconditionally and guiding us to a safe and secure adulthood. In all the years that the five of us played sports, participated in 4-H and school events, or (the three of us girls) were cheerleaders, I don't think my mom or dad *ever* missed an activity. They were the one couple that every kid could count on to be in attendance and to cheer us on. Mom lavished praise, encouragement, and lifetime skills on her children. Most of all, she gave us her time.

When my brother David was killed, her hosannas dimmed. She had lost a child to embrace and feed. When my dad died, we wondered if Mom would survive. Her zest for life was nearly extinguished. Her children were already grown, and now she had no one to cook for, no one to admire her handiwork in the garden. The recipients of her hosannas had gone, and she wondered why she was needed on this earth. It took time and effort, but with the love of her children, their spouses, and her eleven grandchildren, she accepted at last that we still cherished her and looked forward to seeing her beautiful gardens, tasting her wondrous dishes, and hugging her. She rediscovered her hosannas.

Hosannas are those things in life that earn you a pat on the back, the special talents that make you unique and proud. When you share those gifts with those you love, good fortune comes back to you a hundredfold. My mother's hosannas were her cooking, gardening, and children. They gave her great pleasure because she possessed natural talents in these areas. Shared moments in Mom's kitchen, surrounded by the aromas of her cooking, absorbing her gardening wisdom and parenting expertise, have shaped me into the woman I am today. Her hosannas became my bounty.

Each of us is different. Your hosannas can be in any area of your life—your job, family, garden, creativity, knowledge, skills, handiwork. Value your hosannas. They are your unique gifts and are part of your purpose in life. Acknowledge them and enjoy the satisfaction you get from sharing them with others.

Our hosannas may change occasionally. Things change, people grow, and we need to let go of past applause. If your hosanna no longer brings you joy, find another. Glory in it, share it, and congratulate yourself!

Cynthia Brian

Hosannas in the Highest

A hosanna is a gift to be shared with those around you. What are your hosannas? What special talents do you possess that enrich the lives of others while bringing you great satisfaction?

Sit down with your journal, and write whatever hosannas come to your head. You have a special gift, even if you haven't recognized it yet. Like my mom, one of my hosannas is sharing my knowledge of gardening. For my husband, it's communicating his expertise about fine wines. Give yourself permission to praise yourself. Hosanna in the highest!

Sing the praises of others joyfully.
Recognize and honor their hosannas.

The Gift of

HUMOR

Life is funny. Even in the saddest of times, we can discover humor, whether we're looking for it or not.

When the father of my friend Steve died at age eighty-three, Steve followed his dad's wishes. The old soldier, a World War II veteran, was cremated in preparation for interment at Arlington National Ceremony.

A week later, the call came that arrangements had been completed, so the ashes could be shipped to their final resting place. Steve's wife, Trish, had never shipped human ashes before. But she carried the beautiful pewter box to the post office and asked the best way to pack it.

The clerk sold her a cardboard box, bubble wrap, and several different kinds of tape. But when she returned to the window with the package and asked to insure it, a different clerk told her she had used the wrong kind of tape. He also asked a simple but disturbing question: "What is the value of the contents?"

Trish hesitated, embarrassed. "It has no value," she finally replied.

"Well, if you want to insure it, you have to state a value," the clerk replied sensibly. "What is it worth?"

"I'm not really sure," Trish said. "To me it is invaluable."

Sighing, the postal clerk tried to be helpful. "I need a value to put on the form. What's in the box?"

"A very personal item," Trish replied, becoming more and more flustered.

By now the line was getting longer behind her, and the postal worker was starting to eye the bomb-sized box suspiciously. "*What* is in the box?" he insisted. The other customers and clerks also began staring at the package.

Trish grew more and more distressed. "Something of value just to my family," she muttered, turning red and starting to tremble.

Her obvious nervousness alarmed the postal clerk. He stepped back from the counter and the ominous package. "If you won't tell me what is in this box," he said loudly, "I'll have to call the police! *What is in the box?*"

Startled, Trish shouted back: "My father-in-law!" The entire post office fell silent. Trish felt humiliated and ridiculous. Then a woman at the back of the line stepped forward. "What's your father-in-law's name?" she asked softly.

"Ray," Trish replied.

"Okay," the woman said, addressing the package, "Come with me, Ray, and we'll get you fixed up. I'm in the import-export business, and I'll wrap you up perfectly."

She took Trish and Ray to her nearby office, wrapped Ray appropriately, and sent him off to his hero's burial at Arlington.

When Trish and Steve told me their story, we all laughed so hard that we cried. All this occurred a week after Ray's death, so finding humor in their sadness was a great gift. It lifted everyone's spirit. Ray had been a prankster, full of mirth, so he surely would have relished the story too.

Humor keeps us young and vibrant. Humor can relieve tense situations, fear, and anxiety. Having a good chuckle releases healing endorphins into the bloodstream, which energize us and make us feel great. Real life is often funnier than fiction. Enjoy yourself; it is later than you think!

EXERCISE

Whatever You Do, Don't Laugh

Stare hard at a cooperative friend, telling yourself, "Whatever I do, I mustn't laugh." How long can you keep from giggling?

We don't stop laughing because we grow old. We grow old because we stop laughing. Laugh more!

If you want to know why imagination is important, just ask a child to tell you a story. Children's minds are filled with chocolate moons, whipped cream clouds, cows that fly, dogs that talk, and many invisible friends.

As soon as we could reach the pedals, my brothers, sisters, and I learned to drive in a 1930s Ford jalopy. It had three gears and a maximum speed of about thirty-five miles per hour. My dad had cut the top off it so we could call it a convertible. We loved to drive it up and down the ranch roads and through the vineyards, pretending we were traveling in faraway lands.

One afternoon, my sisters and the children of the ranch hands decided to go on an adventure. While driving through the fields, they spotted a deer and wanted to play with it. The deer started running. The jalopy, with about six little kids in it, followed in rapid pursuit. When the deer jumped over a small ravine, the kids thought the car could jump too. After all, didn't Fred McMurray's car fly in the movie Flubber?

The jalopy flew all right. Over the ravine and right into several grapevines, throwing the kids, seats and all, out of the car. (There were no seat belts in those days.) The muffler was broken off and the windshield cracked, but amazingly no one was hurt. The jalopy came to a halt, the deer pranced away, and the kids wiped the dirt off their faces and assessed the damage.

"*What* are we going to tell Dad?" they wondered. They had to come up with a believable story so they wouldn't get in trouble for damaging his grapevines and the jalopy. As the kids were walking home, they hit on a foolproof idea. They marched together into the tractor barn and began telling Dad their story: "We were out on a drive inspecting the vineyards, when, out of nowhere, a big train came and plowed into the jalopy. The train knocked down the grapevines, and we were lucky to escape with our lives."

My dad listened intently, asking for more details. The kids went on and on, spinning the tale until the story had grown to such proportions that my dad could hardly contain himself. Finally they finished, certain they had convinced him.

Dad told them how much he appreciated their honesty and how happy he was that they had survived the ordeal. However, train or no train, they were grounded and would not be allowed to drive again until they understood the responsibility of being behind the wheel of a car. In addition, they would have to pay off the damages by working in the fields.

The wonderful part of the story is that it was several years before the kids realized that my dad had not bought their story (there wasn't a train track for fifty miles)! He had so enjoyed their enormous communal imagination and was so relieved to know that everyone was all right that he had the good heart to play along.

Telling a lie is not okay. But the beauty of childhood is the unlimited scope of imagination. These kids didn't recognize the tale they invented for Dad as a lie, instead they considered it to be a creative solution to a very profound problem. They were too young to realize that as imaginative as their story was, it was not logical. It is a good idea to use common sense even in the most fantastical situations.

Dad's reaction to their fantasy speaks volumes on his sagacity and acumen as a father. Instead of accusing the children of lying, he wisely appreciated their wild imagination. He enjoyed the fact that they were thinking "out of the box," and he played along with the ruse. Of course, he also made sure the children understood the ramifications of their actions and had them make amends. Dad's understanding is a testimony to excellent parenting skills.

Children constantly remind us what it is like to be free, innocent, and playful. I know that's why I enjoy working with them, helping to ensure that they don't lose their sense of wonder and magic when they enter the grown-up world of acting. My daughter, Heather, has always had an active, frolicking imagination. As a young child, she would draw funny pictures and ask me to write down the story that went with the picture. I saved most of them, and today we reread the stories and laugh. The stories make no real "sense," but they are original, usually about animals teaching humans important life lesson's. Heather's goal to work with animals was created first in her imagination.

The next time you come up against a brick wall, let your imagination run wild and ponder the potentialities. Think like a child who knows no boundaries and be aware of possible solutions to what seem like impossible challenges. Our experiences are only limited by the quantity and quality of our imaginations. Imagine!

EXERCISE

Just Imagine

Children are great at imagining they are someone or something else. Become a child for ten minutes. Find a room that has a full-length mirror. Lock the door, look in the mirror, and become the person you most want to be. Is it a rock star? A pro ball player? Miss America? An astronaut? Or president? Do you want to win an Academy Award, a Nobel Prize, or the love of your life? Sing, dance, applaud, scream, yodel, or travel to distant shores.

We are only limited by our imaginations.
Imagine your reality.

Cynthia Brian

IMPROVISATION

The Gift of

Will you be ready when your fifteen minutes of fame arrives? My husband and I were on a three-day trip to New York City and decided to see as many Broadway plays as we possibly could. We were able to secure last-minute orchestra seats for a Mother's Day matinee of the popular Dame Edna and the Royal Tour. Dame Edna Everage (actually actor Barry Humphries) is billed as "Australia's First Lady" and touts herself as being the most popular and gifted woman in the world today.

During the second act, Dame Edna began addressing individuals in the audience, most of whom were embarrassed and shy. Suddenly, she looked down at me and asked my name. We began a fast-paced and exciting exchange. I'm sure it was the actor in me coming alive, but I immediately started improvising and just having fun. Obviously, Dame Edna was enjoying our tête-à-tête as well. She invited my husband and me to join her on stage. Actually, she insisted. She kept calling my husband "Ryan," and, since his name is Brian, he and I began an improvisation with that.

Once on stage, we had a grand time, bantering away as if we were a regular part of the performance. Dame Edna asked her photographer to take a picture of the three us, sprinkled us with sequins, and I left the stage bidding the audience to "Be the stars you are!" I'm sure the audience thought the entire episode was rehearsed.

Actually, in an odd way, it was. I have been preparing my entire life to be on Broadway. I just never thought it would happen on Mother's Day at a Dame Edna matinee. What a great adventure in improvisation!

Improvisation means inventing solutions on the spur of the moment, winging it, and going for the gold without preparation. With the materials available to us, we create something where nothing was before. The best improvisation is done with total confidence and no apology for any lack of readiness. Improvisation incorporates many other gifts: faith, energy, enthusiasm, hope, patience, perseverance, spontaneity, and, most of all, a willingness to risk being laughed at and with.

Actors learn improvisation, and so can you. Improvisation starts with confidence in yourself, trusting yourself to make smart decisions most of the time. Accept yourself as you are, with all your inadequacies, idiosyncrasies, and shortcomings.

Start small. For example, if you usually follow recipes, throw something together tonight. It might be terrible, but you might create a new culinary sensation. When carefully laid plans go awry, think on your feet and improvise a new plan. In stress-filled situations like job interviews or meeting future in-laws, stay loose and ready to extemporize. Few things are the end of the world. Stay flexible and alert, like a skilled dancer, ready to follow whatever the band plays next. Improvisation is an invaluable gift in our everyday lives. Sometimes we need to just "fake it 'til we make it!"

I stress improvisation for my acting students who get nervous before auditions. "This is no big deal in the grand scheme of things," I assure them. "There are only two truly important things in life—birth and death—and both are highly unlikely to occur during your interview. Either you get the job or you don't. If you don't, there is always tomorrow. Relax, lighten up, do your best, and be kind to yourself." Improvisation can save the day.

Acting is behaving believably in imaginary circumstances. Improvisation expands the possibilities for different outcomes. Improvising in your daily life develops your imagination, courage, and flexibility. You'll be better equipped to handle job interviews and challenging business situations, and best of all, you'll be a lot more fun at social gatherings. You never know when your improvisational skills may result in your own fifteen minutes of fame.

Cynthia Brian

What's Next?

Get a radio, turn it on, and make sure no one can see you. Turn the dial to the next station and improvise a response to what you hear. Sing, dance, make a speech, pray, or act out a commercial. Keep moving up the dial, and see how quickly you can react to each new program. Can you get your response time down to less than a second?

Life is 90 percent improvisation. Stay loose, breathe deeply, and go for it.

The Gift of
INGENUITY

My brother Fred is the most ingenious person I know. Growing up, we thought he'd be a famous inventor one day. He was always creating some useful and imaginative contraption. One of his chores was to empty the wastepaper baskets and kitchen garbage cans into the big bin behind the shed, near the creek. It was quite a walk, and he figured there must be a better way. He invented a container attached to a pulley system of ropes and chains. All we had to do was dump the garbage into the container and wind a crank. The container would glide to the bin, dump itself, and return. Fred was eight years old at the time.

As a prank, Fred once tied all our bedroom doors together so when one person opened theirs, it closed another door. We were all trapped in our rooms with doors opening and slamming until he kindly gave us the secret to get out.

When I was a teenager, Fred invented a spyglass to see through keyholes and around corners. With this invention he could keep tabs on my activities with my friends and boyfriends.

"What's she doing now?" my younger brother, David, would ask.

"Making another strawberry milkshake," Fred would respond. Fortunately, we were all very innocent in those days. Also, we knew we were being watched and got a big kick out of Fred's creations.

Years later, Fred built a river in his backyard, complete with live fish. He encircled his garage with an elaborate train system, which has numerous tracks, tunnels, and mountains. After my dad died, Fred took over the ranch full time and expanded the farm, again using his creativity and ingenuity to improve irrigation systems and planting techniques. He also re-created his train track, built a fantastic pool house, and installed marvelous outdoor lighting, fountains, and landscaping. Fred can design and build anything. There isn't a

Cynthia Brian

tractor, trailer, truck, cycle, or building that Fred can't fix. He's resourceful and is always figuring out ways to do something more efficiently, and for less cost. Best of all, he has fun with his flights of fancy and shares his gift of ingenuity when any of us need assistance. He has truly become a famous inventor!

We can all be ingenious. Use your imagination. Be resourceful. Strive to be innovative and adroit with the tasks at hand. There is always a better, faster, cheaper, easier way to do something; we just have to discover the method. Be willing to err, be open to ideas, try everything. Your next blunder could be a brainstorm and the contraption you develop may become a timesaving invention.

I'm sure Fred tried many ways to get that garbage emptied, before finding one that worked. Happily, we always remember the successful inventions. The ideas you generate and cultivate will help you overcome obstacles, solve challenges, and achieve goals. And who knows, maybe you won't have to take out the garbage either!

EXERCISE

Book a Flight of Fancy

Pick any challenge you have faced recently. Write it down in the form of a question. Then go into your spontaneous, ingenious mode. Write nine possible solutions. Don't worry if the ideas seem crazy or impractical. For example: Question: "What can I do about a commute that has become a stressful nightmare?" Your answers might include

☆ *Use commute time for business projects.*
☆ *Use commute time for personal projects or extra sleep.*
☆ *Speed up the journey. (Travel by helicopter?)*
☆ *Change my work schedule; for example, fewer but longer days, or arrive and leave when traffic is lighter.*
☆ *Quit, and find a job closer to home.*
☆ *Move to live nearer my job.*

☆ *Move the job facility closer to my home.*
☆ *Telecommute.*
☆ *Retire.*

   Most of your answers won't be immediately practical, but they'll trigger new ways of looking at things, revealing new solutions. You'll be amazed at the quality and quantity of ideas that pop into your head. Repeat this exercise regularly with different problems. When problems overwhelm you, book a vacation on a flight of fancy and use your ingenuity.

You have all the answers already.
You just have to match them with the right
questions.

                     Cynthia Brian

The Gift of
INSPIRATION

I look for inspiration every day. Inspiration is all around us. We just have to open our eyes and our hearts.

I interview a lot of extraordinary ordinary people for my radio and television shows. One was Deane Hawley from San Diego. As a young man in the 1950s, he had majored in marketing and sales at the University of Southern California in Los Angeles. However, he was bitten by the songwriting bug and was constantly running over to Hollywood to pitch his songs. He ended up with a record contract and made a hit record, "Look for a Star."

But the music business changed, and Deane settled for the more stable world of corporate pharmaceutical sales. Decades later, a midlife crisis put him back on his dream path. Deane started writing and producing insightful music with another angelic person, Zannah Castenada. When I heard the music from their CD, *Angel Light,* I asked Deane, Zannah, and their talented vocalist, Molly Passutti, to talk about their mission on my show. They described their determination to bring positive messages to the world through their songs. Shortly after that, they wrote an inspirational theme song for my program, *Starstyle—Live Your Dreams!*

Deane and I spoke often on the phone about doing what you love and helping others to find their purpose. One day he said to me, "I'm working on a great project right now with a living legend." He and Frankie Laine, the famous singer of the 1950s, were putting together a new CD.

"Frankie Laine?" I said. "Is that the same Frankie Laine that sang "Mule Train" and the theme song for *Rawhide?"*

"The one and only," said Deane. "This man is truly amazing."

It took me a few seconds to process this information. Then I told Deane how my grandfather Fred Abruzzini had often spoken of his wonderful friend Frankie Laine, who he had come to know through the winery at Beringer. As kids, we had even listened to recordings of Grandpa and Frankie singing together. It was ten years since Grandpa had died, and it was difficult to imagine that Frankie was still alive.

"Oh, he is very much alive," Deane told me. "In fact, our new CD is called *It Ain't Over 'Til It's Over*. I learned that Frankie Laine was an energetic eighty-six and was working with the same passion he had years ago. Deane told Frankie about my grandfather, and Frankie invited us down to San Diego to visit him.

Sitting on his patio overlooking the beautiful harbor vistas, Frankie told me stories of Grandpa and recalled the fun they had shared. He considered my grandfather an original, an honest, truthful, trustworthy, irreplaceable buddy. I felt honored and grateful to be listening to Frankie's remembrances and for this chance opportunity to connect with Grandpa's friend.

We began discussing Frankie and Deane's project. The songs from the new CD are a senior's celebration of life. Frankie believes in living life to the fullest and being present in the world. He sings about giving back to the community and having a sense of humility about the many blessings bestowed on us in our lives. Take life a day at a time, he says, and don't be afraid of love, no matter how old you are. He even speaks of facing death, losing a loved one, and allowing time to grieve and heal one's heart. Frankie also offers a musical tribute to couples whose long relationships still have the glow that brought them together. In the first half of our life, he says, people use their five senses to understand the world. In the second part of life, the senses are pathways to the soul. Best of all, Frankie sings about living your dreams, continuing to grow, and pursuing your passions at every age.

Frankie doesn't believe in retiring. He believes in rediscovering your purpose and coming back strong for that final "third act." Deane and Frankie have become huge inspirational beacons in my life. They are both back in the game, not living in the past, but constantly in the present with an eye toward the future. Joy is in the moments, not the hours, days, or years.

Frankie Laine's first wife died some years ago. He remarried a wonderful woman about a year and a half ago. He is touring, singing, and creating new music with that ever-youthful, melodious voice of his. He embodies the ingredients of a Super Senior, a group that Deane developed for the art and science of optimistic living.

Frankie and Deane continue to entertain, inspire, educate, and participate in life. They graciously presented me with a theme song for the charity I founded for positive programming. Their song will inspire the world to live fully. Thank you, Deane and Frankie, for lighting the flame of inspiration in me.

Inspiration can come from people, places, ideas, events, even things. My kids always know exactly what I'm going to say at a certain time of day. Just as the sun settles low on the hills, burning bright red and orange, I call to them, "Come on! Let's go outside and sit on the swing." It's my favorite time of day. Sunsets inspire my spirit. The warmth, the colors, the ending of a day, and the promise of another spark my enthusiasm and my creativity. At sunset, I feel energized, happy, and full of gratitude. Sunsets remind me that we have spent another beautiful day on planet Earth.

I feel the same way about moving bodies of water, whether it is the ocean's crashing waves or a lake's lapping ripples. I am rejuvenated just being around it. I do my best writing at sunset and especially when I am near water. My thoughts flow easily, and my fingers type all by themselves. I am filled with purpose and the potential for action.

Frankie and Deane are inspired and inspiring. They celebrate living and seek opportunities to encourage others. Their legacy will be that of both entertainment and inspiration. And it won't be over until it's over!

Seek inspiration. Use it. Give it. Surround yourself with people and places that are enlivening and stimulating. Weed out the counterproductive naysayers in your life and replace them with people who electrify your dreams and energize your spirit. Spend time in a place that rejuvenates you and amplifies your ideas.

Commit yourself to worthwhile activities and causes that enrich and uplift yourself and others. Find meaning and value in all your interactions. Don't make excuses and say, "No one and nothing inspires me." If you want to improve your life, concentrate on creating the cast of characters you want to play with. It is never too early or too late to be inspired.

Inspiration is your life force. With continuous inner development and growth, you will become an inspiration to others. To be inspired and to be inspiring is the ultimate goal. When we light the way for others, we are truly enlightened ourselves.

EXERCISE

Twenty-Four Hours to Live

Imagine that you have been told you have only twenty-four hours to live. How would you spend those hours? Write this question in your journal. Ask yourself: Who would I want to talk to? What would I say or not say? What kind of legacy do I want to leave? What inspiration can I give others?

Would you watch another sunset, smell the flowers, eat your favorite foods, or write your loved ones? Revisit this page of your journal often. Fine-tune your answers.

Cynthia Brian

Be the star you are
Light the flame that burns
Deep within your heart
Where the real you yearns

To spread your wings and fly,
Though the journey's long.
Keep your love alive
And your spirit strong.

You're a seeker, a dreamer
With courage to give
Every precious part of you.
You're an artist, a poet
Who will never give up
Till your dreams come true!

Let go of your fears
You've traveled so far
Show the world your smile
Be the star you are.

—Words and Music from the song "Be the Star You Are,"
by Deane Hawley and Frankie Laine,
Innertainment Music. Sung by Frankie Laine.

The Gift of

INTERDEPENDENCE

When my kids were younger, we loved to hike in the surrounding hillsides in the spring. The meadows were ablaze with poppies, and the grass was the greenest green imaginable. We'd picnic and go on scavenger hunts for treasures like feathers, acorns, rocks, and other gifts of nature. One evening in early May of 1988, our hike yielded a living gem.

We had just visited our favorite olive grove and were climbing a hill on our way home. "Shhh, what's that sound?" whispered Justin. Heather's eyes widened, and we strained to listen but couldn't hear anything. "Quiet. Listen. There it is again," said Justin. He started tiptoeing carefully through the grass.

Then we heard it too. It was a whimper, a cry like that of a small baby. We moved quietly toward the sound. There in the brush was a still-bloodied newborn baby goat. "Where's the mother?" I said to no one in particular.

"Don't touch the baby," Justin advised, "or the mother will never take her back. I'll run and get some towels." We stayed with the crying baby, wanting to comfort her, but knowing he was right. Justin quickly returned with some clean towels, and we wrapped the kid carefully.

"We have to get her to Kenny right away," Justin said. "She needs her mother's milk." The city had recently commissioned a goat herder named Kenny to graze his goats on open land as a fire prevention measure. The goats kept the dry grasses and weeds trimmed, which was invaluable during the dangerous fire season. Justin knew Kenny and had been working with him after school, moving fences to redirect the goats.

We carried the newborn to Kenny's trailer. "I know exactly who the mother is," Kenny told us. "Unfortunately, she has no desire to have a kid."

"What will happen to her?" asked Heather.

"If the kid doesn't get some colostrum and mother's milk immediately, she'll die. I'll try to get one of the other mothers to take her, but if they won't, I'll have to put her down."

With one voice, we cried, "No, don't kill her!" We couldn't imagine this precious baby being killed just because her mother wouldn't care for her. We asked if we could come by in the morning to check on her. Then, if none of the other mothers had accepted her, we'd take her ourselves.

"She probably won't live until morning," Kenny told us, "but if she does, and she hasn't been adopted, you can take her."

We couldn't sleep that night. We watched the clock, eager for morning. At seven o'clock, we literally ran down the road to Kenny's trailer. "How's the baby?" we panted.

"I was able to get some colostrum for her from one of the other moms, nothing more," he told us. "But she's a fighter. She definitely wants to live. If you're willing to take her on, you can have her." We thanked Kenny, got care instructions, and took our new baby home. Heather named her "Mini," as in miniature goat and Minnie Mouse. She was truly a mini, fitting easily in the palms of my two hands. We bought goats' milk from a feed store and fed her a bottle every three hours around the clock.

Mini followed us everywhere and slept in a comfortable nest the kids built for her in the laundry room. She was so adorable and loving that we took her with us on excursions. Sometimes she went to school with Heather and Justin or to softball games with Brian and me. Our coed adult softball league made her its mascot. Justin became an entrepreneur, renting Mini for two dollars a day as "an environmentally correct weed-eating and fertilizing machine."

Mini grew larger, and we built her a doghouse to live in. She grew more, and we built her a goat house. She grew even more, and we built her a barn. What we thought was a mini-goat turned out to be a maxi. We adored her and gave her a huge fenced-in barnyard to protect her from coyotes and mountain lions. Goats have an average life span of seven years, but our Mini is still with us and thriving after thirteen years.

Mini was the first animal in what would become known as "our rescued menagerie." Since her adoption, we've supplied her with lots of animal friends who we also rescued from death and destruction. We often joke that we must have a welcome banner at our home that only animals can sense, because every stray and abandoned creature seems to find its way to our door and our hearts. We posted a wooden sign on the barnyard gate that reads "Mini and Friends." She is definitely the grand dame, a real old goat and queen of the barnyard kingdom.

Mini would have died if we hadn't rescued her and showered her with food, shelter, and love over the years. We have received much from her in return. She taught my children responsibility, gentleness, and the importance of all creatures. She taught them how to play and frolic. And she has kept our weeds trimmed. Although we never imagined we'd be raising goats, we can't conceive of our lives without Mini.

There is a difference between interdependence and dependence. Interdependence means having the courage to stand on your own two feet, while allowing others to help you and nature to shape you. We are all interconnected. Whether we like it or not, we are a part of a larger whole, an inescapable "one." No one can be an island. We may be nonconformists or mavericks, but we are still part of a universal community of humans, plants, animals, water, sky, and stars. As astronomer Carl Sagan liked to say, "You are star stuff."

You can't start living your dreams until you see yourself in everyone and everything around you. Often we reject in others what we most dislike in ourselves. Some of our most special gifts are lurking under a protective layer that we've built up over the years. Cynicism, negativity, and lack of purpose can be excellent defense mechanisms, shielding us from feelings of failure: "If I never try, I can never lose." But these comforting barriers also keep us from the connectedness that lets us experience life and feel fully alive.

Treasure your interdependence because it emphasizes how extraordinary you are, not how ordinary. You can't be interdependent

Cynthia Brian

alone. We all interact, and we are interdependent from birth until death and beyond.

One Word at a Time

Gather at least two other people, and sit together in a circle. Each person in turn says only one word. The purpose is to create an interdependent, coherent story using your listening *skills. Start out with, "Once upon a time…" Most stories turn out humorously, which works wonders for the soul. Have fun, and say the first word that comes to mind. This is a really fun game to do after a dinner party while you are still sitting around the table. Try it! You'll like it!*

See yourself in everything
because everything is already within you.
Take care of your world; life is precious!

The Gift of
JOY

This is about a fish that not only got away; a big crowd waved it good-bye. When my friend Scott Sunkel was a boy, he and his dad enjoyed hiking and fishing together. It was their special time, and Scott learned to love the outdoors and the pleasures of fishing. After Scott married and had his own children, he passed on his love of nature to Cody and Shauna, taking them hiking and fishing as often as possible.

Then Scott's dad became very ill with diabetes. "Poppy," as the grandchildren affectionately called him, began discussing the concept of life after death with his family. He questioned the existence of heaven and was skeptical about spirituality in general. Still, he asked his family to scatter his ashes on the small, tranquil lake in the woodland where the family had enjoyed so many walks. Poppy died, and his relatives fulfilled his wishes. On days when Scott felt sad or needed to feel his dad's presence, he went to the lake for a walk, fresh air, and sometimes a good cry. He envisioned his dad as the guardian of this peaceful lake, protecting the wildlife, birds, fish, and children who came to play.

One hot afternoon a couple of years later, Shauna and Cody asked Scott if they could go fishing at the lake. The sun was at its highest, not the best time for fishing, but the kids were insistent. Scott and his wife, Nancy, thought it would be nice to be together for a few hours. Their busy carpet cleaning business usually kept them apart.

When they arrived, a park ranger gave them the bad news that fishing was very poor right then. The lake hadn't been stocked in months. "But," he continued, "maybe you can catch a small catfish or a few crawdads." Nancy decided to rent a pedal boat to get some exercise, while Scott and the kids baited their hooks and flung their lines into the water.

Cynthia Brian

"Daddy," said Cody, "do you think Poppy is watching us fish?"

"Of course," said Scott, "he's going to help us catch the big one." Just then, Scott's line went taut, and his reel started spinning. Scott's first thought was that his line had caught on a log being moved by an underwater current. But no log ever moved this fast.

"Nancy, bring the boat over here," he called. "We're going for a joy ride."

The kids were grinning from ear to ear. They grabbed their poles and jumped into the pedal boat. Nancy pedaled as fast as she could toward the moving line. A wild goose chase followed that lasted for more than an hour without anyone knowing what they were following. Then, *splash!* The monster leapt from the depths of the lake.

Their eyes grew as large as saucers when a four-foot sturgeon arched and dove back into the dark water. The furious pedaling began again. "What am I going to do now?" cried Scott. "My line's only an eight-pounder, and this baby must weigh at least forty pounds. I need a steel cable line or a fifty-pound test line! The ridges on his back are like razors; he'll cut the line. We have to keep up with him!"

"No way, Jose," exclaimed an exhausted Nancy, and she pedaled to the dock. Two teenage boys had been watching the chase and ran down to help. Nancy jumped off the boat and ran to ask the ranger for rope, a stronger line, a net, steel cable, or anything that would help to land this prize. The teenagers leapt on board just as the sturgeon unspooled Scott's line, taking the rest of it from his reel.

Nancy described this monster sturgeon to the ranger, but he didn't believe her. "We only have catfish and trout in this lake, ma'am," he smiled. "Our biggest fish is about eight inches long, so we don't have any nets or ropes and *especially* no steel cable." He chuckled. "But I appreciate your imagination."

For two more hours, the troop paddled excitedly around the small lake, pursuing the sturgeon, anticipation competing with exhaustion. Scott had never caught a sturgeon big enough to keep. Now he had a monster on the other end of his line.

A rowboat approached the strange scene. Fortunately, they had a length of rope and threw it to the pedal boat. Dusk was coming on. The ranger yelled from the shore that it was time to come in. The park was closing. Scott began to apologize to the teens for wasting their time. At that moment, he looked down in the water and saw the white of the sturgeon's belly. The fish was exhausted too. The teens, Boy Scouts both, tied a slip knot in the rope. Then, gently, the line was pulled taut. When the fish reached the surface, the boys lassoed the sturgeon, and everyone pulled it into the boat.

By now, a large group of people had gathered on the shore. As the pedal boat neared the dock, the onlookers were astonished. Soon the press arrived. History was being made at this small lake. Sturgeon live in the ocean. Yet here was one in a lake—fifty-four inches long and weighing forty-six pounds. (The world record was fifty-two pounds.)

The rangers reviewed their logs and found no report of anyone sighting a large fish in this lake. Flashbulbs flashed while Scott was thinking about all the people he would invite to share in the meal of a lifetime. Nancy grabbed his arm. "You know you can't keep him," she whispered, pointing at the still-gasping fish. "You have to throw him back. He's the king of the lake."

"What do you mean?" Scott choked. "We spent the entire after-noon chasing this guy. It's the first sturgeon I ever caught and the biggest fish I ever caught. I'm eating him! No way am I throwing him back."

The normally shy Nancy pressed her lips together and squared her shoulders. She leapt on a box and addressed the crowd. "What should we do with this fish?" she shouted. "Cut him up and have a celebration? Or throw him back?"

One by one, the people responded. "I guess you have to throw him back." "Yes, he's the granddaddy of the lake." "He's the king; let him go." Scott turned to the Boy Scouts, sure *they'd* agree with him that the sturgeon was dinner. The boys stared at the fish they had fought so hard to catch. "You have to throw him back," they said. "He's God's gift to the lake."

Everyone helped return the dazed sturgeon to the dark water. Scott stood gazing at the water as the monarch swam away. A peacefulness and magical feeling came over him. Somehow, he was sure, his father had brought this big one to the lake to let the family know he was okay, still fishing in the next life. Poppy had found heaven and had made himself the guardian of the lake. No one has seen the sturgeon since that day, but the legend of the Big One continues to captivate visitors.

The joy of fishing, the joy of family, the joy of life. When we can be spontaneous and joyful, tranquility will replace fear and doubt. Work or play we love—a sense of purpose and total involvement and challenge in a project—makes us happy. Close relationships make us happy. Happiness and joy are side effects of relishing your daily life with all its imperfections. Don't search for joy, just recognize it when it hits you, and revel in it.

EXERCISE

Wave

Remember how you used to sit on the bus or in the backseat of your car when you were a child and wave to the cars, keeping score of how drivers waved back? Well, do it again today. Just for the pure joy of it, stand on a street corner this afternoon and wave to all the passersby. You may feel a little foolish too, but, ooohh, the fun you'll have! Be childlike, and wave joyously to the world!

Joy is contagious.

The Gift of
KNOWLEDGE

During the Great Depression of the 1930s, my godmother, Aunt Linda, attended a one-room schoolhouse in Rutherford, California, along with her five younger brothers and sisters. In the fall of her eighth grade year, Aunt Linda was put in charge of decorations for a class party. The class had no budget, and Linda's family, proud but poor, couldn't afford to buy decorations. So my grandparents, Swiss immigrants, Eugenio and Louise Gina Defilippis, suggested Linda do what they would have done in the old country: gather nature's gifts from the autumnal woods and hillsides.

Linda enlisted her brothers, sisters, and friends for a foraging party. Dressed in shorts, the group set out with bushels to comb the hillsides and banks of the nearby creek, gathering branches of black-berries, bunches of grapes, walnuts, wild sunflowers, and boughs of bright red leaves.

Back in the classroom, they arranged their bounty on the tables and made arbors of red leaves and grapes at the doors. Everything was beautiful. "Almost as good as professional," Linda boasted. As each guest arrived, they were given a corsage of red leaves and wild flowers. The fun and festivities began.

Before long, Linda felt feverish. Her brothers complained that they too felt hot. A few classmates left early, saying they didn't feel well. Linda gave each student a bouquet of red leaves to take home.

By the next morning, Linda's parents had six very sick children. Not knowing what was wrong, Louise Gina went to a neighbor's home for help. Her friend's children were also burning with fever and covered with a terrible rash. The country doctor was working overtime. Every party guest was burning, itching, and on fire. Several had to go to the hospital. His diagnosis was simple. The lovely red leaves were poison oak. Although the entire class was sick, everyone survived.

Knowledge is power. The adage "What you don't know can't hurt you" is absolutely false, and as the saying goes, "A little knowledge is a dangerous thing" is especially true when a child decorates a school party with poison oak.

People are often afraid to admit that they don't have all the answers. It is not ignorant to confess that you do not know something. Knowing that you don't know something is the first step toward wisdom. Knowledge and education are different. I've heard people belittle themselves by beginning a sentence with, "Well, I'm not educated, but...." We can learn new things every day. It doesn't require a college degree to become an expert on subject. The high school dropouts who became computer millionaires are proof of this. However, education is the foundation of learning. We should keep learning, keep training, and keep instructing ourselves in the ongoing process of accumulating knowledge. Knowledge is the expertise we develop from our amassed experiences and studies.

When my dad was diagnosed with a rare cancer, I became an expert on his disease. I read every book and medical journal article about it that I could find. I listened to tapes. I spoke with physicians, surgeons, and anyone who had any information on how to combat his cancer. I was not trained in medicine, but I became an informed warrior on my dad's behalf.

You can't become a brain surgeon by reading every book on brain surgery, but we have access to resources that will inform us. We can go to the library, search the Internet, take courses. The irony of learning is that the more knowledge we gain, the more we realize how little we know.

Jim Rohn, author of *The Art of Exceptional Living,* told my radio listeners that "a formal education can make us a living, but self-education will make us a fortune. The higher-priced houses selling today feature a room called a library. That should tell us something."

When I visited *Chicken Soup for the Soul* author Jack Canfield at his home in Santa Barbara, I was not surprised that he has a personal library in a separate building, filled floor to ceiling with books, all of which he had read. No wonder Jack is so successful. And on an architectural tour of the Hudson River Valley, I fell in love with the library in the beautiful summer home of Wall Street magnate Richard Jenrette. He, too, had read every book on his shelves and hadn't become a billionaire by watching sitcoms.

Because of Aunt Linda's misadventure, our family became knowledgeable about poison oak. This expanded to learning about other California wildlife, fauna, and flora. I intend to keep on learning as long as I live, adding to my library and my life experiences. We can not know everything, but we can strive to know many things. "Knowledge is power" may be a cliché, but what you don't know can most certainly harm you.

EXERCISE

Snoop

Nothing makes us more eager to learn about something than the idea that we're not supposed to know about it. Choose a subject you've wondered about, and really check it out. Look it up, read books about it, talk to experts. The word "studying" has onerous overtones, but "snooping" always sounds like fun.

As a long-term project, develop your personal library. If you are a bibliophile, with books covering every surface and stacked in every corner, organize and catalogue your books. Keep the books you haven't read yet in a "To Read" pile. As you read them, transfer them to your library shelf. You might use sticky notes to mark important passages and record your thoughts about the book on a file card, tucked inside the cover. Each book becomes part of your body of knowledge, ready for you to revisit whenever you wish.

"If you think education is expensive,
try ignorance."

—*Harvey MacKay*

Cynthia Brian

The Gift of
LEADERSHIP

As a child, did you ever play the game of Follow the Leader? The leader determined the group's direction and everyone had to follow. Leadership is not something you are born to do. Leadership is an earned skill. Leaders are people who form a vision and convince others to collaborate in implementing it.

People tell me I'm a born leader because I seem so confident, passionate, and optimistic. From the time I was three years old, I was organizing my numerous cousins and giving them parts in performances we'd give on Sundays at our weekly family get-togethers. In spring, this took place at the picnic grounds on our hill; in winter they would be at a relative's home. As the leader, I made sure that everyone participated to the extent they wanted. The cousins were exhilarated at their competence, the parents were proud of their thespians, and I found I liked leading.

My formal education begun in the first grade; there were no preschools or kindergartens in our area. As the eldest in our family, I felt obligated to come home each night and teach my younger siblings everything I had learned at school that day. One day the teacher mentioned the Girl Scouts.

Although I had no clue what the Girl Scouts did, I knew it was an organization for girls. So, with no groups in our area, at age seven I founded our ranch house Junior Girl Scouts. I was the leader of the pack. Members included my two sisters, Patty and Debbie, and the daughters of ranch hands. Every weekend I organized learning expeditions. I would hand everyone a piece of cardboard, some tape, and a crayon, and off we'd go into the hills, scouting for wildflowers, which we would identify using our nature book. Or we would pretend we were explorers discovering new worlds, like Magellan, Columbus, or my personal favorite, Ponce de León. As leader, it was my job to scout ahead and make sure there were no lurking rattlesnakes. An oak tree or buckeye tree would catch our fancy, and one of us would pronounce this her territory. From that day forward, no one could climb that tree without permission from the discoverer.

My sister Patty loved these adventures, and I gave her straight As for her enthusiasm. Debbie, on the other hand, didn't like the history lessons and the wildflower gathering, wouldn't heed my directions, and thought what we were doing was stupid. She was more interested in playing on the tractors, and I routinely flunked her for the day. I didn't realize that, instead of reproaching her for her lack of interest, a *real* leader would have encouraged her, inspired her, and listened to her.

One day, I decided it was time to teach my band of merrymakers how to dive. Everyone was excited. We didn't have a swimming pool so, being creative, we hiked up to the cow trough, which was full of spring water. I announced that this was where we would learn the fine art of diving. Everyone wanted to go first, but *I* was the leader. Or so I thought.

Confidently, I climbed up on the rim of the cow trough and, with much fanfare, dove into the murky water. When I came to the surface, I felt a bit light headed, but boldly announced, "See how easy it is? Now you try it!" Then I passed out.

I had hit the bottom of the trough and torn my chin on a big bolt. Blood was everywhere. That day, at age seven, I learned that leadership is more than being the oldest, the strongest, the tallest, or the smartest. Leadership is not about bossing people around or getting them to do what you want done because you say so. Leaders are not dictators nor are they careless. After that, I was a humble leader and encouraged everyone else to show off her own skills, strengths, and unique abilities. I had learned that authority is not leadership.

Leaders must have the courage to do new things, to take chances, and to endure the consequences of their decisions. Almost by definition, a leader braves strange new territory, dreams bigger dreams, and dares to go where no one has gone before. Leadership also means being responsible for yourself and your charges. A leader's job is to inspire, to motivate, to make it *easy* to do the right thing. A

Cynthia Brian

good leader knows how to gather the most intelligent and knowledgeable people for the task at hand, then get out of their way and let them create magic. Leaders encourage others to break through their barriers, release their fears, and reach for success. A true leader never threatens, but instead offers trust, encouragement, gratitude, and recognition when others do something well. Great leaders let go of ego. Leaders listen to their own hearts and souls and help others do the same. That's why people love to "follow the leader."

Since the cow trough fiasco, I have had other strenuous lessons in leadership and honed my skills. An old Italian proverb says, "Keep the company of good people, and you'll increase their number and accomplish your mission." For my television shows, I do just that, bringing together the best people I can find, exciting them with my vision, and then letting them do what they do best. Together we explore life's issues.

There are no rules for becoming a strong leader. You proceed at your own risk. It helps to look, listen, and think creatively. Leaders design new methods, strategies, products, and solutions. Leaders innovate. Each of us plays many roles in life. Sometimes you will need to be a leader. Sometimes you will need to be a follower. The skills and awareness you learn in both roles can make you a wiser, more effective leader and an enthusiastic, loyal, and judicious follower.

Leading the Pack

When you think of the word "leader," what first comes to mind? Do you picture a real person, an authority figure, a politician? Or yourself? Let's start working on you *as a leader.*

☆ *Write a list of the qualities you admire in someone you feel is a leader.*
☆ *Put a check next to the qualities you now possess.*

Do you have many of their qualities? If so, pat yourself on the back and pledge to keep developing those virtues. If not, choose a quality you will concentrate on improving.

A great leader makes it easy to do the right thing
and difficult to do the wrong thing.
The success of the pack is determined
by the success of the leader.

Cynthia Brian

The Gift of

LIFELINES

An East Coast literary agent and book reviewer named David wrote me one day that "I've just finished a set of reviews, and I'm back in the world of the living. Writing under a last-minute deadline, rushing against the clock, is always the equivalent of a near-death experience for me!"

I was struck by how people equate deadlines with death. The idea of a "deadline" is so destructive that I urged David to look at them as "lifelines." Instead of thanking me for my wisdom and insights, he was furious because I wasn't empathizing with his pain.

Some of us respond to every deadline like a champion racehorse hearing, "They're off!" But most of us occasionally torture ourselves with the effort of getting things done on time and on budget. I am just as guilty as the next person, but life usually goes on, whether we meet our due dates or not. Sometimes we are stressed because we have procrastinated and have only ourselves to blame. That increases our distress.

The mere thought of meeting a deadline used to give me cold chills. "Deadline" meant that if I didn't finish on time, I'd be dead. The pressure and anxiety could be paralyzing.

At one point, I decided that I would no longer have deadlines. No, I didn't stop being a human being or stop completing tasks. I simply changed my vocabulary. I now call my deadlines "lifelines." When a project is due by a certain date, I look forward to that time as a positive thing. My life will be improved when I complete my tasks by my "lifeline," and I will reward myself for finishing the project. This keeps me energized and puts a stop to procrastination.

We all have to meet our time lines. Just change the wording from dead to life, and you'll approach due dates more positively. Deadlines wither. Lifelines enhance.

Turning Deadlines into Lifelines

The next time you are procrastinating or distressed about finishing a project, change your deadline to a lifeline.

Write down a reward that you will give yourself when your project is complete. It doesn't have to be costly or elaborate, just something that enhances you so you will look forward to completing the task. One of the rewards I tantalize myself with in the summer is time to go outside and sit in the garden with a big bowl of ice cream in the middle of my work-day, listening to the birds and smelling the fragrances of the day. In the winter, I promise myself a big cup of hot cocoa, a blazing fire, a good book, and a cozy blanket ensconced in a comfortable chair for an hour of uninterrupted pleasure. Your deadly deadlines will be eliminated, your tasks will be completed with less stress, and your life will become more pleasurable.

For the next seven days, keep a list of actions, big or small, that you tend to avoid. At the end of the week, do you notice any commonalities? Are they boring? Potentially embarrassing or dangerous? Likely to require great effort without tangible results?

☆ *Cross off anything that you can realistically never do.*
☆ *Choose one of the other actions, and do it now!*

A dream is a goal with a lifeline.
Throw yourself a rope.

Cynthia Brian

The Gift of

LISTENING

In nineteenth-century Britain, there were two famous political rivals, Gladstone and Disraeli. A lady who had met both was asked by her friends to describe them. "Well," she said, "when I met Mr. Gladstone, he convinced me he was the most brilliant man in the world. But when I met Mr. Disraeli, he convinced me that *I* was the most brilliant *woman* in the world."

When was the last time someone listened to you like that?

Listening isn't always easy. Our mind races ahead of a conversation with responses to what is being said and points we want to make, so we stop hearing. Listening requires enormous discipline, but it's a learnable skill.

Forget cars, CD players, and the latest designer sports shoes. The best gift you can give teenagers is to listen—really listen—to them. I have two teenagers myself, and I have made many mistakes with them. But one thing I learned from my own teenage years is the value of listening *without* commenting or judging. (Much of the time, of course, I am biting my tongue.)

My son, Justin, has never been one to talk much or to share his feelings. When he does, I have to remind myself to open my ears and let him know I hear him. My daughter, Heather, is just the opposite. She likes to confide in me and tell me everything that is happening in her life. But, even though we are really close, I learned that if I make a comment or suggestion, she will clam up and say, "I can't tell you *anything*. You just don't understand!"

So, I listen quietly. Sometimes kids (and adults) just need to get things out of their systems. They are not asking for advice or comments or strategies to make it better. They just want to be heard. If they do need help, it does no good to offer any until they ask for it. I save my advice for times when they are likely to listen to me.

Our family rules are strict, but fair. One night, Justin exploded because we had said "no" to something he wanted to do. He shouted that we didn't trust him and were being irrational. He was very upset and angry. I could have responded with equally strong emotions of my own, retaliating like a dictatorial parent guarding a power base. Instead, I listened quietly and carefully. What I heard was almost an exact repeat of my own words at his age. I clearly remembered a terrible argument I had with my own parents when I wanted to attend a Jefferson Airplane concert in San Francisco with my high school boyfriend. My parents had real concerns about drugs, violence, sex, and car accidents. But what I heard them saying was, "We don't trust you." I was devastated.

After several days of battling and feeling miserable, we finally listened to one another. I heard their worries and understood their logic. They heard my arguments and acknowledged that I was an honorable and respectable young lady. They allowed me to attend the concert, and I was extra cautious to obey their rules and live up to the responsibilities they had given me. When they had really listened to me with both their hearts and their minds, their fears were minimized. It was the only big argument I ever had with Mom and Dad.

With my son, Justin, I really listened too. I realized he was justified in expecting to be trusted. How better to help our teens know their own self-worth than to give them more responsibility?

A few days later, Justin had several of his buddies over to the house for their weekly guys' event of Monday Night Football. The boys were talking about college plans. All of a sudden, Justin said to one of his friends, "Talk to my mom about your concerns. She'll help you. She really knows how to listen." Then he looked at me. "Mom, you have to help him go for his dreams. Notre Dame is all he's ever wanted, but he doesn't think he's good enough. Talk to him. You're the dream queen." Sometimes, kids hear us when we don't think they're listening.

Whenever anyone says, "You never listen to me!" it's usually true. Someone starts a statement, and our mind rushes to predict what will be said, sometimes so intrusively that we fail to hear the real message. Our minds can process words and ideas at an incredibly

Cynthia Brian

high speed, much faster than speech. That's an explanation for not really listening, but it's no excuse.

Have you ever been in a group and really listened to what others were saying? Almost no one does. People are usually more focused on their own reactions and concerns about what others think of them.

Why stop our own intensely interesting cerebral pyrotechnics and actually listen? Because when we listen, we learn something interesting about others. We also learn about ourselves.

If you can turn off the self-talk in your head and truly listen to someone else, two extraordinary things will happen. First, you'll leave with the feeling that you now know more about that person or situation than before. Second, the speaker will leave feeling that you are a fascinating, intelligent, and likable person because you were so attentive.

EXERCISE

Active Listening Game

You'll need a partner and an egg timer to do this exercise. Grab a friend or family member, and set the timer to three minutes. Designate who takes the first turn to talk on any subject for three minutes. The listener must pay attention without interrupting until the timer dings. The timer is again set for three minutes, and the listener must repeat what he or she heard. The listener begins by saying, "This is what I heard you say. Let me know if I have understood you correctly." The talker has permission to give feedback and correct any miscommunications. Then switch positions and repeat the game. (The former listener now talks on any subject for three minutes.) You'll be amazed at how quickly your listening skills will improve when you actively listen to what others are saying.

We are each blessed with two ears and one mouth.
Listen twice as much as you talk!

The Gift of
LOVE

When I was young, my mom said something that terrified me. She loved her children so much, she said, that she'd cut off her right arm to save our lives. I had nightmares that she might actually have to do it. Then how could she hug us?

It wasn't until I became a parent myself that I recognized the reality of such unconditional love. Mom sacrificed selflessly to give her children great food, a great education, and great self-esteem and self-worth. Because we lived on a farm, she and Dad drove us over a hundred miles a day to school and back. When we forgot our lunches, she'd make another trip to be sure we ate. Mom was involved in all our activities. She attended all our sports, cheerleading, and 4-H events. She volunteered for every parent committee so she would stay involved with her children.

At Christmas, Dad would take us kids shopping, and we'd each buy Mom our favorite present. (Every Christmas, Mom got five flannel Mother Hubbard nightgowns!) For her birthdays, we showered her with homemade gifts such as cookies, colored leaves, knitted items, and hand-framed photos. We cooked her a special dinner, and Dad always made a big to-do about his "queen." We treasured her dearly within the family, but we'd never celebrated her *publicly*.

When her seventieth birthday approached, my two sisters, my brother, and I decided it was time to give Mom a big surprise party to show our appreciation for all those years. Keeping it a surprise turned out to be a considerable feat. One sister insisted we tell her in advance so she could invite the guests of her choice, but the rest of us vetoed that idea.

We divided up the duties. Patty's family worked on invitations and catering. Fred arranged for lighting and the cake. Deb and I handled the decor, choosing a garden theme so Mom could take the decorations home afterward. We booked a rural firehouse and started early on a Saturday morning to transform it into a Garden of Eden. All her children, grandchildren, and spouses came to help set up. Trellises, birdhouses, hoses, water buckets, garden tools, rakes, potted plants, candles, potpourri, garden lights, hummingbird feeders, and all types of beautiful accessories adorned the tables and walls, while hundreds of balloons in wine colors of cabernet, chardonnay, rose, and champagne floated through the air. It was gorgeous. Then the guests started to arrive, hundreds of them, laden with more gardening gifts and bringing their wonderful stories of Mom.

Mom arrived to a fireworks and rocket display, thanks to her grandson Justin, and was totally surprised. The love that filled that firehouse could have ignited a real fire. To have reached the age of seventy and to have so many true friends and loving relatives celebrating her life was indescribably wonderful. As people danced, ate, and laughed, I realized that the only thing in life that truly endures is love.

Love is the deepest of all emotions. Fear and hate are awfully powerful, but love can beat them both. We are shaped and defined by who and what we love. We can never obtain love by asking for it, but we can always give love. Mom had given love all her life, and this day, her seventieth birthday, others paid tribute and gave love to a loving person. As Goethe said, "Love is the reward of love."

Sometimes love may seem a rare commodity, but like a garden, it can be nurtured from the harshest soil. Here are my Seven Rules for a Loving World:

1. Make other people feel good.
2. Make other people look good.
3. Help them meet their needs.
4. Applaud their achievements, no matter how small.
5. Go for win-win solutions.
6. Say "I love you" often and mean it.
7. Expect the best from others. People often become what you believe they are.

Start somewhere, anywhere. French poet Antoine de Saint Exupéry has his Little Prince explain, "We see accurately only with our hearts. The essentials are invisible to the eye."

EXERCISE

Increase Your Lovability Quotient

Nearly everyone says they would like more love in their lives. To have love, we must give love. What can you give? What are you giving? How are you giving? (Love given conditionally is a bribe, not a gift.)

In the Jewish culture, there is a tradition of performing mitzvahs (literally, blessings). Each day, one should do a good deed, preferably anonymously, and with absolutely no expectation of acknowledgment, praise, or being repaid.

Your assignment today is to perform one mitzvah, one special loving act for which you honestly expect nothing in return.

Love is like happiness:
the harder we seek it, the more it eludes us.
Only when we can give it freely can it come
back to us.

Cynthia Brian

The Gift of
MAGIC

Magic happened regularly around our house when I was a child.

My family has always celebrated everything. Because our farm was somewhat isolated, the family traditions that our parents created were the mainstay of my childhood.

As in most households, Thanksgiving, Christmas, and Easter were eagerly anticipated festivities, but we had additional holidays. One of those celebrations was "Three Wise Kings." My mom said because we lived in the country, it was easy for the Three Wise Kings to park their camels outside our house. (Three Wise Kings is also known as Twelfth Night, celebrated twelve days after Christmas on January 6. It honors the Magi who followed the Star of Bethlehem, bringing gold, frankincense, and myrrh to the infant Jesus.)

Because the Three Wise Kings had to travel so far on camelback, they could only bring us small gifts—usually an orange or tangerine, an apple, sometimes an avocado or mango, plus a small sweet and about twenty-five cents in coins. We loved Three Wise Kings Day because it made us feel special.

My parents went all out to create magic in our lives. One year, my mom excused herself during dinner. Suddenly, through the window, we saw a camel. (She had acquired a huge stuffed camel and was outside, moving it up and down.) We shrieked with excitement and awe, knowing the Kings were passing by. The next morning, we awoke to find jewels strung everywhere on the bushes and vines. There were camels' hoofprints and camel dung and a note that this had been a great year for the Magi, so they were sharing their wealth. I vividly remember the sensation of utter delight and can still see the shimmering jewels hanging from the trees. My parents had created the illusion with used costume jewelry from a Goodwill store, horse-made hoofprints, and horse manure posing as camel dung.

At Christmas, we didn't always get something we had especially asked for. Of course, we'd be disappointed. Later in the day, Dad would suggest we take a jeep ride around the ranch to see if anything had fallen off the sleigh. Sure enough! Down at a barn or dangling in a grapevine would be that special gift. Once, a bicycle was sticking out of the chimney with a note attached: "Sorry, it wouldn't squeeze down."

Every holiday provided an opportunity for my parents to be creative. We *saw* the Easter Bunny, we *felt* the tooth fairy's kiss. We witnessed Santa and his elves flying through the sky with Rudolph's red light leading the reindeer. My sister Deb remained an avid believer well into her teens. Eventually, my parents had to tell her that it was all "magic."

As we grew and questions arose, their response was, "If you *don't* believe in magic, magic never happens." I decided to believe. Today, my children delight at the magic they experience year-round in our household and the Three Wise Kings still visit. They remind me that when you believe it, you see it!

In an un-magical world, you create the magic in your life. Find ways to reinterpret your daily routine through the eyes of a child. Children give us a second chance to view the world with innocence and credulity. What magic is hiding in your soul? What simple things can become magical experiences if you use a little imagination?

EXERCISE

Be Your Own Fairy Godmother

Imagine that you are a magician with a magic wand. You can even make a wand from a stick. Add a few ribbons or a sparkling star, and presto! You hold the key to power. Wave the magic wand over your head when you want to change something, even your mood. The magic to create the life you want is inside you. Dream it. Do it.

If you don't believe in magic, magic doesn't happen.

Cynthia Brian

The Gift of
MIRACLES

I remember exactly what I was doing when my sister called to tell me that my father was dying.

When the phone rang, I was at my desk, preparing for the next self-esteem class I was to teach at the Academy of Performing Arts. "It's cancer," my sister Debbie said. "The doctors told him to go home, drink his best wine, and enjoy what was left of his life. There is absolutely nothing that can be done to save Dad. He'll die within three weeks."

I was shaken to my soul with grief. Then the anger set in. How could these doctors just write off my dad like this? This was my dad, whom I adored and worshiped. My father can't possibly have cancer. He is a farmer, healthy and robust. He has always eaten well, including lots of fruits and vegetables we grow ourselves. His one indulgence is a glass of red wine at dinner, made from the grapes of his own vineyards. He works the farm daily in the fresh air, getting plenty of exercise. He has always enjoyed a clean and happy life.

My mind began to review all the special moments I had shared with my dad. I was the oldest of five children, growing up on a farm that boasted grapes, walnuts, cattle, and us kids. My parents worked from five in the morning when the first rooster crowed until seven at night when the last lamb had been put in the barn. My father taught us the value of hard work and the pride it reaped.

I can still hear him in the morning, climbing the stairs to wake us, whistling happily and announcing, "Wake up, sleepy heads, it is a *beautiful* day!" He would lift us onto the caterpillar tractor to plow the fields with him. When we were older, he taught us how to drive. In the springtime, he'd find baby jack rabbits whose mothers had been killed. He would stop the tractor, put the bunnies in his coat pocket, and bring them home for us to raise until they were old enough to fend for themselves.

He was so strong that when we were young, he could lift my sisters and me from the floor with one finger. If anything broke, he could fix it. If we misbehaved, he never yelled, just looked at us with those big brown eyes and let us know that we had disappointed him. He would saddle the horses for us, tighten our wire ski bindings, and make us a special concoction of warm, sweet milk with bread when we were sad.

He'd pile all seven of us in the Willy jeep and drive straight up our steep hill for picnic. Being with my dad was better than being at Disneyland. I remembered how he cried when he walked me down the aisle on my wedding day, and how, at the funeral of my sixteen-year-old brother, David, he supported my mom and the rest of us who were near collapse. He was our tower of strength, our lion in winter, our gentle, patient, loving father. He was only sixty-three years old, still madly in love with my mom after forty-two years of marriage, and grandfather to eleven grandchildren whom he treasured as he had us.

I determined right then and there that my father was not going to die. Not now! Not until we had tried everything. We weren't ready! How can doctors—ordinary humans like you and me—be so sure nothing can be done? In my father's case, they said that surgery was impossible. He would die on the operating table or bleed to death.

I decided to take charge. These were the days before information was readily available on the Internet so I had to do my research the old-fashioned way. At the library, I checked out every book they had on cancer. I bought books and tapes by many authors, including Bernie Siegel, Gerald Jampolsky, Shakti Gawain, and Wayne Dyer. I called all my friends who are doctors or married to doctors and asked for help. I contacted anyone I knew who had struggled with cancer. I wanted experts and answers, and we had no time to lose. Then the miracles began.

Everyone was kind. Everyone I called offered some information. One friend told me about the 800 Cancer hotline. Another told me about cancer societies, the Physicians Data Query (PDQ), research centers, and medical schools. I studied laughter therapy and was encouraged by the work of Norman Cousins, best-selling author of the book *Anatomy of an Illness*. Our first miracle occurred when my girlfriend Eileen was able to schedule a private appointment free of charge with the renowned laughter guru. My mother, father, Eileen, and I flew to meet with the late Norman Cousins, who had cured himself of a life-threatening disease by laughing. I'll never forget Mr. Cousins's words upon shaking my father's hand: "I can see you are a winner. You can beat this." My dad grinned from ear to ear and responded, "Yes, I can."

We began our own therapy of positive thinking, mind over matter, and laughter. Every day I sent my dad a funny joke to give him a good belly laugh. Doom and gloom were replaced by love and laughter.

The harder I fought for my dad's life, the more doors opened. Dad and I talked several times a day, and I could see he was getting as excited and optimistic as I was about possible treatments. "But I'm worried about your mother," he confided, "because she is so afraid that I'll suffer with surgery and that I'll die." I took my mother aside. "Mom, you have to think positively. You have to believe in Dad's ability to heal himself."

She shook her head slowly and tears ran down her cheeks. "I want to believe, but I trust our doctors, and they say there is no hope, that we're wasting our time and giving Dad false hope." I understood her fears, but felt deep in my heart that a miracle would occur.

We found three experts who gave us some great news. They all agreed that my father's cancer was treatable. The treatment would be surgery after all. Now the real fight began. His national HMO insurance carrier refused to pay for any tests or surgery, saying that any treatment for his rare condition was "experimental." This appeared to be a common evasion tactic, and it discouraged most patients from getting help. Not us. We had seven second opinions, all stating that surgery could save my dad's life and that it was a standard procedure. After several conversations with various insurance officers, I asked the CEO of the company why coverage was refused. He urged me to look at the situation from the insurance carrier's viewpoint. It was just too expensive to try to save a dying man. It was more economically responsible to let my dad die. I was astounded! After conferring with my family, I called the CEO back and read him the press release we had composed. I gave him a list of the television stations, radio stations, and major newspapers around the country that would receive this announcement by the next day. The press release simply stated that this HMO had decided to play God and take the life of a "simple farmer" because it would save the insurance company money. It was a portrayal of David versus Goliath, and the CEO knew his company didn't stand a chance of winning any sympathy by battling us in the press. Approval for the procedure was granted the following morning. Knowing the power of these huge conglomerates, I reckoned this was another miracle.

The night before surgery, we met with the medical team. I asked all of them to give my dad positive messages throughout the five- to six-hour surgery. "Please tell him over and over again that he is doing well, and that he will awake hungry, thirsty, and comfortable," I pleaded. They agreed to allow a tape recorder in the operating and recovery rooms that would play soft music and words of encouragement.

The next day, my mom and I made another tape for my dad. We sang some funny Italian songs and told him how much we loved him and needed him in our lives. When we met my brother and sister in the hospital parking lot, they added their own comments: "Dad, you better get out of here soon, because it is a real pain to park here!" But we got some bad news when we went into the hospital. Dad had already been taken into surgery before we could say good-bye. Worse, especially for my mother, was that he didn't have the tapes in the operating room. We both were confident of the surgeons' abilities and my dad's great attitude, but my mother feared that if Dad didn't have the tapes, he would die.

"Don't worry," I told my mother. "I'll take care of it."

The nurses didn't know how to get the tape recorder into the operating room, so I did something I had only seen in the movies.

Cynthia Brian

I happened to be wearing green sweat clothes the same color as the doctors' scrubs. I placed my pager on the outside of my pants, grabbed a mask and rubber gloves from a nearby utility closet, and marched into the surgical center as if I belonged there. With an air of authority, I calmly handed the nurse my son's three-foot-long boom box with five cassettes. She set it up, and my dad was in business.

After a successful operation, my dad kept visualizing his tumor getting smaller. He sent messages to his body. And every day he laughed. He truly believed he would recover. He believed in prayer and miracles. He drew mental pictures of himself growing old with my mother and watching his eleven grandchildren grow up. He made a conscientious decision to live.

He was released from the hospital a week ahead of schedule. He lived happily and healthily with my mom on the farm for three more years. He went to work and was as busy as ever, plowing fields, mending fences, whistling in the morning, and saving bunnies. He still had his glass of homemade red wine every day, and I still sent him a daily joke.

The fact that my dad lived three more marvelous and grateful years instead of three weeks was a miracle—a miracle that he created because he fought for his life. Then one early November day, the cancer reappeared with a vengeance.

It was time to renew our grape contracts with the winery for next season's vintage so Mom would be secure for the following harvest. But the wineries weren't keen on signing a contract. For seven years, California had had little rain. The drought had nearly destroyed the grape industry. The winery representative told Dad they wanted to be fair, but "in reality the vineyards may all be dead by next year if this drought continues." Dad responded confidently: "Don't worry. When I get to heaven, I'm going to open the floodgates, and you'll get so much rain, you won't know what to do with it."

"Al," my mom said without realizing the imminence of my dad's death, "there'll be hundreds of people at your funeral. I don't want a rainy day."

"Honey," he replied, "it's going to rain right up until my funeral, but then you watch. I'll make the sun come out, and you'll have your beautiful sunny day."

The vintner signed an equitable contract, and my mom felt some relief.

I knew we were facing Dad's final days on this earth, but I didn't give up hope for one final miracle. When I asked my dad what more I could do for him in this life, he held my hands and said: "I am dying a peaceful and happy man. I married the woman I loved, and we were married for forty-five years. We had five wonderful children and eleven grandchildren, and I was lucky enough to do work that I was passionate about. I have lived my dreams."

But, he added, he had never had a chance to speak with a man he admired, Dr. Bernie Siegel, whose book *Love, Medicine & Miracles* had given him so much help. Without blinking (and without thinking), I retorted, "Well, of course, Dad, you'll get to speak to Dr. Siegel. I'll make sure of it." Dad hugged and thanked me while smiling broadly. I left the house kicking myself wondering how in the world I was going to make Dad's last request come true. I didn't know Dr. Bernie Siegel. I didn't know anybody who knew him. Even worse, I didn't even have an address or contact number. The only way I might possibly reach him was through his publisher. So that night I wrote an impassioned plea to the name and address that I found inside the jacket cover of Bernie's book and overnight-mailed the letter to New York. With hope in my heart and a prayer on my tongue, I turned my efforts to helping the family cope.

Dad died as he had lived, in harmony and with dignity. He died in my arms, on his farm, in his room overlooking the vineyards he had tended with love for almost fifty years. And his last wish was granted. Dr. Bernie Siegel had actually opened and read my letter from amongst many, and he telephoned my dad on his last day on earth. Dad had been in and out of a coma most of the day, so I wasn't sure he'd understand that Bernie was on the line. I whispered in Dad's ear that Dr. Siegel was on the phone. Dad awoke, took the phone, and listened with that smile we loved so much while Dr. Siegel led him in a beautiful visualization and prayer. He thanked Bernie as tears streamed from everyone's eyes. Another miracle had occurred.

Small miracles? We believe so. And, yes, as Dad had predicted, it began raining less than an hour after he died. It did not stop until the day of his funeral. Then the sun shone brightly on the many hundreds of people who had gathered to celebrate the life of a farmer. Several mourners had hitchhiked from central Mexico to express their gratitude and bid a final farewell to the *jefe* (boss) they had respected so much. The love my dad had planted and nurtured during his lifetime was reaped and harvested at his death.

Miracles do happen to those who believe in them.

EXERCISE

Create Your Own Miracles

Do you know how to recognize a miracle? Think of some extraordinary occurrence that seemed miraculous. What was it and how did it present itself? Lock this in your memory by drawing a picture or writing a poem or story or song about what happened and the outcome. (You don't have to be a poet or an artist.)

Then take the time to say, "Thank you for the miracle of another day on this earth, and may I help others live miraculous lives." Be sure to acknowledge the miracles in your life.

"There is a giant asleep within every man.
When the giant awakes, miracles happen."

—*Frederick Faust*

The Gift of

MODERATION

Moderation is a gift only in certain circumstances. Everyone needs to partake of food, drink, sex, exercise, and work in moderation. But we should never limit our love, devotion, faith, and hope.

My two sisters, Patty and Debbie, and I were most definitely "Daddy's girls." We adored our father. He was our hero, our Superman, the invincible, infallible, bigger-than-life "Daddio," as we liked to call him. In our eyes, our gentle giant was our king. When Dad married Mom, he had a full head of shiny black curls. When the three of us were youngsters, we'd drag our stools behind his chair as he rested in the evenings and fight over who would get to comb his hair. Sometimes we'd take turns: one stroke for you, one stroke for me, one for you, and now it's my turn. Other times we'd divide up his head and all make loop-de-loops with our little black combs. Dad was very patient. Occasionally we even got the combs stuck in his hair and had to cut them out. Then we'd rub his scalp and massage his strong neck. By the time my dad was thirty-five, he was completely bald, and we took full credit. As he told his friends, "My girls loved all the hair right off my head." Just as a child "loves" all the fur off a beloved stuffed animal, we had lovingly rubbed all the hair off our dad's head! There was no place for moderation in our love for and devotion to our dad.

In our family, bald is beautiful. Bald is a badge of adoration and honor. Dad's bald head became our beacon of security. Whenever we were nervous because we had a performance, a game to play, a competition, or a speech to give, Dad would shine his head and remind us to look out into the audience and find him. Seeing our dad's gleaming bald head reminded us of how much we were treasured and cherished. His bald head was our sign that our world was secure because he was here.

Cynthia Brian

I am a very passionate and enthusiastic person. I admit, I'm not very good at moderation. My motto has always been, "The more the better." I'm one of those people who goes to a restaurant and asks for a baked potato with lots of everything on it, a large salad with extra dressing, and dessert, a giant slice of pie with two scoops of ice cream, thank you very much. When I find a sweater that I like, I buy two. When an animal on our farm dies, I adopt three more. I love life, live fully, and laugh loudly. One of my life lessons has been learning to simplify, to modify, and to tone down.

As I was contemplating this gift, I realized that "moderation in all things" is not necessarily a good thing. I don't want to be moderately loved or to be moderately enthusiastic. Who needs moderate praise, moderate understanding, or moderate acceptance?

Moderation means to be mild, temperate, measured, restrained, minimized, or lacking in passion. Those are hardly words in my vocabulary, yet moderation is most definitely a gift and necessary in certain situations. When we are reasonable and levelheaded, we can enhance our lives.

Moderation is about conquering the "all or nothing" mentality. Some people in today's fast-paced world have a tendency to excess, to become obsessed with work, food, exercise, sex, or possessions. Any time that we dangerously overdo, it is time to rediscover self-restraint and prudence. For example, I am learning very slowly to be more economical with my workload. Just because I have the skills, abilities, and talents to accomplish a task, doesn't mean I am the one that must do it. (See the Gift of Surrender.) Sometimes I take on more than I can chew, and because I have an abundance of energy, perseverance, and strength, I will work on a project to the detriment of my health and welfare. I am learning to say "yes" to life while saying "no" to things that won't enrich me. It's a slow process, since I'm not a very good student of moderation.

The worst thing about excess is that it is usually harmful to our bodies. We have only one body. It is our tabernacle and houses our mind and spirit all our days on this Earth. If we don't protect it by acting reasonably, we can lose it.

Here are some recommendations for moderation:

☆ Get professional help if you are overindulging or out of control with work, alcohol, sex, food, exercise, money, drugs, anger, or anything else you are doing in excess to the detriment of yourself and others.

☆ Break your tasks down into small manageable steps. Others have managed to be moderate; so can you.

☆ If, like me, you have taken on too many responsibilities and feel overwhelmed, learn to delegate or to say "no" more often.

☆ Slow down. Don't race through life so quickly that you forget where you've been and have no clue where you are going.

☆ Learn to live in the moment. Life is right now, and success begins this instant.

☆ Take control of your agenda, your health, and your life while you can.

☆ Most importantly, don't moderate the amount of love in your life. The quickest way to receive love is to give love, and the fastest way to lose love is to withhold it. Give your love wings and you, too, will have a shining beacon in your audience to cheer you on.

EXERCISE

Excess and Abstinence

Make a list of all the things in your life that need some adjustment. What do you need more of? What needs to be reined in? If an excess is robbing you of happiness and a fulfilling life, make a commitment to seek assistance today. Acknowledging that you need to modify your behavior is the first step toward a positive outcome.

Take charge of your life before your life
takes charge of you.

Cynthia Brian

MOTIVATION

Sister Mary Germaine was my first encounter with a real teacher. I was a first grader and an eager student. She told me that one side of her head was green and the other purple and that she kept a leprechaun in her pocket. I believed her and was enchanted.

She was my first nonfamily mentor—young, Irish, energetic, athletic, kind, intelligent, with a thick, gorgeous brogue that I loved to imitate. She was full of life; I wanted to be just like her.

A few days into first grade, I decided I was meant to become a nun just like Sister Mary Germaine. I admired the way she always smiled and made every situation fun. Although Sister Mary Germaine returned to Ireland six months later and I did not see her again until I was eighteen, her impact on me was indelible. In her presence, I was motivated to be the best I could be. She encouraged me to be an outstanding student and gave me a love for learning. She showed me an enthusiasm for living and inspired me to participate in sports. (Sister Mary Germaine never hesitated to hike up her skirt and join us kids in a good game of kickball.) It wasn't until later in life that I realized that Sister Germaine was my inspiration for my three rules for living: Smile, have fun, and be wild and crazy. She herself had exhibited these qualities for those few months I had been her student, and her outlook on life contributed to my attitude of "never say never."

Despite the fact that throughout my high school career I was extremely outgoing, never missed a dance or party, and had wonderful boyfriends, I still had a vision of entering the sisterhood. I prayed to have "the calling" and envisioned myself living in a convent like Sister Mary Germaine.

When I was eighteen, I traveled to Ireland with the full intent of becoming a nun. When I told Sister Mary Germaine my plans, she gently suggested that perhaps God's will would be better served using my creative talents in a different vocation. I realized that she was right and returned home with intentions of pursuing my acting career.

Fifteen years passed before we saw each other again, when she visited the United States for the first time in twenty-six years. This time, the dynamics of our relationship had changed. We were now meeting as adults, as equals, like long-lost friends. I was studying architecture, interior design, and landscaping, but was torn between being an actor and an interior designer. Once again, Sister Mary Germaine identified my potential and encouraged me to follow my dreams in *both* entertainment and design. "Just go do it!" she told me. "You have to start somewhere."

When she arrived, I had just booked my first assignment to faux paint the interior of a house. Not wanting to miss either this exciting job or visiting with Sister Germaine, I dressed her in painter's overalls and introduced her as my assistant. (She was an artist in her own right, so she was enthralled with this project.) Together we shared my first interior design project, talking all the while, as we transformed a house into a home. What a shared experience! Of course, I wouldn't expect anything less from this fun-loving friend.

Sister Germaine is still a nun, a director of a school in Ireland, and we have become motivators and mentors to one another through our letters. Since that day of house painting and soul sharing many years ago, we have not seen one another again, yet we help each other navigate life's back roads and highways, knowing that we trust one another and can turn to one another.

We all have someone who has inspired us at some point in our life. Maybe it was a police officer, a mail carrier, or even the aerialist at the circus. Perhaps it was a teacher like Sister Germaine. Although I have been in her physical presence only six months and two days in my entire life, I know she believes in me. That knowledge has kept me going during difficult times, rejections, and failures.

Cynthia Brian

Motivation is the motor that gets you started and keeps you going. It is the energy source that puts you in gear. A few rare souls can jumpstart their own engines, motivating themselves without any outside support, but most of us benefit from finding someone who believes in us. It is essential to have at least one support person on your team. On days that I have no one in whom to confide, I pretend that one or more of my support team is with me, and I carry on a conversation with my pretend motivator until a solution presents itself. These motivators give us a push when our battery runs down. They whisper or shout in our ear, "Just do it!"

In the final analysis, we have to motivate ourselves. The easiest way to get motivated is to believe in yourself, your dreams, and what you are doing in life. Don't limit your capacity to achieve. Develop the habit of motivation, and you will develop unshakable self-confidence and fear failure less. Instead of saying: "I can't, I can't," shout, "I must, I must!"

EXERCISE

Motivation Boosters

When everything seems to be going wrong, here are three strategies to boost your motivation:

1. Make a "The world is an okay place" list. At the end of the day, write down everything that went right, such as

☆ *There was plenty of hot water for my shower.*

☆ *My car started.*

☆ *I had time to eat lunch.*

☆ *I made a great business contact.*

Every day, add more things that you usually overlook. Review your list once a week and don't stop writing until you convince yourself that you have many things to be grateful for.

2. *Find someone to be a mutual motivator, and help each other through life's rough spots.*
3. *Reflect upon an important role model from an earlier period in your life. Think about how they would have operated in your situation. If necessary, use this person as your "pretend motivator."*

Any time that you need a stimulus to go into action, look at your list and talk to your mutual motivator for a quick hit of motivation.

The best way—the only way—to start is to start!

Cynthia Brian

The Gift of
OPPORTUNITY

The inventor of the telephone, Alexander Graham Bell, wisely said, "When one door closes, another opens. But we often look so long and so regretfully upon the closed door that we do not see the one which has been opened for us." I agree with Mr. Bell.

For three months, I had been booked do a scene in the movie *Jack,* starring Robin Williams. It was a simple scene where Jack's photographer dad was shooting an ad for the Carrot Advisory Board, and I was a model, prettily posed on the giant carrot. The dates to shoot the scene kept changing. Any time would be fine, I told the production company, except Thanksgiving, when I was booked to spend a much-needed one-week vacation with my family in Mexico. My special time with my family is nonnegotiable.

Twenty-four hours before our flight, the casting director called. The shoot was now scheduled for the two days before Thanksgiving. "Sorry," I told her, "but I'll be in Mexico with my family." She suggested that I shoot the scene, then try to fly to Mexico on Thanksgiving Day. I repeated to her that my time with my family is nonnegotiable and that, regretfully for both of us, they would have to recast the part.

I made a choice; I chose to close a door. As difficult as it is to turn down an acting job, I chose to be with my husband, Brian, and our two kids on our long-planned trip. We had rented a condo on the beach in San Jose de Cabo, away from the crowds of the more popular Cabo San Lucas. What a wonderful week. Warm sunshine, warm weather, warm family reunion time, and virtually no people. But as I snorkeled and frolicked on the beach, there was a part of me that wondered what it would have been like to work on that film. But I had made a decision to be with my family, and I honor my promises. Always.

A few days before we left Mexico, a young couple, Mark and

Simone Levinson, arrived to stay in the condominium next to ours. They asked me whether it was safe to swim in the ocean. I said we had been swimming all day, every day, and were about to go for a sunset dip. Would they like to join us? They did.

The water was wonderful, the waves were invigorating, and we fell into such lively conversation that we stayed in the ocean until the moon was shining in the heavens and the night sky surrounded us. Simone was from Germany, so much of the talk was about traveling and Europe.

We decided to go together to a local lobster house for dinner, still enjoying our new vacation pals. It wasn't until we were getting ready to go to the airport that we began discussing what we all did in our real lives back home. I volunteered that I had given up a role in the movie *Jack* to be there. Mark's eyes lit up. He said he was being considered for the job of additional replacement dialogue (ADR) supervisor on that film. He, too, was in the movie business! We exchanged addresses and parted.

Back home, I found a message from the casting director. The shoot date had been changed yet again, and would I still be willing to do the part? The opportunity was still there. I was cast in the movie after all. The scene went fabulously.

Some time later, I got a phone call. "Hi, Cynthia, I am now looking at you on the big screen, and you are *not* going to end up on the cutting room floor." It was our friend Mark from Mexico. He *had* gotten the job as ADR supervisor and was now editing my scene. A few weeks later, he called to ask whether I would be interested in casting children for a looping session, dubbing voices on the soundtrack of *Jack*. I was able to refer several of my child clients for the job.

In this case, my courage in turning down an initial opportunity opened doors to additional opportunities. Mark was a guest on my television series a week before he shared the Academy Award for editing *The English Patient,* for which he was ADR supervisor. Mark and Simone have become our very good friends, and we enjoy visiting one another's homes for dinner parties. Mark's culinary talents are a perfect compliment to Simone and Brian's wine expertise. I provide all the fresh eggs from our hens and organic homegrown vegetables and fruits plucked from my garden. Our chance meeting resulted in a solid friendship, and it turned out to be a profitable and exciting opportunity for all of us. Soon Mark will be directing a new film called *Goddess,* which he has written, and I will be auditioning for a prime role.

We never know what accepting or rejecting a particular opportunity can lead to. Fortunately, we always make our own "luck"—with our talent, hard work, passion, perseverance, and openness to opportunities.

To enjoy the fruits of opportunity, you have to be willing to take risks. Sometimes you'll win and sometimes you'll lose, but if you never put yourself out there, you won't go very far. Before you take any actions, though, be sure your core values are not compromised in any way.

When someone tells me that they have no luck or good fortune, I offer them an attitude adjustment. The golden opportunities you seek are all around you. You alone are responsible for creating your own luck, your own chances, your own future. Every day proffers opportunities if you are willing to see them and welcome them.

Motivational speaker and best-selling author Tom Peters says it best: "When the window of opportunity appears, don't pull down the shade."

EXERCISE

What I Don't Want

Make a list of all the things you don't *want to do. For example:*

☆ *I don't want any job that requires getting up before dawn.*
☆ *I don't want to marry anyone who hates animals.*

☆ *I don't want to live in an apartment.*

Your list defines opportunities you don't want to create in your life. Then get out another piece of paper. Using your first list as a reference, write down things you do want to happen. For example:

☆ *I want a job with flextime.*
☆ *I want a spouse who loves animals.*
☆ *I want to own my own house.*

After you know what you don't want and what do you want, focus your energy on creating opportunities to achieve your desires. If you want flexible hours, you can research and zero in on companies and jobs that offer them. If you want a mate who loves animals, you can volunteer at an animal shelter or wildlife center.

Don't wait for opportunities to appear. Make *them!*

Every event, however terrible or ordinary,
conceals opportunities.
(Often they are disguised as hard work.)

The Gift of

OPTIMISM

It is during the greatest tragedies and most trying circumstances that we must be idealistic and optimistic. On October 17, 1989, at 5:04 P.M., San Francisco came uncomfortably close to the long-awaited "Big One." The Loma Prieta earthquake registered 7.1 on the Richter scale and was responsible for 66 deaths, 3,757 injuries, and $10 billion in damage.

Other parts of the world have to deal with tornadoes, hurricanes, floods, and freezes, so we Californians usually feel fortunate to live here. However, Nature occasionally reminds us that she is boss. In fifteen seconds, the 1989 earthquake made the preciousness of life immensely clear.

I was on the fourth floor of our design center in San Francisco, helping a client choose some mirrors. Suddenly, the building began to rumble and shake violently back and forth. Glass shattered all around us. Unable to stay on our feet, we plopped down on all fours and crawled for cover. The sound was deafening, but we stayed surprisingly calm.

When the shaking stopped, we worked our way cautiously down darkened stairways to the street. We emerged into bright sun and the frightening sight of scattered bricks and broken glass everywhere.

My first thoughts were for my young children at home on the other side of the bay with a baby-sitter. I dashed to a pay phone, but it had no dial tone. (These were the days before the ubiquitous cell phone.) My client and I headed for our cars, planning to get out of the city as quickly as possible. At this point, we had no concept of the destruction caused by the biggest earthquake to hit northern California since 1906.

As we neared the Bay Bridge, we saw cars trying to back down the approach ramps. We assumed there was a traffic jam, not knowing that a portion of the bridge had collapsed. My client suggested we try an alternate route out of the city, driving through the Marina and over the Golden Gate Bridge. We didn't know the Marina was on fire. It took us six hours to travel a distance that usually takes twenty minutes.

The scene became even more surreal. Geysers were shooting up from broken water pipes. Sections of the streets were either raised or lowered several feet. Power was off, and no traffic lights worked. Volunteers were directing traffic at major intersections. A frightened woman in the car stopped next to us called over, "I've been in hurricanes, tornadoes, and fires, even robbed at gunpoint, but I've never been in anything like this!"

"We'll be all right," I reassured her. "Just keep going."

We stopped several times to try to phone home, but without success. I tried to be optimistic, but as darkness fell, we saw flames rising in the distance. The air smelled sharply of acrid smoke, and helicopters rumbled endlessly overhead. It felt like a war zone. Broken gas mains began spewing gas and mud several feet in the air. Firefighters were shouting, "Go back!" Buildings were collapsing. It was as if I was acting in a bad disaster movie, but this was all real. As we struggled with the here and now, both our thoughts were across the bay with our families. Were they all right? Was everything okay there? Or worse?

When my client and I reached an area where we could receive radio transmissions, we learned that the Bay Bridge had been severely damaged and the Cypress Freeway had collapsed, killing several people. People were trapped in the rubble, and rescue teams were valiantly trying to reach them. Perhaps it was fortunate that so many people had taken the afternoon off to attend or watch on TV game three of the World Series being held here in San Francisco. More people in office buildings or on the roads during rush hour might have meant more lives lost.

Twelve hours later, I drove up my driveway. My home was still standing, and my husband and children were alive and well. There was some damage inside the house, but nothing compared to the ruin and chaos in San Francisco. I hugged my children like I'd never hugged them before. Justin, who was nine, said he had not been scared. He saw the earthquake as a good chance to practice the survival skills he had been taught. When the earthquake started, he sprang into action, grabbing his little sister and going to the center of the lawn where no trees or electrical wires could fall on them. The baby-sitter quickly followed, ready to calm them, and found Justin definitely enjoying being in charge.

Once the shaking stopped, Justin said they must assess the damage and make sure there were no water or gas leaks. Then he carefully set out our emergency earthquake kit just in case.

Heather, just five, was interviewed later by a local newspaper reporter. "Were you scared when you heard that the Bay Bridge had collapsed? Did you think that maybe your Mommy was there?" she was asked.

"No, I wasn't scared for Mommy. I knew that if the bridge fell down and her car fell into the water, she would just swim home." Heather has always been an optimist.

Optimism doesn't mean life will be perfect, just that we can imagine positive outcomes. It is in the most dire tragedies and circumstances that we must be idealistic and optimistic. Optimists live longer, healthier lives than pessimists, even though the pessimist may have a more accurate assessment of the situation. Every day around the world ordinary people are dying in wars and catastrophic acts of nature. Without optimism how can they pick up the pieces of their lives and have faith in the future? Optimism offers the hope of a tomorrow in the face of uncertainty. Given a choice, we all have the power to write a happy ending.

EXERCISE

Heaven or Hell?

☆ *My students can get very dramatic with this favorite exercise. Stand up tall. Reach as high as you dare. Stand on your toes, and reach for the stars. Imagine yourself flying to the stars and landing on a twinkling surface of heavenly light.*

☆ *Now, bend over and fall limply to the ground. Imagine yourself continuing to fall, being sucked deeper and deeper into the earth's molten core.*

☆ *Stretch upward again. Make circles in the air with your arms, sweeping them around as you jump high off the ground.*

☆ *Which feels better? Do you want to reach and soar? Or fall and sink? In life, you can be an optimist and reach for the stars, or be a pessimist and collapse into the earth. That's your choice.*

An optimist sees a potential opportunity in every calamity. A pessimist sees a potential calamity in every opportunity.

Cynthia Brian

The Gift of

PASSION

Are you familiar with those florid covers on popular romance novels? Real artists paint them, and these artists hire real people to pose for the iron-jawed heroes and the doe-eyed heroines who cling, trembling, to those incredible biceps. I was one such model, booked by the renowned illustrator, Kazuhiko Sano. As he painted me, I learned his fascinating story, one not unusual for people who are following their heart but still have to struggle for survival.

Kazuhiko was born in Japan, the son of an architect. He loved to draw from an early age. The older he grew, the greater his passion for art, and he resolved to be a professional artist. His parents were pleased, but didn't want him to starve. Obviously, he should be an architect like his father. But Kazuhiko had no heart for the intensive math and science necessary to design a successful building.

His parents, concerned for his future, told him all the things parents tell children as they set off to follow their dream. In this case, the litany included: "An artist can rarely make a living; artists become beggars on the street or worse; artists lead eccentric lives and often are involved in highly inappropriate activities." I hear similar stories all the time, especially from people working in the arts.

Kazuhiko was crestfallen, but obeyed his parents' wishes and applied to architectural schools. Three different universities turned him down. Kazuhiko felt this was an omen and decided to follow his passion. He saved up and moved to California where he attended art school part time, working as a freelance illustrator to support himself. A noted artist took an interest in the talented young man and became his mentor.

A few years later, Kazuhiko got married, and the couple honeymooned in New York City. His mentor arranged for Kazuhiko to meet with the head of a publishing house in New York. The editor looked at Kazuhiko's portfolio of illustrations and announced, "As your wedding present, I'm offering you a job." That was more than twenty-five years ago. Since then, Kazuhiko's work has appeared in all kinds of books and magazines. Besides romance novels, he illustrates histories, scientific books, *National Geographic* articles, CD covers, and creates artwork used in films. He is living his dream because he recognized his passion and his gift. He followed his heart, despite dire warnings that he wouldn't succeed. I felt it was an honor to work with him.

I hear stories like Kazuhiko's all the time. Despite what people tell you, despite what your parents want for you, you alone have the right and the responsibility to use your God-given gifts. Once you recognize your passion, you will yearn to follow it.

After my dad died, I found that my passion was to produce a television series about people who were doing what they loved in life. I didn't know the first thing about producing. I only knew I had to do it. I enlisted the help and expertise of experienced crewmembers. My passion for my project brought many people into our production company, all volunteering their time and talents to benefit the viewing audience. Their "pay" consisted of monthly doses of inspiration and hope, along with fresh fruits, vegetables, herbs, and eggs from my farm. We joked that we were the only TV company in the world whose salary was passion.

There was once a man with a passion for show business. Unfortunately, he couldn't act, sing, dance, write scripts, or design sets or costumes. So he decided to direct others in creating his vision. His "lack of talent" turned into a lifetime of movie-making magic and monetary rewards. Film veteran Stanley Donnen directed the classic films *Singin' in the Rain, Seven Brides for Seven Brothers, Charade,* and *Two for the Road,* and went on to win an honorary lifetime-achievement award at the 70th Academy Awards in 1998. In his acceptance speech, he commented that if you want to be a successful Hollywood director, "All you have to do is hire the best actors and technicians, and then stay the hell out of their way." He had found the perfect way to express his passion.

What is passion? It is a flame in the soul that commits you to being and doing something profound. It is a zest, hunger, craving, yearning, longing, an enthusiasm, a fervor, gusto, zeal, an eagerness, and an alacrity.

My passions have been many and varied. My resolve has always been to follow my passions and make them profitable if at all possible. I can think of few things more fulfilling than to be passionate about what you do every day. My various businesses have always reflected my love of what I do: acting, teaching, gardening, designing, writing, producing, and animal husbandry. Passion provides an energy and focus that make you almost unstoppable. When you know where you are going, it's amazing how people help clear a path for you. When you are passionate and dedicated, it shows.

What is your passion, and how can you access it? Identify what you *love* to do. What activities, people, or situations are you naturally drawn to? I am not talking about addictions and obsessions that can be detrimental to your physical, emotional, or spiritual growth. You'll recognize your passion not only by the incredible energy it gives you, but also by the way it enhances your life and the lives of those around you.

Your passion is unique to you. It doesn't have to be something that others aspire to do. For example, kids want to grow up to be firefighters, astronauts, president, teachers, doctors, movie stars, and sport heroes. Because my dad's passion was farming and ranching, my son, Justin, has always wanted to be just one thing: a farmer and rancher. In today's technological society, farming is not a booth at career day. Yet Justin followed his heart to an agricultural college and then to work on farms and ranches.

Deep inside, we all have a dream. Our challenge is to identify the dream and follow it, despite the naysayers who may include those we love. They may tell us we'll never be a success or make money (which, in some minds, is the same thing), and that we should try something else. Don't listen. Follow your heart, and live your passion. Then figure out how to make a living at it so it doesn't have to remain a part-time hobby.

Don't apologize for your God-given gifts. You are one of a kind, and your skills must be shared. Erma Bombeck wrote: "When I stand before God at the end of my life, I would hope that I would not have a single bit of talent left, and could tell him, 'I used everything you gave me.'" Use your gifts in a life of passion.

EXERCISE

Turn Passion into Profit

Can't make a living doing what you love? Try the following simple strategy.

1. **Dream the dream.** *Write down everything you love and everything you have ever thought about doing or becoming. Take your time. Dig deep. Don't leave something off the list because "everyone says" you'd never be able to make a living at it.*

2. **Identify your path.** *If your passion hasn't yet become obvious to you, take an aptitude test, read books, or talk to a career counselor. Don't be discouraged if you have several passions that seem unrelated. Life has a way of merging our talents in remarkable ways.*

3. **Assess your talent.** *Talent doesn't always come with its own passion, and passion sometimes lacks the talent to back it up. (If you have to choose between talent without passion or passion without talent, go for passion. Its energy can develop your talents and abilities in incredible ways.)*

4. **Write a plan.** *Now that you have determined what you love, write your plan. How will you know which road to take if you don't know your destination?*

5. **Get educated.** *Decide what skills you will need to acquire before you can become proficient at your chosen passion.*

Cynthia Brian

6. Ask for support. *Surround yourself with friends, relations, and mentors who realistically believe in you and your dreams. Never ask for or accept false hope.*

7. Believe in your ability to make it happen. *It is up to you to do the hard work, take the risks, and reap the rewards.*

Do what you love. Live your dreams.
(Then turn your passions into profits.)

The Gift of
PATIENCE

We are already running late for midnight Christmas mass when we hear the crunch in the drive. A Jeep Wagoneer looms out of the darkness, followed by a horse trailer hitched on behind. Suddenly our son, Justin, vaults into our arms. It is five months since we've seen him, since he waved good-bye and went off for his first year of agricultural college.

Here we are, in a tumult of hugs and hellos, all together as a family again. Welcome home, Justin! Take off your boots; tell us all your news. But my eye keeps wandering to the clock. (Patience, I whisper to myself, he is just arriving home after a long journey.)

Although I'd heard all the stories of kids coming home from college with mountains of laundry, turning the household upside down with their new *bon vivant* agenda, I am not completely prepared for Justin.

Christmas morning is spent by the fire, opening gifts from each other and Santa. When we finish, Justin asks us all to come outside so he can give us his presents: eighteen bales of hay, both alfalfa and oat, that he has grown, cut, and baled himself; ten pounds of honey that he has harvested; and, surprise of surprises, a newborn baby lamb with a gallon-size feeding bottle and a sack of powdered formula. (Did I mention that Justin is attending an agricultural college where he is one of six students chosen to live on and run the college farm?)

Once we recover from these unexpected and wonderful gifts, Justin starts unloading the rest of the Jeep. First come the two biggest bags of dirty laundry I've ever seen. I didn't know he owned so many clothes. "Don't worry, Mom, I'll take care of it." Of course, that means I have eight loads of wash to do. (Patience, Mom, he's home for the holidays.)

Two more humongous bags are hauled to his bedroom along with

Cynthia Brian

two horse saddles and bridles, piles of books, and miscellaneous farm equipment. I suddenly realize that the "bags" are actually tractor covers, so huge they almost fill the room. "This one has dirty clothes, Mom, and I put clean clothes in the other, just in case I need them." His once orderly room is now completely filled with everything he had at college. (Patience, Mom, patience.)

But I am not a patient person. I am very much a "let's do it, and let's do it *now*" person. Procrastination is not a word in my vocabulary. Organization, organization, and more organization are my keys to success and getting everything done on time. Patience is a virtue I must constantly work on.

Okay. I take a deep breath and savor the fact that my son is safely home. Now I have eighteen bales of hay, ten pounds of honey, and a baby lamb. So what are a few days of laundry and mess? Then Justin's friends come over.

"It's Monday Night Football, Mom. I *always* have the Monday Night Football parties at our house." I had forgotten, probably on purpose. Hot dogs, hamburgers, chips, drinks, and big, big college guys (they used to be boys), all crowded into our family room for a raucous night of shouting and cheering while I try to write in the next room. Actually, they are all very nice guys. Just so *big* now. How did they grow up so fast? (Patience, Mom, life goes on.)

College kids home for the holidays sleep until noon. Justin is extremely tired, I guess from all those 5:00 A.M. wake-up calls to feed the sheep, cattle, and hogs on the college farm. Of course, now it's me with the 5:00 A.M. wake-up call. A baby lamb needs her milk.

Justin's been home a week, and the eighteen bales of hay are still in the horse trailer. He'd promised to carry them to the barnyard, 165 steps straight up a steep hill, but he's sprained his ankle doing tricks on his motorcycle. Each bale weighs 150 pounds, and I'm not up to hauling a ton and a half of hay on my back. (Patience, Mom, it'll get done somehow, sometime, by somebody.)

"Take off your boots in the house, please, Justin," I say in my sweetest mother voice. "Too hard with my sprained ankle, Mom.

Don't worry, I wiped off most of the mud and manure." His sheepish grin reminds me that the lamb needs another bottle.

Well, we are all together for the new year, the turn of the century, and the next millennium. We're safe, we have plenty of supplies, and the laundry is now done. The hay may be especially handy if the nonstop winter rains cause a mud slide. The honey is delicious, and that baby lamb is the cutest thing on this planet. (She calls me "maa.") Justin has given me three pairs of slippers and my daughter, Heather, gives me a fourth pair. They want me to relax for the millennium, they say. Good idea! I always did think that patience is merely the art of concealing impatience.

Practicing patience is difficult. Fortunately, we don't have to buy expensive equipment or go to a designated practice site to do so. All we have to do is choose which battlefield we want to die on. When I'm in traffic, it is difficult to have patience, but what other option is there? If I yell and scream, I don't go any faster. I just raise my blood pressure.

The same is true with raising kids. Even college kids. Oddly, I am most impatient when I think about nature. Nature is all about patience and order, everything in its time and place. Leaves change color, snow melts, bulbs sprout, darkness falls—all on nature's clock and without help from us.

Would I trade a lifetime of perfect order for having my children around me, muddy boots, noise, and all? Not on your nelly! Justin is a great young man, and I am very proud that he's creative, independent, unscheduled, and a farmer like my father. What do a few bales of hay matter?

Patience. I'm working on it. But don't ask our baby lamb to be patient when she's hungry! She'll be hoarse from calling to me. Sometimes patience means now.

Stop-and-Go Traffic

Here's a great exercise in patience. The next time you are in a stressful situation like a traffic jam, imagine a huge billboard that says "Patience." Let in the driver next to you. Don't rev your engine. Put on some good music and sing. If that tries the patience of fellow passengers, imagine a "patience song" in your head. Every few minutes, breath in three deep, cleansing breaths and release slowly. Send patient thoughts to all the frazzled travelers around you.

"A handful of patience is worth more than a bushel of brains."

—*Dutch proverb*

PERSEVERANCE

A successful businessman named Laren decided he was itching for a career change and came to me for a consultation. He was tall and handsome with slightly graying hair, and people often asked if he was a model or actor.

His natural abilities were immediately obvious. He had a great look that was currently in demand. He was also organized, businesslike, personable, and willing to take direction. We mapped out his acting and modeling future, and he followed through on every instruction exactly. Even before his publicity head shots were back from the photo lab, casting directors were clamoring to hire him for print jobs, those photos you see in newspaper and magazine ads. Every talent agent in San Francisco wanted to represent him.

Laren and I began polishing his acting skills so he would perform well at those terrifying but essential actors' job interviews called auditions. An actor is considered truly hot if he lands one job for every thirty-six auditions. Laren didn't like those statistics.

Laren's new agent immediately sent him out on auditions. When he interviewed for a print job (requiring no acting ability), he was booked almost every time. His look was just what the clients wanted. But auditions for TV commercials, film, and industrials (in-house training videos)—anywhere acting was required—were a different story. He would get callbacks, meaning he was being seriously considered for the job, but never landed a performing job. I quoted the statistics to him and tried to encourage him: "One day very soon, you will be exactly what the producer wants! Persevere!"

When Laren was called back three times on his thirtieth audition and still didn't land the job, he was definitely discouraged. He came to see me and told me he was thinking about quitting. "What's wrong with me?" he asked. "How can they see me four times, tell me how great I am, and then pick the other guy?"

"Nothing is wrong with you, Laren," I explained. "Keep at it. You are very, *very* close to getting the next job."

On Laren's thirty-third audition, he got a TV commercial. Right after that, he was booked to appear in a film, several industrial shows, and more commercials. Laren was on a roll. He had persevered and earned the rewards. Today he continues to thrive.

But what if he had given up? So often, the dream is right on the other side of the hill, but we quit one step too soon.

When I got my first big-time talent agent in Hollywood, I asked him what I needed to succeed in the entertainment industry. I expected him to say something about unparalleled talent, unequaled beauty, and unbelievable connections. Instead, he said, "Cynthia, you need only three things to succeed. Perseverance, perseverance, and perseverance." As I now advise my acting clients, the person who gets the job is the last one still standing.

Perseverance is tenacity, persistence, better-than-average drive, holding firmly to beliefs, and never giving up. Think of a time in your childhood when you were incredibly stubborn, refusing to eat your rutabaga or to sleep without your favorite toy. Applying that same level of resolution to adult activities practically guarantees success.

When my husband and I were first married, we had big dreams about building a house together. We thought it would be an easy thing to accomplish and figured that we could afford to start within the next three years. We were wrong. Three years became six, then eight, then twelve, but we never gave up our dream. The more obstacles that were put in our path, the more fervent we became. I was inventively tenacious. As we saved, I collected photos of rooms and homes I admired, made files, took classes in architecture, design, color, and landscaping.

Then one day we found the perfect piece of land and broke ground. In nine months, we would move into our dream home. But nothing went as we had meticulously planned. The framers ran away with the money we had paid the contractor. Our old home didn't sell, so we couldn't get the urgently needed loans. The windows arrived late, well after the start of the rainy season. Then it rained so hard that the subcontractors wouldn't come to work at all. Nine months quickly turned into two years. The house was half finished, and we were broke.

We could have given up, sold out, and run for the hills. We didn't. We hung in there because we knew, deep in our souls, that we were meant to build and live in this house. The process was challenging and exhausting. I'm not sure I could go through it again, but now we can laugh at our money pit. Now, we're happy that we persevered.

Give yourself the time you deserve to get what you want. Latch on to that streak of childhood stubbornness that drove your parents and teachers crazy. Persistence prevails when all else fails. Just ask Laren.

EXERCISE

Just One More Step

Envision yourself climbing to the crest of a mountain. You can see the top and you know you can get there. You just don't know how long it will take. Push yourself to take just one more step, then another step and another step. Don't give up until you have a view of the world. It's just a step away! Persevere!

Your detractors will call it pigheadedness.
You call it tenacity.
Your rivals will call it obstinacy.
You call it determination.
Your opponents will call it stubbornness.
You call it perseverance.

Cynthia Brian

The Gift of
PLANNING

In the early 1980s, a leading talent agent asked if I would develop a program to train young children to "act for the camera" so they'd be more effective in film, television, and commercials. At the time, I had been acting professionally for several years and had been in numerous workshops, but I'd never taught acting.

Although flattered, I was somewhat daunted. However, I decided to accept the challenge and spent three months creating a comprehensive lesson plan. Every exercise, every song, every word was carefully choreographed, leaving nothing to chance. The plan adapted the most effective and enjoyable techniques I had learned over the years, working with many teachers, coaches, and directors.

The talent agent looked over my plan and hired me, starting my long career as an acting coach, teacher, and consultant specializing in children. Since then, I've taught for many prestigious performing arts academies and am very proud of my clients' successes.

However, creating my dream job of helping others succeed as actors would never have happened if I hadn't overcome my insecurities by carefully planning every detail.

When you have something you want to do and somewhere you want to be, here's how to get there.

1. Start with what big business calls "strategic planning." Draft a plan that considers all probable eventualities—everything that might go wrong—and decide the best actions to take. This will take some research and thinking. Try to benefit from the mistakes and achievements of others. There is no need to reinvent the wheel. Find people who have done what you want to do and decide which of their strategies would work for you.
2. Write down your final plan, combining your thinking, research, goals, and gut instincts.

3. Acquire the skills you need. Everyone is born with innate talents, but skills are learned and developed. You may be a natural born actor, but that won't help you work with a camera. You'll still need to learn about blocking, lighting, movement, and inflection for today's sophisticated technologies. You may need managing or bookkeeping skills to run a business. You'll need special training to be a dentist, firefighter, or circus clown. Don't expect your doorbell to ring with the offer of a lifetime until you know what you're doing.
4. Find support. Surround yourself with people who support your desires and believe in your ability to prevail. Just one person is enough to start with. No one ever succeeds alone.
5. Believe in yourself. No plan can succeed if you lack faith in yourself. Conceive, believe, achieve.

Once you have developed your plan, stop worrying about things you can't control. Work hard, but remember to enjoy the moment. You have a great plan. All you have to do is follow it.

EXERCISE

Before Tomorrow Is Yesterday

If you plan your destiny carefully, you'll succeed beyond your wildest dreams. Here's a quick practice to familiarize you with realistic planning.

☆ *At the top of a sheet of paper, list three goals for today. (They can be three errands or phone calls or letters you want to do, or even just the task of eating breakfast, lunch, and dinner.)*

☆ *Below them, write an Action Plan. How will you achieve these three goals? What steps will you take? What is your timetable?*

☆ *Write a Resources List. What help, tools, backup, or input will you need? Whose support or encouragement will you seek?*

Cynthia Brian

★ *Finally, determine how you will know when each goal is achieved, and write that down too.*

Easy? Okay, let's keep going. Get four more sheets of paper. At the top of the first, write "Goals to achieve by a week from today." Label the others, "By a year from today," "By five years from today," and "By ten years from today."

Expand your Action Plan and your Resources List. Do you need to change something you are doing or something in your surroundings or circumstances to meet these goals? If so, do so.

If you fail to plan, you plan to fail. Plan your work and work your plan.

The Gift of
PLAYFULNESS

We lived out in the country on a big ranch, with lots of rolling hills, vineyards, trails, creeks, and rattlesnakes. My mother's flower gardens were a wonder to behold. My dad's domain was three hundred and sixty-six acres of farmland. My mom had two acres of color. Azaleas, roses, wisteria, bougainvillea—you name it, my mother grew it.

The one-room schoolhouse in our area covered grades one through eight, so my parents decided to enroll us in the newly built parochial school in town. The teachers were all young Sisters of the Holy Faith order who had just arrived from Ireland.

One day Mother Superior asked my parents if she could bring the Sisters to our ranch to stroll through the gardens, smell the roses, and get some fresh air. "They miss the gardens and countryside of Ireland so much," she said, "and it sounds like your ranch is a Californian paradise. This will be their playtime."

"It would be our honor," responded my dad. "Just watch out for the rattlers!" Mother Superior misunderstood, thinking Dad had said "antlers," as in deer. (How could she know what a rattler was? There are no snakes in Ireland!)

She had one request, that no one from the parish should ever know about their visits. In those days, nuns were not allowed to socialize or eat with nonclergy. We were all sworn to secrecy.

Soon, the nuns were making regular visits to the colorful and restful gardens around our home and walking in the hills and vineyards of our ranch. They would hike their skirts, tying them in the back, and frolic like young girls. They adored the ranch and especial-ly Mom's beautiful flower patches. My mom joked with them that it was the "faeries" who tended her gardens. We picked magnificent-smelling bouquets and brought them to the Sisters at school.

Our Sisters told Sisters in other convents of the great peaceful

Cynthia Brian

walks on the Abruzzini Ranch and the glorious gardens, which were tended by the faeries. Some of these Sisters taught my cousins in other parishes. Before long, we had three different orders of Irish nuns from three different counties enjoying our property. My uncles, aunts, and cousins were also sworn to secrecy.

It was time to organize a play day for our holy friends, and we affectionately nicknamed it "The Nuns' Picnic." For months we planned the event. We decorated our hot rod, a 1930 Model A Ford with a chopped-off roof, to give the nuns rides through the vineyards and to teach them how to drive. My cousin, Linda Sue, and I produced the entertainment. Dad built us a stage for our performance by the creek under the shade of several walnut trees near the food tables. He also leveled a field so we could play the American game of baseball. Mom, Auntie Bern, and Auntie June prepared an Italian menu featuring fresh ingredients from their gardens, while Dad, Uncle Joe, and Uncle Frank barbecued steaks and burgers.

The big day arrived. Over 125 nuns came to the ranch for a homegrown feast, entertainment, baseball games, sack races, and wild rides in our hot rod and the Willy jeep. All my cousins dressed as their favorite nun or priest in honor of our guests.

Late that afternoon, it was time for the kids' performance. Our special presentation was a skit of the old camp song "You Can't Get to Heaven." (We wanted some religion in our act. Remember I was planning to be a nun.) We were halfway through the song and dance, when I glanced down at the stage. To my horror, a huge rattlesnake was coiled, ready to strike my year-old baby brother. With a calm that only a child director can possess, I sidled over to the edge of the stage and whispered to my dad that we had a problem. As if he were part of the act, he grabbed the oar that was part of our next scene and climbed on stage. As we kids sang, "Oh, you can't get to heaven in a rowing boat, 'cause the rowing boat, it just won't float," my dad, with a grin on his face, was using the oar to kill the rattlesnake. Of course, the Irish nuns from snakeless Ireland were electrified. They saw my dad as the star of the finale and went wild with clapping, whooping, and hollering. As we took our bows, Dad held up the four-foot rattlesnake draped over the oar and playfully asked, "My dear Sisters, where is St. Patrick when we need him most?"

The Irish nun picnics continued for over twenty-five years, and never once did anyone from our family peep a word about the Sisters' play days. Those times of laughter, food, fun, and frolic were one of the highlights of our childhood and an anticipated respite for the nuns. Now forty years have gone by, my dad and Uncle Joe have died, the baseball field has become a vineyard, the Sisters no longer wear habits, and the veil of secrecy has been lifted. In fact, it was the nuns themselves who decided to "let the snake out of the bag."

I will never forget the playfulness of the nuns' picnics. It was a day to feel young, carefree, boisterous, and wild. We laughed at the way the nuns drove our hot rod and marveled at their baseball prowess. The walks through the hills were sacred times of discovery, and games of hide and seek, tag, and king of the mountain. We were all playful.

As I have grown older, I have learned the necessity of playtime. I play working in my garden or going for walks or just sitting with the kids telling family stories. We may dress up in costumes, singing at the top of our lungs, or pretend to be wild animals. Playing is like praying. Both enhance the mind, body, and spirit and make us feel better. When we lose our sense of play, we lose our childlike qualities.

Take time to add playfulness to your busy agenda and watch how much your productivity will soar as you are rejuvenated.

Cynthia Brian

Cobra Slithers

Lie on the floor face down and do a standard push-up. When you are fully raised, think of yourself as a slithering, slimy snake. Hiss and wiggle on the way down. Do this as many times as you wish while you get in touch with yourself on a primal level.

Now, imagine that you are a snake pretending to be a person. Isn't that a wild thought? Laugh at yourself. Roll over, extend your arms, put a big smile on your face, and yell, "I love to play!" *Say this three times, and follow it up with a belly laugh. Don't you feel better after playing?*

Your "to do list" for today:
laugh, pray, and play!

The Gift of
PRAYER

Prayer was always part of our life and was as important as eating, sleeping, and brushing our teeth. We did it every day, whether we needed to or not. We called it "talking to God," and it seemed as normal as talking to Grandma and Grandpa. Instead of making wishes, I made prayers, which were wishes aimed toward Heaven. One of my favorite authors, Kahlil Gibran, says, "You pray in your distress and in your need. Would that you might pray also in the fullness of your joy and in your days of abundance."

I learned to give thanks when I heard a mockingbird's song or witnessed a lamb's birth. I petitioned God for sunny days, rainbows after storms, and wind so my kites would sail through the sky. I counted the food in our bellies and creeks to explore among my blessings. And I felt no guilt in asking for what I wanted: "Please God, let me win cheerleader." "Help me get an A on the test." I also made bargains: "If you'll let the bunny live, I promise to wake up and feed it by five o'clock every morning." As I've grown older, I've understood that prayer is much more than bargaining with God.

When my niece Marlina was eleven months old, she ran a high fever. "It's just the flu," the doctor said and prescribed cool baths, fluids, and aspirin. That evening, Marlina began having seizures and stopped breathing. My brother-in-law administered CPR as my sister hastily drove them to a nearby hospital. (There was no 911 in those days.)

Marlina was diagnosed with bacterial spinal meningitis and was given less than a 1 percent chance for survival. The doctors suggested that we pray. Marlina hovered near death for nearly a month in the intensive care unit. Our family never stopped praying to the Divine to save this precious child. My dear brother, David, had been killed only eighteen months earlier at age sixteen. How could we cope with another child dying? We enlisted the prayers of everyone we knew and everyone we met. We wanted Marlina to live, but we held tightly to our faith that God's will would be done.

Our prayers were answered. Marlina survived. She continued to have seizures until she was about twelve, and she has had to struggle with various learning disabilities, but today Marlina is a beautiful, healthy twenty-year-old college student, enjoying life in every way. Although she could still suffer setbacks from the meningitis, Marlina has a positive, confident attitude and looks to God to help her overcome her challenges.

Was it the prayers or pure chance? We have no doubt that it was the innumerable invocations for God's love, help, and compassion that saved this lovely child, and we give thanks for his great gift of life.

I don't know how prayer works. I just know that it does. Prayer doesn't have a religion. Prayer crosses all boundaries, all faiths, and all beliefs. Somehow, prayer makes a difference. Prayer changes people, or perhaps because of prayer, people change themselves or the circumstances around them. When I pray for someone or something, I do everything I can to help ensure that positive outcome. There have been studies indicating that when people pray and are prayed for, they heal faster, do better, and are happier. Subjects tended to improve more than a control group, even if they didn't believe in prayer or know that anyone was praying for them!

But sometimes, even though we pray from the depths of our souls, a tragedy befalls us. Our family has endured its share of grief and pain. It is at these terrible times that Robert Louis Stevenson's prayer is most urgent: "Lord, give us the strength to encounter that which is to come, that we may be brave in peril, constant in tribulation, temperate in wrath and in all changes of fortune, and down to the gates of death, loyal and loving one to another."

In hard times, prayer sets the problem outside of ourselves and allows us to let go. It's a wonderful relief to turn your pain over to prayer. I have literally thrown up my hands and said, "God, *you* take this. I can't deal with it anymore!" In that instant, my entire being feels lighter. There is a gentleness and reverence in prayer that invokes peace. Just the act of praying is a release.

I believe with all my heart that our prayers are heard and answered. Though the outcome is not always expected, praying brings its own rewards. Prayer connects our inner spirit to the spirit of the universe and brings people together in thanksgiving, praise, hope, and faith. Welcome the power of prayer into your life and enjoy inner peace.

EXERCISE

Pray

☆ *Some people find it comforting to pray in a special sanctuary in their home. You can create an altar any place you wish, as large as an entire room or as small as a table. The important thing is that this place is meaningful to you and helps you talk to your god. You may want to display special mementos, such as photographs, flowers, or scented candles, that help you feel spiritually connected. I have two sacred places, my garden where I interact with nature and my barnyard where I commune with my creature friends. Give thanks at your altar for the incredible gifts within you and around you.*

☆ *If you have friends and family with you, hold hands and exclaim: "We thank the divine spirit for one another."*

☆ *Each day for a week, ask family members and friends to take turns offering a different "thank you" or asking for help. Soon, praying together will become a habit.*

"The family that prays
together stays together."

—*Father Patrick Peyton*

The Gift of
PURPOSE

My dad died in my arms. He was only sixty-six, a robust, salt-of-the-earth man, whose life was dedicated to tilling the earth and loving his family, not necessarily in that order. On his deathbed, he gave me a great gift. He said "My end is your beginning." I asked him if there was anything more I could do for him in this life. He held me close, looked in my eyes, and smiled the warm smile I adored.

"I am dying a happy man," he said. "I married the woman I loved, and we have been together for forty-five years. We've had five fabulous children and have eleven grandchildren. Every day I worked at something I felt passionate about. I have lived my dreams."

Although it took a while for me to implement it, at that moment I knew my mission in life: to communicate the importance of living a life of purpose, of being the person you were born to be, and of doing work that you love. When my dad stood alone in one of his fields, he was the absolute star of his world. I want others to enjoy this same happiness.

Whatever your life's mission, it starts with short-term and long-term goals. All formal goal-setting programs require you to write down a timetable or schedule for performing the steps necessary to achieve your goal. I do this, and you may too. However, while I've achieved nearly everything I set out to achieve, I've never yet met any of my schedules.

I have accomplished my tasks, but not in my planned time frame. I think the universe has a different clock. It doesn't measure time in the same minutes and months and years that we do, but it recognizes our purpose nonetheless. Don't think that reaching my goals was easy just because I have a purpose. It still takes hard work, using all the ninety-nine lessons in this book. Being passionate about my mission and enthusiastic about turning my dreams into reality helps. Direction and working for a higher good is an unbeatable combination.

A purpose must come before a plan, and you must believe that your direction is inevitable. Then create and follow a schedule, but accept that your clock and that of the universe may not be synchronized.

Have faith in your abilities. People become high performers by being themselves, not by imitating others. Be true to your purpose. Then exceed it whenever you can.

What if you can't quite get your purpose into focus? I recommend the "sweat equity" principle used by service organizations like the Be the Star You Are! charity or Habitat for Humanity. Put your energy into other people's projects. Involve yourself with other people's good works and positive endeavors. Volunteer somewhere until you discover your own passion and purpose. The paradox of life is that by serving others, you serve yourself best.

EXERCISE

Discovering the Purpose of Your Life

Have you already discovered your passion or calling? If so, congratulations! If not, get out that pen again, and write down all the things that could help you live your life as a champion. What new things would you like to try?

At least once a week, do something on your list. Include activities that will make the world a better place or provide value to someone less fortunate. Experiment with new foods, fashions, people, places, sports, charities, and activities. Don't forget to laugh, cry, dance, and sing. Soon your passion will be revealed to you.

"To live, you must have a purpose to guide you."

—*Nido Qubein*

Cynthia Brian

The Gift of
REFLECTION

Raymond Ramirez was the foreman on our farm for over twenty years. His kids were our play pals as we grew up, and our moms even got pregnant around the same time. We thought it a funny coincidence that their mom was named Alicia and our mom Alice. The same name, just different cultures. Rachel Ramirez and my sister Debbie were the same age and best friends. Rachel was tall and slender with beautiful coffee-and-cream skin and long chestnut hair that brought her some modeling jobs. She had an irresistible laugh, an intelligent sense of humor, and a gentle spirit.

As teens, Rachel and Debbie loved to hang out at the Ramirez family restaurant, El Tapitio. There, they'd eat hot peppers and salsa, retell stories of their childhood, and discuss their plans and hopes for the future. Then, at twenty-two, Rachel was struck by a rare cancer. She lost her gorgeous hair and fought for her life. She had near-death experiences where she was enveloped in radiant light, heard music, and was visited by relatives who had died before.

Rachel lived long enough to be a bridesmaid at Debbie's wedding. Although her hair was very short, she was excited that it was her own. She whispered to Deb that this might be the closest she would ever get to the matrimonial altar. Eight months later she died, telling her mother that she had loved her life and had no fear of death. She had already seen the heavenly light.

The Ramirez family lost their daughter to cancer in the spring. In the summer of that same year, we lost my youngest brother, David, to a tractor accident. Our two families mourned the deaths of our precious children and reminisced.

Before my dad died, I remember him looking out the window at the sunshine and reflecting that he had lived a life of joy and love. He also had no fear of death. He was at peace with a life of no regrets. But there is never a good time to die.

The deaths of loved ones have led me to reflect on my life. When I become introspective, looking back at what I have accomplished and looking forward to what I still want to do, my life choices seem clear. I want a life of no regrets. When my life is being examined in the final analysis, I want to say that I have loved and been loved, that I have pursued wisdom while committing myself to excellence. I have decided to live a life of passion and to reach for the stars.

Every moment of every day, I have made choices that have dictated my path. Some were poor. I've made tons of mistakes and plenty of U-turns. I've jumped on trains going in the wrong direction and said some things I wish I hadn't. I alone made these choices, learned their lessons, and took responsibility for my actions.

My hands are rough and callused from years of cutting peaches, apricots, and pears and from picking prunes, grapes, and walnuts to earn money. I've learned that money doesn't grow on trees, but cherries do, and they need to be picked and processed to get that money.

Traveling around the world has taught me that there really is no place like home. Back-stabbing "friends" have taught me that true friendship is based on mutual respect, love, and support. I've been guilty of feeling guilty when I took leisure time, afraid someone might think I was lazy. Now I've decided there is no time for guilt. It is okay to be tired, to have a few down days, to take a rest. I have learned that I serve myself most and best when I can serve others. I have cleaned stables and I have cleaned my soul.

The tragic deaths of many loved ones have given me the impetus to "live in the moment," long before it was fashionable to do so. I know sorrow and grief firsthand. Suffering, anguish, and heartache have been regular visitors, as they are for all of us.

It helps to keep your eyes on the road ahead and not in the rearview mirror. The past is history; we must live in the present while preparing for tomorrow. Following is my original recipe for a life of no regrets.

CYNTHIA'S RECIPE
FOR A HEALTHY
BODY, MIND,
AND SPIRIT

☆ Blend together generous amounts of

spontaneity	joy
forgiveness	challenges
giggles	integrity
serendipity	humor
appreciation	acceptance

☆ Add walks on the beach, good books, piggyback rides with the kids, sunsets, the wild kingdom, mangoes, and lemonade.

☆ Stir in smiling attacks, daydreaming, back rubs, angel dust, starlight, and sheer delight.

☆ Bake for a lifetime while slowing topping with

a quest for knowledge	choices
unconditional love	gratitude
freedom	generosity
inspiration	prayer

☆ It is normal for this recipe to encounter pain, sorrow, disappointment, discouragement, and dismay. This is not a sign of failure. Every batch is special and creates change, growth, and learning.

☆ Serves one or a multitude with confidence, happiness, and fulfillment of life's purpose.

☆ Share and be prepared to cook up more!

Take some time to reflect on this life. Give thanks for daily blessings. Listen to the silences that set off the music in your soul. Life is a gift. No one has proven there is life after life, but no one has proven that there isn't. I believe Rachel and Dad. I want to witness the light and dance until my soles wear out. I want no regrets.

No Regrets

Reflect on this: If you had your life to live over again, what would you do differently? We are taught by the past, but we can never live there again. Think about the size of your car's rearview mirror. How big is it? Small, right? And how big is the windshield? Windshields are large so we can clearly see the road ahead. Don't look back; always look forward.

Reflect on your future. How will the lessons you have learned direct your path? How does your life need to be so you will be a fulfilled and have a life with no regrets?

You are your own destination.

Cynthia Brian

The Gift of
REJECTION

"You're too tall, you're too short, you're too pretty, you're too ugly, you're too young, you're too old, your hair is too blonde, your hair isn't blonde enough, your eyes are too blue, your eyes need to be brown, you have too much experience, you're not experienced enough." How many times over that past twenty-six years of my acting career have I heard these words?

Rejection is one of the most unpleasant words in the dictionary—refusals, repudiations, turndowns, rebuffs, renunciations, disapproval, snubbing, dissing—basically people are shouting, "I don't want you! You're not good enough!"

And what have I done with all that rejection? I have included it among my gifts for being the star you are.

You are probably thinking I'm crazy to consider rejection a gift, but I can tell you from firsthand experience that it is. From birth until death, we are going to be rejected thousands of times for one thing or another. It's a good idea to get used to it early on and to make rejection our friend.

When I was growing up, my parents instilled great confidence in me that I could do and be whatever I put my mind to. What I didn't realize was that other people were also putting their minds to similar things. This led to a lot of disappointment when I was runner-up instead of queen, or took second place in a talent contest or third place for my jar of jam at the fair. But none of this compared with the rejection that actors must learn to accept.

As an actor, every new day means interviewing for one or more new jobs. Sometimes weeks or months go by with every door slammed in our face.

Over the years, I have perfected the art of auditioning. I learn the script and prepare carefully. I dress for the part, I pump myself up, and I walk in that door knowing that *I am a gift!* Then I do the best audition I possibly can on that day. I leave the room, refuse to replay the interview in my head, and go buy myself an ice cream to celebrate my achievement. If I get the job, it's icing on the cake. I'll celebrate again.

I teach my acting students to realize that it isn't "Cynthia, the person" who is being rejected. It is "Cynthia, the actor." As the actor, I probably am too tall, too short, too pretty, too ugly, too young, too old, too blonde, not blonde enough, too blue-eyed, too brown-eyed, too experienced, or too inexperienced. None of us can be right for every situation, every relationship, every job.

Most people are crushed by their first rejection. My daughter, Heather, told me her philosophy that rejection is a revolving door when it comes to relationships. The first time a boy expressed his undying devotion, she was shocked and uninterested. Therefore, she rejected him. A year later, she found herself in the same position, expressing her undying "love" for this same boy. This time, *he* said he was not interested. She was devastated, but, after several discussions, she realized that sometimes rejection is all about timing. So her remedy was to give herself time to grieve and to get over her sadness at being rebuffed, then get on with her life. That is excellent advice for all of us.

We won't get out of this world without experiencing rejection sooner or later. The secret is to embrace it and never give up. Rejection is a numbers game. For every "no" we get, we are closer to a "yes"—but only if we keep going, keep giving, and keep improving. When you are feeling down and out, it's hard to get up and get going, but believe me, you can do it. Go for it, and keep going for it.

This is my favorite poem. I have it posted in my office and in my home, and have included it in all the books I have written. The author is anonymous, but his or her legacy is a great defense against rejection and an aid for being the star you are. I suggest you copy it and post it in your home and office also.

DON'T QUIT

When things go wrong, as they sometimes will,
When the road you're trudging seems all up hill,
When the funds are low, and the debts are high,
And you want to smile, but you have to cry,
When care is pressing you down a bit,
Rest if you must, but don't you quit.

Life is queer with its twists and turns,
As everyone of us sometimes learns,
And many a failure turns about,
When he might have won had he stuck it out.
Don't give up though the pace seems slow,
You may succeed with another blow.

Success is failure turned inside out,
The silver tint of the clouds of doubt,
And you never can tell how close you are,
It may be near when it seems so far.
So stick to the fight when you're hardest hit,
It's when things seem worse,
That you must not quit.

—Anonymous

Success rarely comes on the first, second, third, or even fourth try. It may be the hundredth. Keep trying and don't give up. Even when you are rejected unnecessarily, consider each rejection as character building. You are a miracle of life, and you can do it. Give yourself a break, but never quit. You are a star!

"Only Thirty-five to Go"

I tell my acting students that an actor is really hot if he lands one job for every thirty-six auditions. Life is the same. You may have to date thirty-five duds, look at thirty-five prospective homes, apply for thirty-five jobs before hitting the jackpot. As hard as it is, try to see each "no" as tremendously positive because you are now that much closer to a "yes."

There is a "yes" around the corner.
Embrace each "no" and exclaim, "Thank you, I am
now that much closer to a 'yes'!"

Cynthia Brian

The Gift of
RESPONSIBILITY

I still remember my embarrassment vividly. I was out in the fields plowing, pulling the old disk behind the red Ford tractor when it ran low on gas. My dad called over from the next field that I should take the tractor back to the tractor barn and fill up the tank. I drove off hurriedly, eager to finish so I could go to a school dance.

"Make sure you put gas in the right tank," he called after me. But when I got to the tractor barn, my mind was firmly fixed on the exciting evening ahead. When I focused on what I was doing, I realized I had put the gasoline in the oil compartment. The tractor wouldn't budge. Now the oil tank would have to be drained and cleaned before the tractor could operate again. My irresponsible behavior would cause more work, money, and time.

Humiliated, I walked back to the vineyard where Dad was working. I admitted my mistake and waited for his rebuke, but he didn't yell at me. Instead, he gave me credit for being accountable for the error. However, he was disappointed I hadn't been responsible for what I was doing as I did it.

"You could have asked me for help," he said, "but you were thinking about the dance. This is what happens when you hurry without thinking." He was right. I had wanted to finish my chores quickly and show how reliable I was, but I had been undependable. Feeling remorseful, I stayed to help drain the tank and get the tractor running. I wasn't much help, but it was the responsible thing to do after my irresponsible behavior. I was definitely late for my date.

Being the eldest child in a family of five children meant that I had to be "the responsible one." I had to be a role model, set the standard for my siblings to follow, toe the line, walk the talk, and lead by example.

It's not easy to always be that responsible, but it leads to success. The great American dream is to be your own boss, to have control, and to be in charge, but what you really have control over is your own life. When you can look at every situation as an opportunity for growth, learning, and serving others, you become your own boss—the boss of your own soul. You become the star you are.

No matter what we do, we are all self-employed. No matter who hires us, it is our responsibility to treat the job as if we own the company and the company's success depends on our contributions. (It does!)

What we do every day has a direct connection to what and who we are as people. When we give less than our best, we make it impossible to value our own integrity. Some people think they can punish uncaring bosses or crabby co-workers with slipshod, halfhearted efforts, but their souls and their conscience are the real victims.

As long as we blame others and complain about our lot in life, we can evade responsibility for our own actions and words. Such liability can be a terrifying prospect for some people, but consider the benefits. When you take responsibility for the bad stuff in your life, you also become the proud owner of the good stuff. It wasn't luck, it wasn't someone else; it was *you*. What a terrific trade-off!

The word "responsibility" has onerous overtones for some people, implying restrictions and a loss of joy. I choose to think of responsibility somewhat differently. We are all one—the planets, stars, galaxies, earth, water, elements, plants, animals, and humans—and each of us contributes to that one. What an enormous responsibility! Fortunately, they are all responsible for us too. It is a mutual admiration society, and we have to keep up our end.

What can you take responsibility for that will bring you joy? Start with simple things like saving water, recycling, composting, and being kind to animals. Accept people of all ages, races, religions, nationalities, political and social belief systems, and sexual orientations. Extend love to others, and accept love in return. When the natural universe is at peace with itself, we will know peace within ourselves.

Responsibility connects your life to a bigger story. It's okay to say, "I'm scared, and I've made lots of mistakes." Vulnerabilities and

Cynthia Brian

frailties are human; admitting to them is superhuman. We all have mountains to climb. Blaming and complaining slows the journey.

The lesson I learned that day on the tractor was to take action responsibly and to be responsible for my actions. "Do it right the first time" is a slogan I now live by. It may take a little longer to figure out the instructions, but time will be saved in the errors you don't make. For the record, no one in my family has ever let me forget that reckless incident. A favorite family joke is that "even the responsible one makes mistakes." That's for sure. We are all human.

EXERCISE

Don't Feel Your Big Toe

Reread the name of the exercise above. What are you feeling right now? I bet it's your big toe! It is our responsibility to phrase our sentences with positives instead of negatives. Be careful what you say because your brain will believe you. A statement like "I will not get sick" translates subliminally as "I will get sick." Instead, tell yourself, "I am healthy." Reprogram negative statements into positive ones.

Here are some common negative statements people make. Use this exercise to reframe one or more positive versions for each, then implement them in your life.

☆ *I shouldn't eat that.*
☆ *I never get anything right.*
☆ *I mustn't be late.*
☆ *I can't do that.*

It's okay not to know all the answers, so ask whenever you aren't sure. It's okay to make mistakes, so 'fess up when this happens. Take responsibility.

When you own up, you own your destiny.

The Gift of
REST

When we were teenagers (and remember, there were five of us!), somebody asked my dad why he never missed church. "So I can rest!" he said. As I grow older, I am constantly reminded of the importance of taking a break and resting—usually because I'm totally exhausted.

One typical day, I taped an interview for my radio show, rushed to eleven consecutive business meetings, zoomed home to drive the evening car pool to gymnastics, returned to my office to reply to e-mails, and finally collapsed in bed at 1:00 A.M. By 6:00 A.M the next morning, my computer already held more than twenty-five incoming e-mails, the answering machine was full from East Coast callers, and a barrage of meetings loomed in the hours ahead. All this business stuff had to be squeezed in between obligations to children, husband, animals, home, and volunteer work. Suddenly, I felt completely overwhelmed.

So I picked up a pencil and took inventory of my schedule. I write and host two national cable TV series and a weekly radio show. I also produce them, which means booking guests and editing, marketing, publicizing, and distributing. My daughter and I do radio and TV versions of a show about animals. I write books and articles, run a national nonprofit volunteer organization, and coach children and adults in acting for TV and film. I am a certified interior designer and still fulfill special jobs for longtime clients. I am the poultry leader for the 4-H club, a lector and Eucharistic minister at our church, a wife, and a very involved mom of very active and involved kids. Then there are our animals, which I tend twice a day, cleaning the barn once a week. Plus general housekeeping and maintenance, major gardening responsibilities, chauffeuring, and the list goes on.

Cynthia Brian

Once I took the time to write this down, I realized it was no wonder I'm burned out and exhausted. It was definitely time to take a break.

So I stopped and literally went out to smell the newly blooming roses. I brushed my horse and climbed on his back for a bareback ride, leaving the answering machine to cope. It was hard to let go, but like my dad, I needed rest.

Not long ago, my computer kept freezing up on me just as I was trying to meet a lifeline (I don't call it a "deadline"). My persevering side kept telling me to hang in there, that eventually I'd find a solution, but my intuition told me it was time to "chill out" and sleep. Struggling when I was going nowhere only made me angrier and more frustrated.

When we are tired, we become depressed, self-doubting, and less productive. Once I stopped and decided that I didn't need to know everything about computers (or anything else), I gave myself permission to go to bed. I awoke calmer and realized I could do other projects while the computer went to a pro for an adjustment.

My work is always better, cleaner, more intelligent, and more creative when I have had enough sleep. In fact, when I am working on a big project, I try not to make any major decisions until I can literally "sleep on it." My clients know that my best ideas come to me in my dreams. French philosopher René Descartes wrote of a "fiery angel" that brought him blinding insights at night—in other words, inspiration. My joke has always been that my creativity is not all mine. A dozen little angels go out into the universe, collect information, and bring it back to my brain while I am sleeping. How often I've solved challenges simply by going to sleep! So many new ideas crowd my brain when I wake up in the morning that I keep a pen and notebook on my bed table.

Sleep refreshes and gives the body time to heal and regenerate. Rest offers revitalization, rejuvenation, invigoration, and renewal. So why do so many of us can-do people resist getting enough of it? Even God rested after seven days!

Brain Breaks

In 1910, Americans averaged nine hours of sleep each night; today it is seven. Schedule rest periods as carefully as appointments. If you can't get a full night's sleep, you can still refresh yourself with quick brain breaks.

☆ *One way to get extra oxygen to your brain is a great big yawn. Stretch out your arms, open your mouth, and yawn. By faking it the first time, you'll begin a yawn. Suck in the air, let your eyes water, and yawn big. Feel the new energy.*

☆ *Every day for the next week, grab quick brain breaks. Shut your eyes for five minutes whenever you can. Take three deep, cleansing breaths and sit down in a comfortable chair (outdoors if you can). Better yet, lie down, shut your eyes, and tell yourself that you are going to feel refreshed. Turn off the clutter in your head, and let your mind float. See yourself in your special, private place where all is happy and peaceful. When you are replenished, take three more deep breaths, open your eyes, and thank your body, mind, and spirit for being.*

Never apologize or feel guilty for resting.
Running with your gas gauge on empty works for
only so long.

Cynthia Brian

The Gift of
RISK

When my oldest child, Justin, was just a year old, I was cast in a TV commercial because I was an accomplished motorcycle rider. (Throughout my career, I've landed numerous jobs because of my athletic or multilingual abilities.)

The "plot" of this commercial had a handsome young man landing his World War I biplane, hopping on the back of a motorcycle driven by a lovely young woman (me), and riding off into the sunset with her. Sounded great to me. When I arrived on location, the director told me there had been a slight change in the script. It would be much more modern if the lovely young woman flew the biplane. "We'll put an actual pilot in the plane with you," he said, "but it will look like you're flying it." Still sounded great to me. I had never flown a plane, but I'd done a lot of skydiving, and I am always adventurous. After all, one of the requirements for Being the Star You Are is willingness to be wild and crazy—having the guts to stretch, reach out, and risk making a fool of yourself.

"Tell me what to do, and I'm your gal!" I told him. The plane was a vintage biplane from 1917. The pilot gave me my instructions. "But," he confided, "sometimes the old engine stalls. In an emergency, we might have to bail out." That didn't frightened me, I thought he was joking.

Wardrobe outfitted me in a great-looking "Red Baron" outfit—goggles, helmet, leather jacket, long scarf—the works. Plus a parachute. As soon as the director cried, "Action!" we were off. Up, up we flew. This was fun. Then the stunts began, with loop-the-loops, twirls, tumbles, and falls. The plane would shoot straight down toward the ground. Then the pilot, sitting behind me, would pull up, and we'd shoot for the stars. A moment later, we'd be doing rolls. It was a thrill, and all this time, they were filming us. We landed to great applause.

"Do it again," shouted the director, and we repeated the entire scene. By the third take, I was feeling pretty queasy. I was doing my best to portray the hot-shot aviatrix, but I began to feel hot. Then I felt like I was on fire. The actor's voice inside me said, "Don't blow the shot. Stay cool, and hang in there," but the disciplined practical side of me, the wife and mother, told me to get down to the ground. Now!

I signaled the pilot to land immediately. During our descent, I felt so hot that I was ready to parachute out of the plane. As we landed, I was throwing off my goggles, helmet, and scarf while screaming, "Get me out of here! I'm on fire!" The crew pulled me out of the plane. I *was* on fire. The engine had overheated, and my seat was in flames. My leather jacket was literally burned off my back. Thank God I was wearing it, though, or I would have suffered severe burns.

The plane was retired to the hangar for repairs, and since I wasn't hurt, the shooting continued with little fuss. Wearing a similar leather jacket supplied by the wardrobe department, I leaped on the back of the motorcycle with the handsome young man, and off we rode into the sunset.

The commercial won a prestigious award, and I learned a valuable lesson. There are risks in acting, as in all aspects of life, and we have to evaluate them. Fortunately, I listened to my inner voice and escaped with my life.

On the way home, I kept thinking about how my year-old baby might have been motherless. I decided to delete some of the more dangerous athletics from my résumé, things like scuba diving, sky-diving, motorcycling, and hang gliding, and focus on abilities that didn't have such a high potential for danger.

I've always advocated thinking big and being willing to risk. Risk can be a great energizer. It gets your blood pumping, produces a pleasurable high, and can bring unexpected dividends. But "risk" is not a synonym for idiocy. It doesn't mean jeopardizing the things most important to you for the sake of money or glory. Before you take a risk, figure the worst possible outcome and decide whether you could live with it. This holds true even if you put yourself in danger to rescue a loved one. Although the decision process may only take a split second, you are subconsciously weighing the potential peril against how you could live with yourself if you stood by and did nothing.

Risk is a two-faced gift. Like fire, it can warm and brighten our lives, but it also has the capacity to destroy. We stretch and grow when we can distinguish between true courage and simple daredevilry.

EXERCISE

Risky Business

Calculated risktaking is a great way to operate if you want a life of enjoyment, growth, and satisfaction.

☆ *For this acting exercise, dress up like a person that is totally out of character for you. For example, you could dress up like a fisherman or a business executive. Go to the place where your character would frequent and walk around for one hour. (Be aware of your safety at all times while acting the part.) The point of the exercise is to feel real in this new character, while knowing in your heart that you are still you, only taking risks that you would not take naturally.*

☆ *Notice how people react to you and how you respond to them. Are you more bold, brave, and intelligent? Or are you behaving in a manner that attracts negative attention?*

☆ *What does this exercise tell you about your ability to balance risk with clear evaluation of possible outcomes?*

Dare not to dare when it would be truly dumb.

The Gift of

SERENDIPITY

In Denver I boarded my plane and turned left, through the curtains, into first class. This was a big treat. My TV production assistant had graciously turned over flying miles to upgrade me as a morale boost while I traveled to promote my television show.

The effect of luxury was somewhat marred by my pack-mule appearance. Slung over my shoulders were a laptop, a sack of videotapes, and a portfolio crammed with publicity materials from the show. To get to my seat, I had to climb over a relaxed, nice-looking gentleman who immediately made me feel comfortable. We introduced ourselves, and what followed was pure serendipity.

Do you know the story of *The Three Princes of Serendip?* When these fortunate gentlemen looked for anything, they invariably stumbled across something unrelated but much nicer. Thus the wonderful word "serendipity."

In my serendipitous encounter, I found myself chatting with resiliency expert Roger Crawford whose most recent book, *How High Can You Bounce?,* had just hit the bookshelves. We soon realized our missions were identical: to help people become the best they can be.

Roger is an amazing human being. Born with physical disabilities that included an underdeveloped leg that had to be amputated below the knee when he was five and hands that boast only thumbs (the medical explanation is ectrodactylism, Roger's term is "inconvenienced"), Roger was told he would never walk. Doctors recommended institutionalizing him. With love and support from his family, he overcame his "inconveniences" not only to walk but to become a professional tennis player and instructor. He became the first person with a physical challenge affecting two or more limbs to participate in Division I NCAA athletics. He even played John

McEnroe. (He lost, but so did a lot of other tennis players.) Roger's fascination with human potential led him into professional speaking; his topic: how to overcome challenges. Today he is among the top speakers in the country, his calendar crowded with Fortune 500 companies.

Here was a man who walked his talk. He told me how enthusiastic he was about my television series and asked why I hadn't written a book on the subject. Actually I *was* writing a book, I said, but hadn't had the time to look for a literary agent or publisher. Roger generously shared his knowledge and contacts with me, and I shared my media contacts with him. We left the plane that day with pages of notes and a list of phone numbers, as well as the knowledge that we had both found a new crony. I also invited Roger to be a guest on my show.

What a coincidence that we ran into each other, but both of us feel there are no coincidences, only divine synchronicities. The publication of this book is the result of our plane ride together, and Roger was the first guest on my new radio program. Serendipity at work.

There are no coincidences in life. Everything happens for a purpose at the time it is supposed to happen. Our job is to be open to the possibilities presented to us. Anything is possible when we open our hearts, ask for support, then let the universe take care of the details. We seem to become "lucky," have good fortune, bump into someone we need to meet. Our intentions, both conscious and unconscious, are connected to an invisible world.

Before my serendipitous meeting with Roger, everything my assistant planned for me had gone wrong. Her original intention was to have me ride in first class from Los Angeles to my television convention in New Orleans on the happenstance that I might meet a buyer for my new program. When the ticket came, the first-class seating was not on the outward bound portion of my trip, but on the return, and instead of it being via Los Angeles, it was departing from Denver. "I'm so sorry," Becky said to me before I left. "I really wanted you flying first class from Los Angeles. What Hollywood TV buyer is going to be flying to San Francisco from Denver?" "Hey, don't worry about it! I'm just thrilled to fly first class at all. *Que sera sera* (what will be, will be), as my mom always said." I retorted, even though I was disappointed too. When I boarded that plane in Denver, the last thing on my mind was writing a book. All I wanted to do was sell my television show. But talking with Roger changed the direction of my life. Because I appreciated the fortuitousness and followed up on the literary leads Roger provided, I present my life's purpose in a new medium to people all over the world.

We are all magnets, and we all have the ability to draw to us that which will fulfill our mission. Whether we believe it or not, we are all spiritual beings born with a driving force to succeed during our life on this earth. Invite your angels into this moment and experience the energy of serendipity. Stay open.

EXERCISE

Coincidences

Have you ever known someone who is "lucky"? Parking spaces magically open up before them. Dimes glint on the ground in front of them, and taxis appear during rainstorms when they need them. Opportunities constantly present themselves to these people. Are they just lucky? Or do they see opportunity all around them? Do they notice and react?

What positive coincidences have you experienced recently? Jot down three. Read them aloud three times. (This may sound silly, but it helps you focus.) What happened as a result of these accidental occurrences? Were they truly "coincidences"? Or moments of serendipity that you recognized?

There are no coincidences in life, only divine
serendipity. Wherever you go, you are there!

The Gift of
SIMPLICITY

Living on a farm is simplicity at its most magnificent. Our modest farmhouse had basic amenities, and we lived in close communication with the earth.

Sometimes a bit too close. We didn't particularly like using the outhouses out in the fields around the ranch because rattlesnakes and black widow spiders resided in them, so we usually chose to squat behind a tree.

We weren't materialistic. Everything we used was recycled again and again, but we were abundantly rich in spirit and had every creature comfort: peace of mind, love, wonder, happiness, responsibility, courage, faith, discipline, and more love. And we lived according to the rhythms of the seasons.

Our favorite season was springtime. Spring meant lavish picnics on our hill with all our aunts, uncles, cousins, and grandparents. When we were just toddlers, Mom and Dad designated the best location on the highest mountain as "The Picnic Grounds." The views were forever. We could even see San Francisco Bay sixty miles away. A giant old oak tree provided shade, surrounded by hundreds of trees perfect for climbing. Using the scraper on the tractor, my dad leveled a huge space where we could play silly games and have plenty of open space to run, do sack races, and play ball. Fallen tree trunks offered places to build forts and do tightrope routines.

The hill itself was perfect place for sliding down on a piece of corrugated cardboard or rolling down in an old wine barrel. Every Sunday, most of our relatives gathered at our house for the bumpy ride up the hill in our Willy jeep. Some of us walked when the wildflowers were in full bloom.

Our picnic food was never sandwiches and chips. No way. My grandmother, Nonie, my mom, and the aunties made every type of Italian culinary delight: platters of antipasto and prosciutto, whole chickens roasted in garlic and rosemary, bowls of polenta and spaghetti, plus numerous salads, cheeses, and fruits. And don't forget the vino. Lots of vino. "Pa," my mother's father, sat, cane in hand, as *patrone* on his wicker throne underneath the magnificent oak, keeping an eye on everyone and everything. Nonie supervised spreading blankets and quilts on the grass. The three sisters—Aunt Linda, Aunt Helen, and Alice (my mother)—would start the singing and dancing. My brother David would play the accordion, and the rest of us would join in. The festivities lasted until the stars came out.

One Sunday stands out above all others. It was the day of "The Great Kite-Off." For weeks, we'd brought kites to the hill and flown them with modest success. But that day, the wind was absolutely perfect. We all had our kites in the sky by midday. Then Uncle Joe and Uncle Frank came up with the idea of having two teams compete in a "kite-off" to see who could fly the highest kite. We divided up, and each team started making one giant string ball. Uncle Joe and Uncle Frank were the team leaders, and everyone took turns flying a kite.

The wind stayed steady, and soon both kites were racing each other through the skies toward the Blue Ridge Mountains. My dad and Uncle Bob had to make an emergency run to town, a twenty-four-mile round-trip, to buy more string. All afternoon, those kites kept flying, looking smaller and smaller until they were barely visible. We started making bets. Members of the winning team would get an extra helping of ripe Bing cherries (for the kids) or a glass of grappa (for the adults). We all whooped and hollered and cheered on our team. Soon Dad had to make a second trip to town for string, and then Uncle Bob a third to get binoculars.

By our calculations, we had added more than five miles of string to those balls, and both kites were still in sight, faint specks reflecting the setting sun. When darkness fell, we could still see two dots through the binoculars, making their way in the heavens like two twinkling stars. No one knows who really won The Great Kite-Off.

To this day, we kid each other about who won and where the kites finally came down. Just recently, at my niece Betsy's wedding, Uncle Frank hugged me and clowned, "Hey, Cyn, it was our team that won that great kite-off! Remember that day? Wasn't it great?" "Absolutely, Uncle Frank! We won!" I responded, unable to truly recall which team I was on. It didn't matter anyway. The simplicity and pure delight of those Sundays will always be with me and with our family.

There is so much clutter today in our fast-paced, technological lives. "Back to basics" seems so attractive, but what are the basics? I am a firm believer in living in the present and being in the moment. I feel very privileged to have lived an earthy life, drenched in simplicity, fun, family, and frolic. I enjoy reminiscing and retelling the old stories, but pining for the past is a waste of time. What matters is doing what we love with the people we love today. Yesterday is gone. Tomorrow never comes.

You can live in a mansion or a monastery and still lead a life of simplicity. By "simplicity," I don't mean austere, severe, spartan, lacking in complexity, or boring. Simplicity is living with authenticity, living your truth, and expressing and accepting love with joy in your heart. In actuality, there are few things more complicated than leading a truly simple life. We are constantly bombarded with advertisements that encourage us to be the ultimate consumer. We become so involved in keeping up with the trends that we forget who we are and why we are here. We are never far from our computers, e-mail, voice mail, cell phones, pagers, remote controls, and fax machines. Are you feeling overwhelmed by your "always accessible" factor? It's time we remember that we have the power to unplug ourselves once in a while.

Stop for a moment and take a deep breath. Inhale the sweetness of nature. Listen to the chirping of the birds and the sighing of a breeze. Throw pebbles into a pond. Collect polliwogs and watch them grow into frogs. Go for walks in the hills; bring a blanket and a basket and enjoy a relaxing picnic. Give thanks for this magnificent day, for the sunshine, the dew, the clouds, and the rainfall. Be your authentic self. Being your authentic self means allowing yourself to be in the moment, to take time out to enjoy the simple things in life.

If you love the city, your idea of simplicity may be the sounds and sights of a bustling urban area. Grab a sandwich at a deli and find a place to people watch. Resonate to the vitality of rumbling traffic and honking horns. You are part of it, yet detached and observing. As the sun sets, relish the twinkling city lights against the night sky. Simplicity is time out for a minute, an hour, a day, a week, or a lifetime.

Find your simplicity. Rejoice! Go fly a kite!

EXERCISE

Go Fly a Kite!

Do you own a kite? If so, get it out. (You'll probably need to make some emergency repairs, since they tend to get battered in the back of the closet.) If you don't have one, make one. You can buy kits or materials at a hobby shop. Get some extra string too.

Investigate the best kite-flying spot in your area, and arrange a kite day with loved ones. Be sure to bring a scrumptious picnic.

Simplicity is magnificence!

Cynthia Brian

The Gift of
SOLITUDE

My dad spent endless hours alone on the tractor every day as he plowed his fields. He was a strong, quiet man, and when he spoke, his words were wise and weighty. As kids, we always punned that he "stood alone in his field," being both a farmer and unique. The reality was that he enjoyed solitude.

In solitude, he received inspiration, guidance, and a sense of purpose. Of course, there were five boisterous kids in our household, so having a farm to tend must have been a great way to get some peace.

As I grew up, I discovered the importance of solitude for my mind, body, and spirit. Being alone and being lonely are not the same. I'm rarely lonely when I'm alone because I enjoy my own company. In silence, I am the most creative and can experience true tranquility.

My favorite retreat has always been my garden, a smaller version of the ranch and farm I grew up on. Digging in the dirt, pulling weeds, pruning trees, mending broken irrigation pipes, or picking a bouquet of spice-scented roses for the kitchen table helps me focus and connect to God and the universe. When I've had a bad day, I go into the garden. And when I've been rude or impatient with my family, they banish me to the garden to regain my equilibrium.

You don't need a garden to experience solitude. Wherever you find a sense of peace and stillness is the place to plant your seeds of creation. I often meditate, imagining my quiet place as a sandy beach at sunset with gentle breezes swaying the palms and rippling the aqua lagoon. Once the solitude has quieted me, I am ready to be a better friend and companion.

Solitude and friendship are the twin foundations for inner peace. Ultimately, we are all alone, but we are also social beings. As philosopher Kahlil Gibran said, "Let there be space in your togetherness."

People who have chosen lives of solitude still need companionship for growth and sharing. Interaction and communication are essential human functions. People who have chosen lives of companionship still need solitude to nourish and renew their relationships.

The world today is full of noise and distractions. Sometimes we need to make the quietness we need. It's the contemplation and reflection of solitude that give us strength and compassion.

EXERCISE

Shhhh!

Think of a space where you feel completely nurtured, relaxed, and rejuvenated. Close your eyes and take a deep breath from your diaphragm, inhaling slowly, then exhaling even more slowly. Now, envision becoming aware of your imaginary retreat and everything around you. Listen to the sounds, see the colors, feel the warmth, taste and smell and touch your surroundings. Be present in your body and your mind.

Open your eyes. Acknowledge where you really are, but hold the sense of peace from your special place. Savor the stillness. You can do this exercise anytime in any place, even in the midst of hectic and stressful situations.

It is the pauses between notes that make the music.
Make time for the sounds of silence.

Cynthia Brian

The Gift of
SPONTANEITY

It was a Thursday night, and I was doing my radio program, *Starstyle—Be the Star You Are!* when my pager vibrated. At the next break, I returned the call. It was my friend Carol, excitedly inviting my husband and me to join her and her husband on a private jet to Montana. "We need to be at the airport at 6:00 A.M. tomorrow morning," she said.

My cue music began to play. "I'll call you back after the show," I gasped. It was difficult concentrating for the next hour of interviews, as I wondered what on earth was going on.

When we connected again, she explained, "We were invited a long time ago to fly to our friends' Montana ranch for the weekend. They just rang to say that two guests canceled, so we could bring along two fun people. Immediately, we thought of you and Brian. Come on! Do it! It'll be fun!"

My mind raced with a thousand reasons why we couldn't possibly go. Takeoff was eight hours away. Who would care for the kids and the animals? How could I get packed so quickly? How could my husband get away? Friday is the busiest day in my office, and I had so much to do. How would I ever catch up afterward? And flying in a private plane was more dangerous than flying on a scheduled carrier, right?

At first, I said "no" automatically. Then a feeling of "Today is the first day of the rest of your life" came over me. I realized what an incredible opportunity this was. The jet part intrigued me and scared me at the same time. I had only flown on private jets for model shoots. I wasn't sure what to expect, but knew that fear isn't an excuse. Brian and I had never been to the wilds of Montana. And we both needed a break badly.

I picked up the phone and called my husband. "Get packed. We're leaving the house at 4:30 A.M. and flying on a private business jet to

Montana with Carol and Lance." Of course, he thought I was mad. He began to protest, reciting the same mammoth list of what we were supposed to do over the weekend and reminding me about the number of small plane crashes. "Carol told me they have two professional pilots, so it's as safe as other airlines, " I responded. As quickly as I had changed my mind, he did too. We decided to be spontaneous.

In the next few hours, I prioritized my workload and arranged care for our children and the animals. The next morning, as the sun began to glow in the eastern sky, we drove up to the tarmac. Our bags were loaded, and we were off on an incredible adventure with old and about-to-be-new friends.

We flew on a corporate nine-seat jet, thanks to our new friends Lisa and Randy. In Montana, we were whisked off to a rustic lodge, located on the ranch of two more new friends, Loretta and Larry. The ranch was located in the middle of a forest near the Continental Divide. Beavers swam in the creeks, herds of deer paraded in the meadow, songbirds filled the air with melody, and wildflowers blanketed the prairie. It was truly God's country!

We spent the weekend walking in the woods, reading, talking, eating, and forming a bond with gracious people who have since become good friends. It was a time we will never forget.

How long it had been since I was totally spontaneous! I remembered how, when I was working for the airlines in my twenties, I could just hop on a plane and fly to Hawaii for the weekend on the spur of the moment. Or when I lived in Europe, I'd wake up one day and decide to board a train for somewhere, anywhere, just *away* into foreign territory. What had happened to those carefree days of exploration and adventure?

Over the years, I had become so entrenched in my routine of family, auditions, work, house, garden, animal care, volunteering, and social gatherings, that I had truly forgotten how to "be in the moment." Our trip to Montana turned out to be an awakening, heightening our awareness and appreciation of both everyday pleasures and the joys of spontaneity. Sometimes we get so stuck in the

Cynthia Brian

routines of our life that we turn down a chance for unscheduled fun and relaxation. Sometimes we let fear of the unknown shadow our opportunities for adventure. Being spontaneous is a great spirit lifter and energizer. It doesn't mean being rude or irresponsible, just being in the moment, letting go of concerns about tomorrow, and living authentically right now. It means doing something unpremeditated, unrehearsed, impromptu. We can always find excuses for not being spontaneous. There is always too much to do and not enough time or money to do it. Saying "I can't" is all too easy.

The truth is that you could be dead tomorrow, and the world would go on without you. Once in a while, let loose. Take a chance and be spontaneous. What a stroke of luck that I listened to my inner voice saying, "Go, girl, go!"

Since that spontaneous getaway, I have made a conscientious effort to do things extemporaneously whenever possible. After all, actors must be great at improvisation to survive auditions, so why not ad lib with life once in a while too.

EXERCISE

Just Do It!

Today is the day you are going to do something unplanned, something not in your routine. It can be anything: Go for a swim on your lunch hour, say "yes" to that tennis match that you've put off for a year, take the time to have dinner with a friend, get a massage, or hop a plane or train for anywhere. Just do it! It will put a smile on your face and a new bounce in your walk. Being spontaneous is its own reward.

Let go, let go, let go. Just do it!

The Gift of
SUCCESS

My definition of success is being happy in the moment, doing what you want to do, living the way you want to live with the people you want to live with, having peace of mind and spirit, and enjoying life to the fullest, whatever the circumstances.

Most people equate personal success with money. Financial success can be useful and is usually welcomed, but it is totally unrelated to your being the star you are. Money has never been my measuring stick, and I have always been wildly successful.

☆ When I learned to tie my shoes, I was a success.
☆ When I took my first photograph with my own camera, and it wasn't blurry, I was a success.
☆ When I learned to disk the fields, I was a success.
☆ When I won the "Make It with Wool" contest by designing and sewing my own wool suit at age fourteen, I was a success.
☆ When I helped a friend through a difficult situation, I was a success.
☆ When I studied hard for a test, I was a success.
☆ When I harvested my first tomato plant, I was a success.
☆ When I financed my college education by raising chickens and selling the eggs for thirty to fifty cents a dozen, I was a success.
☆ When I smiled at the sad-looking person on the street and she smiled back, I was a success.
☆ When I wallpapered my first room, I was almost a success.
☆ When I kiss my children good night, I am a success.

Success is not measured by the dollars we earn, but by the value we get from life. When my husband and I were first married, we rented a tiny house. We weren't sure we'd be able to keep up with the equally tiny rent, but we felt very successful. We had a house.

Later, when we bought our first small bungalow, I thought it was a castle. I termed my style of decorating "old attic, early basement" because I furnished the home with flea market and garage-sale finds. We also traveled extensively on standby tickets, staying in hostels, camping out, and living out of a backpack, but we felt privileged to be able to see the world.

Measure your own success by your contentment with who you are and where you're going. Success means having dreams, goals, and desires, and striving to make them come true. When you recognize that you already have everything you need to be the star of your own life, you are a success. Success is being grateful for what you have, not jealous of others or resentful for what you don't have. We are all absolutely responsible for our individual successes.

Take an inventory of your daily activities, and ask yourself whether you are content with what *you* have created for yourself. If you're not, what changes are you willing to make to achieve your personal definition of success?

If being a millionaire (or billionaire) is essential for "success," and you're sure you can't be happy until becoming one, then you are probably doomed to failure. Possessions can bring excitement, stimulation, and comfort, but they provide only a false sense of self-worth. However, if wealth is merely a convenient measure of your skill and hard work, if you'd be just as happy without it as long as you knew you were doing your best, then by all means incorporate it in your personal definition of success. But it's entirely unnecessary.

My dad lived a life of meaning as a farmer. He was extraordinarily successful because he was the best farmer he could possibly be, the best dad, the best husband, and the best friend. He lived a life of no regrets and died knowing he had lived a fulfilling and meaningful life.

You are a success when you take ownership of your life and your work. It doesn't matter whether you are an artist, entrepreneur, CEO, or assembly-line worker. All of us are really "self-employed."

If there is any secret for success, it is this: You are one of kind. You are you. You have the ability to do whatever you want in life if you are willing to work hard enough and long enough to achieve it. You are unique, a wonder of creation.

Take a look in the mirror and admire yourself. Enjoy each moment of your life. When you fall down, get back up and keep going. We only fail when we don't do our best.

EXERCISE

Play the Success Game

In the game called "Success," the prize is Life. Your object is to get out of jail free, pass Go, and collect your $200. Here's how to play.

☆ *Draw a square for each year of your life. In each square, write one thing you are very proud of accomplishing that year. Your victory can be large or small (highly relative terms that mean different things to different people).*

☆ *For example, someone might write, "I learned to walk" or "I won Outstanding Teenager of America" or "I told the truth every day" or "I am a recovering drug addict." Once you have completed the boxes of your life so far, draw more squares for the years ahead.*

☆ *As you look back over your life's work, are you happy with what you see? Have you been of service to others? Are you grateful for what you have earned? If you can answer "yes" to these questions, you are a success. Congratulations, you have won the grand prize, a life of no regrets.*

Success isn't about possessions.
Success is about being happy!

Cynthia Brian

The Gift of
SURRENDER

The week had been a hectic one for me. Shoots were scheduled for five different television shows, plus I was doing a special promotion for the Academy Awards. And everything was going wrong. Trusted collaborators failed to keep their promises, deadlines (lifelines to me) were missed, equipment was misplaced, and carefully prepared plans crashed. I was stressed, angry, disappointed, discouraged, embarrassed, frustrated, and disillusioned.

The weather wasn't the only thing that was gray, stormy, and miserable that evening when I came home. My kids took one look at me and said, "Mom, you need to go in the garden." Knowing they were right, I grabbed my rain slicker and flashlight and pulled on my mud boots. In the darkness of the dismal moonless night, I sloshed out to the garden to eradicate something, hopefully weeds.

With rain and perspiration sliding down my face and mud under my fingernails, I felt a calm slowly settling over me. Once again, I felt connected with life, humanity, and our godliness. The garden nourished my battered spirit. I stuck my nose in a creamy white narcissus while my eyes dripped with rain and tears. With their glorious fragrance in my nostrils, I knew "This, too, shall pass!"

Sometimes I get going so fast that acquaintances have jokingly nicknamed me "Skater." Friends no longer ask politely what I'm doing. They know they'll become tired just hearing about my day. At times I've used my body like a workhorse and have paid the price of physical pain. I get so busy "doing" that I stop "being." Who can forget the Wicked Witch of the West whisking across the sky, writing, "Surrender, Dorothy." How often have I been forced to surrender and then remembered that surrendering was the best remedy?

I have learned the hard way that I am human—no more, no less. But I am a slow learner and am guilty of repeating the same mistake of overdoing many times.

It is okay to surrender sometimes, to slow down, to take it easy, to take a break, to halt. What I've learned by surrendering is that the world goes on. When we stop and keep quiet for a while, we can see our problems and challenges in a different light. Sometimes a solution appears as if by magic. It was always there, of course, but our busyness kept us from receiving the message clearly.

The gift of surrendering does not mean giving up or caving in, or abandoning your dreams or goals. Rather, you yield to your higher power, relinquish control, and admit that you deserve a break. No matter how much energy we have, unless our bodies, minds, and souls are frequently refueled, rested, and refreshed, we will break down. Now when I start feeling wound up like one of my former toys, I surrender, throw my arms in the air, and exclaim, "God, you're in charge. Thy will be done. You take it from here. This, too, shall pass."

EXERCISE

Cleaning Closets

Take the time to understand where you are overextended. List and eliminate from your life all the stressful "should dos" and "must dos" that have no value for you and your family. Prioritize. Look closely at your alliances with people who no longer share your vision. Maybe it is time to develop new friendships. Stop doing what you are doing long enough to take inventory of your life. Find some green grass, stare up at the clouds, and dream.

Be willing to surrender
to nature, God, your own limitations,
and the inevitable
(but never surrender your dreams).

Cynthia Brian

The Gift of
SURVIVAL

A romantic weekend! My sister Patty and her husband, Marlin, were on a long-awaited break, relaxing alone at the family's remote hunting cabin. The first evening, they gazed out at an idyllic meadow, sipping cold drinks, and watching the sun set. Far off in the distance, a thin column of smoke rose into the pink clouds.

It had been a hot, dry summer. The worst forest fires in thirty years had destroyed more than four million acres of northern California forest. But those fires were too remote to concern Patty and Marlin.

At dawn the next morning, several firefighters stopped by the cabin. The fires had spread into the forest a few miles away, but the winds were blowing away from the cabin. There was no immediate danger, but everyone in the area was being warned anyway. The firefighters anticipated having everything under control within a few hours. Hundreds of fire engines, bulldozers, air tankers, helicopters, and water trucks had come to the Mendocino National Forest from all over the country to do battle with the forces of nature. (Many of these strike teams were from urban and suburban areas, unaccustomed to forest conditions and unfamiliar with the tangle of pines, oaks, and manzanitas that feed a fire frenzy.)

By midafternoon, the sky was dark and the air was acrid with smoke. The temperature had risen to 105 degrees. A distant roar like a waterfall reached their ears. Patty and Marlin were hurriedly throwing things in their truck to leave when two fire trucks sped up the dirt road and stopped abruptly next to the cabin.

"You're not going anywhere," Captain T. J. Welch shouted. The wind had shifted. A firestorm was coming their way at more than seventy miles an hour. All exits out of the canyon were blocked.

Battalion Chief Chris Pollack had devised a plan. The sixteen civilians trapped in the valley were being gathered in the meadow around the cabin. This acre of lush green grass would be the safety zone, everyone's last hope of survival.

Ninety firefighters had been spread out along the roads, trails, and hillsides in the fire's path. Their orders were to stay put until the fire was upon them, then to light a backfire and escape to the meadow.

The wind-driven flames raced south and east, sucking the oxygen out of the air and scorching everything in their path. The intensity of heat and smoke must have been terrifying. If a single firefighter had panicked and lit the backfire too early before fleeing, lives would have been lost.

The sound was deafening as the retreating firefighters and their trucks began arriving at the meadow safety zone. Marlin and several others had sprayed fire-resistant foam on the cabin and nearby area. Now they pumped water from the creek to keep the surrounding ring of trees from exploding in a fury of flames. Ash billowed up, coating everyone's teeth and burning their throats. The civilians were ordered inside the cabin and told to lie on the floor. Patty calmly distributed wet towels to breathe through, but they dried almost instantly. Marlin was still outside, pulling fire hoses until they melted from the intense heat. He returned to the cabin to hold Patty close one last time. Patty thought of our father, Al Abruzzini, who had been a volunteer firefighter for forty-six years. He had been honored as Captain of the Gordon Valley Fire Department just before he died a few years earlier. "Daddy," she prayed, "please don't let us die like this."

A crown fire came rolling down the hillside toward the cabin, moving faster than any human could run. Trees vaporized. The energy released was a hundred times that of a normal forest fire, with an explosive force nearing the intensity of a small atomic bomb. Everyone prayed. Death seemed seconds away.

Then, almost imperceptibly, the roar began to diminish. The smoke thinned slightly, and they could see each other. Finally, someone rose and peered out through the heavy storm shutters. The fire had passed.

Cynthia Brian

Everyone stayed at the cabin for two more days until rescue workers could clear an escape route. Instead of evacuating with the others, my brother-in-law and sister drove to the top of the canyon where they could use a cell phone to call my mom and my brother Fred for supplies. Mom and Fred, my son, Justin, my sister Debbie, her husband, Terry, and their two daughters, Amber and Lacy, hurriedly filled several trucks with supplies—food, water, beverages, toilet paper—all the necessities to care for the firefighters over the next ten days.

The fire continued to rage for fourteen days in nearby canyons, ultimately burning over eighty-two thousand acres. It became the second-worst firestorm in United States history, but not a single life or home was lost because of the discipline and courage of these firefighters. They stuck to the main plan exactly and concentrated on survival for all, not just for themselves. As a television reporter said later, "They had to look the devil in the eye and not blink." Of course, as everyone will admit, a little prayer didn't hurt either. Our family believes that my dad heard Patty's pleas and did his part to save lives.

Afterward, our family made a sign saying, "Thank You, Firefighters. God Bless You," and signed it, "The Abruzzini Family." God did indeed bless them that terrible day.

Since then, my sister and her husband hold annual reunions at "the safety zone" with the firefighters who saved their lives. (This extraordinary combat between man and nature was cited in a special national training video for firefighters. The story is being considered for an upcoming movie.)

Survival can be highly dramatic, worthy of the front pages. It can also be ordinary, something we do daily almost without taking notice. We should celebrate both. Acknowledge your major victories, but don't forget to salute each small triumph. Each time you remain positive in the face of adversity brings you one step closer to being the star you are.

Your Survival Kit

You're not a hero? Think again. You probably do dozens of heroic things every day. Here's a sample checklist. Give yourself credit for each brave deed you did today:

☆ *Stayed calm in the face of provocation.*

☆ *Stayed positive and focused amidst confusion.*

☆ *Accepted criticism graciously and used it to better myself without feeling hurt or defensive.*

☆ *Helped someone who cannot possibly help me in return.*

☆ *Did a boring or tedious task that could have been left undone.*

☆ *Stopped myself from saying or doing something I might regret later.*

☆ *Separated myself from the pressure of immediate deadlines (lifelines) long enough to consider the big picture and to plan ahead.*

☆ *Stopped what I was doing and really listened to someone who needed a listener.*

☆ *Reached out to encourage someone.*

☆ *Did an anonymous good deed.*

☆ *Did the best I could in a difficult situation.*

With each heroic deed, you are demonstrating and strengthening your survival skills.

To thrive, strive to stay alive.

Cynthia Brian

The Gift of
TRANSFORMATION

Everyone is born to be magnificent. Every person is unique and has something special to offer the world. And every day is an opportunity to learn to dance to the music.

Rebecca is a beautiful woman in her early thirties. I was introduced to her through her sister-in-law, Terri, who was in one of my acting classes. "Rebecca wants to make a difference in people's lives. She'd be interested in interviewing with you to work on your television series," Terri told me.

Rebecca and I met, and she was indeed a splendid young lady, bright, talented, and shy. She began working as a part-time volunteer on *Starstyle—Live Your Dreams!* Soon she confessed to me that she envied the men and women I was interviewing, people who were following their hearts and doing what they loved in life. "How I wish I could find a meaningful way to make a living," she often lamented. She felt her day job was a dead end.

"You *can*, Rebecca," I'd tell her. "You just have to make the decision, and do it! Nothing is easy. It may be rough going at first, but you'll be happier." Like most people, though, Rebecca was apprehensive about following her passion. Would she be able to pay the bills? What about medical insurance? Could she survive? What would her family think? Worst of all, what if she failed?

She was like a lot people who know their lives should change and who keep hoping somebody else will do it for them. Fear of life's big decisions—how to handle relationships, what jobs to take, and where to live—can paralyze us. For the next four dismal years, fear controlled Rebecca. She stayed in a job she disliked, but was afraid to leave because she feared rejection in job interviews. She lived in an apartment she disliked because she thought there wasn't anything better. She was in a constant state of turmoil and indecision, frequently sick, sad, and depressed. She had signed up for evening classes toward a business degree, but she was so drained after a hard day at work that her studies suffered. She was overwhelmed and felt she was getting nowhere. Then the universe gave her a really big kick.

Her father was diagnosed with cancer. She went to be with him, to talk things through, forgive the past, and express her love. He died, surrounded by his family, and Rebecca underwent an epiphany.

The death of a parent is a painful turning point. My own father's death gave me a gift with a sense of purpose that forever changed my life. Rebecca had a similar experience. She realized how very precious life is. There is no time to waste being miserable or feeling sorry for ourselves. Rebecca immediately transformed her life. She moved to a more cheerful apartment. She quit her job and found one that is fulfilling her dreams of making a difference in people's lives. She had to take a cut in pay, but now she has flexible hours, less stress, and more freedom to express the beautiful person she is. Knowing Rebecca, I'll bet she'll create a way to earn more money than she was earning before while doing what she loves. She is a woman with great ideas. Now she has a chance to implement them. Her transformation is ongoing. She's working on her personal relationships and honing her communication skills. Rebecca is metamorphosing before our eyes, growing, changing, and becoming the woman she always knew she could be: magnificent, intelligent, and wise.

My friend Linda has just been diagnosed with breast cancer. Linda has always been a powerful executive, vice president of a Fortune 500 company where all the other officers are men. For years, she had to be invincible, battling with the big boys and making difficult business decisions. Now, she has to transform invincibility into vulnerability as she allows medical experts to dictate her treatment, and loving caregivers to offer advice, support, prayers, and assistance. She has transformed herself into a warrior, doing everything possible for her own health so she will be around to love her husband and watch her children grow. Linda is a strong woman, a survivor, and she will beat this.

Transformation is about changing and moving from one form to another. It might mean losing bad habits and routines that have kept us stuck, or it could be adapting to new circumstances in positive and creative ways. Transformation is an acknowledgment that you are a wonder of creation and deserve love, enlightenment, happiness, joy, and all things bright, bold, and beautiful.

The keys to transformation are these:

☆ Believe in yourself and your worthiness of all the possibilities open to you.
☆ Love yourself and others.
☆ Believe that you have the power to create the future of your dreams.
☆ Know that you can make the jump to a new beginning.

Others can give you advice, support, and encouragement, but they cannot transform you. You do it yourself. Sometimes transformation is a natural evolution. Sometimes it is the result of a sudden realization or catalyst. Transforming yourself can be like jumping off a cliff that you've been standing on for a long time. You may be a little stunned by the changes at first. Take time every day to laugh and pray. Give yourself permission to yearn for the old and familiar, to be afraid, and to cry as often as you wish. See a bright future where you are doing what you love, with whom you love, and when you love to do it.

Transformation is change at a spiritual level. We each have just one life, so why not live it with integrity and without regret. Transform the ordinary and dreary into something precious and fine. And to Rebecca and Linda: You go, girls!

Transformers

What one thing would you do if you knew you couldn't possibly fail? Even better, what one thing would you be sure to do if you knew you had only one year to live?

No one knows the future, so today is the day to transform yourself into the person you want to be. Answer these questions honestly:

☆ *Is my life fulfilling?*
☆ *Am I with a partner who loves and cherishes me?*
☆ *Am I doing work that I love?*
☆ *Do I live in an atmosphere that nourishes my spirit?*
☆ *Do I have friends who value me as I really am?*
☆ *Am I the person I want to be?*
☆ *If I die tomorrow, will I have achieved what I want to achieve?*

If you answer "no" to any one of these questions, you may want to make some changes in your life. Only you can live the life you love. Only you can make the changes necessary to follow your heart and live your dreams. Get going! What are you waiting for? You were born to be great.

Each ant thinks itself a giant and so moves
mountains. Live every day as a giant and
discover what you can do.

Cynthia Brian

The Gift of
TRUTH

Actors sometimes lie. Or rather, they are often so desperate to get hired that they don't exactly tell the truth. They'll claim they can high dive, ride a bucking bronco, or drive a tank if that's what the casting director wants to hear. Now I consider myself a truthful person, but early on in my acting career, I learned my lesson the hard way about fibbing.

I had been modeling for only two years when my agent sent me on an audition for a cigarette commercial that would be shot in Japan. I have never smoked in my life and abhor everything related to tobacco, but the allure of the big money, a trip to Japan, and the glamour associated with this production got the better of me.

My first audition was a breeze. The casting director took several Polaroids of me smiling and looking sexy. I walked out of the advertising agency office with no regrets. A callback followed, with more people in the room, and a professional photographer took 35mm shots of me in the same poses. This was no big deal, I thought. I wasn't actually associated with tobacco, I told myself, because I didn't have to hold the cigarette. I wanted this job, and I was willing to rationalize the truth in order to get it.

A few days later, my agent called with the good news. The advertising agency liked me very much and wanted to fly me to Los Angeles to meet the clients and rehearse the scenes before making the final shoot in Japan. Wow! I was being paid to fly to Los Angeles!

I arrived at the audition, ready to shoot more smile photos. To my surprise, the Japanese director asked me to hold a cigarette in my right hand while giving a very alluring smile to the camera. "I can do that," I thought. Everyone seemed pleased with the shot. I assumed I was finished and began to leave. "No, no, get back under the lights. We want you to light the cigarette, inhale, and then blow the smoke toward the camera while giving us your sexiest look!" Oh my God, what horror! How was I going to accomplish this?

"Can't I just hold the cigarette and give you the look?" I asked meekly. "I really don't feel like smoking right now."

"You *do* smoke, don't you?" the director said. "Just light it up and smile!"

My first mistake was that I lit the filter end. As they laughed and corrected me, I tried to bluff. "I'm just a bit nervous," I told them. Once the cigarette was lit, I took a big puff, inhaling as instructed while staring sexily at the camera.

The next thing I knew, I woke up on the floor, surrounded by twenty people fanning me. I was forced to admit that I had lied. Of course, I was fired ignominiously and sent back to San Francisco in disgrace, but I learned an invaluable lesson. Never, never, never lie about your abilities. Telling the truth is the only way to make it through life.

In acting, lying to producers seems to be a natural extension of creating imaginary characters for an audience. It is a slippery and dangerous line to cross. Whatever is needed for the part, actors reply automatically, "Yes, no problem!" Can you fly a plane? Of course! Hold your breath for a hundred minutes? Certainly! Jump from a tenth-floor window? Sure! After the debacle of my smoking audition, I made a commitment to truth and authenticity in all my acting and modeling assignments. I also decided that, since I am opposed to the tragic health effects of tobacco, I will never do a cigarette ad or commercial. My decision has cost me thousands of dollars and many career opportunities, but I am being truthful to myself.

When I coach my acting students, I emphasize the importance of being truthful on their résumés. This holds true for the business world too. Lies come back to bite you on the butt, often at the worst possible time.

My truthfulness was a great asset on one job. Another model had lied about her roller-skating abilities for a big billboard campaign.

The ad agency had booked her because her brunette hair matched that of the little girl playing her daughter and because her résumé said she roller skated. But she didn't. She was fired, and the agency lost a lot of time and money while they searched for another actress. I was sent to the emergency auditions. It had been a long day for everyone, and tempers were flaring. When I walked in the door, the photographer took one look at me and yelled, "Get out of here. You're a blonde." I had driven three hours in rush-hour traffic and wasn't about to be sent home without exhibiting my skills. I shouted back, "Forget my hair. Look at my feet!" He was taken aback and said quietly, "Let's see you skate." I put on my roller skates and raced in circles around him. He looked me over closely. "Okay. Be a brunette, and be here at eight o'clock tomorrow morning." I booked the job because I was telling the truth (and had one-day hair rinse in every color, an actor's best friend.)

The truth isn't always easy, but it makes life much easier. There is a beauty in truth, an inner peace and a power that truly does set you free. When you tell the truth, there's no worry that you'll be caught in lies later.

Over my lifetime, I have come to understand that there are three sides to every story: yours, mine, and the truth. Our perceptions vary, and we all tend to make ourselves the hero or heroine of our own experiences. Our truths may differ, but we should each acknowledge what is true for us. Honor that truth, and you'll never be sorry.

Truth or Dare?

How truthful is your résumé? This is a great opportunity to go back over that dusty sheet of paper and clean it up. Whether you are an actor or an archeologist, dare to list only the skills and talents that you actually possess and the experiences you have actually had. Don't shade, embroider, exaggerate, minimize, or omit. Don't lie. If you have never needed a résumé, make a list of skills in which you excel and experiences from which you have learned. Perhaps your truthful new résumé will land you a great job. At the very least, you'll have a new appreciation of your own honesty and the qualities that make you a star.

"The cask can only yield the wine it holds."
—*Italian proverb*

Tell the truth!

Cynthia Brian

The Gift of
UNDERSTANDING

"Ich bin ein maedchen auf Kalifornien!" I studied German my senior year in high school because I had applied to be a teenage ambassador to Germany. Only forty of the top teens in America were being considered for this prestigious and demanding job abroad to promote understanding between the world's nations. I had already been an exchange student in Mexico, which I had really enjoyed. Now I looked forward to learning a new language and getting acquainted with a new culture.

Late in the spring, the precious acceptance letter came. I was elated. But five days before I was due to leave for Germany, my destination was changed to Holland. I was leaving for eighteen months to represent America, and I spoke no Dutch.

My entire family—grandparents, cousins, aunts, and uncles—came to the airport to bid me farewell. It was the first time I ever saw my dad cry. It was a huge send-off, but then I was the first member of our family to return to Europe since our grandparents and great-grandparents emigrated to America.

In Amsterdam, I was greeted by my host family who took me to their beautiful home in Breda, in the south of Holland. We smiled and nodded a lot, since I couldn't yet communicate with them. Just as we were getting to know one another, I was whisked away to Bergen aan Zee (Mountain by the Sea) in the north for two weeks of intensive language training.

Dutch is considered one of the most difficult of Western languages because it is a combination of many different languages. After ten days of intensive studying, I decided to write to my new Dutch family. Using my translation dictionary, I *thought* I was telling them about how I was learning Dutch, enjoying the ocean and sunshine, missing them, and looking forward to returning to live with them. What I actually wrote was that I had sunstroke and was in the hospital! Alarmed, they rushed to Bergen to be at my side. This was just the first of many mistakes I would make while living abroad. Obviously my Dutch family had to be very patient and understanding with me while I developed a comprehension of their language and customs.

Not long afterward, when I had returned to their very formal household, I was asked whether I wanted more to eat at dinner. In Dutch, I replied, "No thank you, I'm full." However, what I actually said was that I had just had sex and was pregnant. Everyone at the table was shocked and immediately left the room without a word. I had no idea what I had done to deserve such scorn. Finally, my Dutch brother, Stan, explained my mistake to me, and we were all able to reach an understanding. But that was far from the last of my errors.

Soon after, we went on a month-long holiday to the beaches in Belgium. Being a gregarious teenager, I put on my bathing suit and frolicked in the North Sea. I was quickly surrounded by young men who all vied for my attention. It was common in California to go to a beach and have fun with everyone there, so I thought nothing of this incident. After a jolly good time playing in the surf, I returned to our flat. To my astonishment, my Dutch family were all looking at me with grave concern. Again, I had no clue what I had done. Again, it was my Dutch brother, Stan, who took me aside and gave me the news. In those days in the Low Countries, nice girls didn't shave their legs or frolic on the beach, much less with strange men. I had broken all three rules! The giggling guys who romped with me had assumed I was an American trollop.

Me! The American girl who was going to be a nun! If I was supposed to be one of America's outstanding youths and my behavior labeled me as a promiscuous woman, what was my host family thinking about the rest of the teenagers in the United States? I was astonished when I realized that my conventional American behavior was unacceptable in sophisticated Europe. A great deal of new awareness was needed on both sides. My host family and I met with the program director, and we worked hard to expand our mutual understanding of our cultural differences. Although I made many more mistakes, my time in the Netherlands was one of the most blessed in my life, leaving me with a profound sensitivity for the differences in cultures and nations.

All people are unique, with their own problems, agendas, and viewpoints. Every group has its own culture, traditions, rules, and perceptions. If we are to live compatibly, we must try to understand and respect these differences, worldwide and in our own backyards. Comprehension does not assume, however, that we will always agree with one another.

It is crucial that we make an effort to understand and comprehend the customs of other countries and other cultures. When we don't grasp the meaning of a conversation, an action, or a gesture, it is best to ask for an explanation or an interpretation. Wars have been caused by misunderstandings.

When Dr. Bernie S. Siegel, author of *Peace, Love, and Healing*, was on my radio program, he told me about his own lesson in understanding. One day, he angrily phoned an airline about a mixed-up reservation. He was shouting at the clerk when she said, "Why are you yelling at me? You are Dr. Bernie Siegel, a spokesperson for compassion and understanding, and you are supposed to be loving me. I'm dying of cancer, and you are worried about a plane reservation." Immediately, he realized how unfeeling he had been. He was demanding that the clerk understand his problem, but he had failed to comprehend hers. She was not responsible for the error and had her own problems. He apologized and was grateful that she had helped him understand his own anger.

We are all human. We all make innocent mistakes, which humor and acceptance can help resolve. Even when we really blunder, mutual understanding can heal the wounds and bring down the barriers. Staying open to true understanding is an enormous gift to ourselves and others.

A New Language

How you respond to other people can make a huge difference in their lives. For the next twenty-four hours, concentrate on those around you, recognizing everyone's need to share something about themselves and to be appreciated and loved for themselves. Understanding will be your new language.

Expanding yourself through understanding
makes you truly larger than life.
When you don't understand, say:
"Please explain!"

Cynthia Brian

The Gift of

VISUALIZATION

"There is nothing so real as a dream," says author Tom Clancy. In my acting classes, we do a powerful visualization exercise much like dreaming while you are awake. I am fascinated by the power that visualizing can give to the person doing it. My clients have imagined themselves triumphing at auditions or playing difficult roles, and then gone on to do just that. There's no hocus-pocus or magic about it. It's just a mental rehearsal for the real thing, which lets you step out, calm and confident.

The first time I read a *Chicken Soup for the Soul* book, I was sitting in a hammock, gazing out over the blue Caribbean. The whole family was vacationing in a rented cabaña in the Cayman Islands, a respite from our fast-paced lives back in California. The book, coauthored by Jack Canfield and Mark Victor Hansen, was a gift from my husband, and he'd written a dedication inside the cover: *"You* could have written this!"

As I read the 101 stories selected to open the heart and rekindle the spirit, I couldn't have agreed more. My television series was a visual counterpart of these inspirational tales. "I should be a part of this family," I murmured to myself.

Immediately, I decided to begin visualizing myself as one of the *Chicken Soup for the Soul* authors. The first thing I did was to write down this new dream in my journal in the first-person present tense: "I am an author of *Chicken Soup for the Soul."* My next step was to visualize in more detail so my wishful dream would become a concrete goal with steps to achieve it.

Because I am drawn to positive works, I began to fill my library with each new *Chicken Soup for the Soul* sequel that hit the bookstores. One day, as I was planning the six-month lineup of motivational guests for my radio show, a flyer came in the mail. It said simply:

"This Christmas, inspire your listening audiences with stories from the *Chicken Soup for the Soul* series by inviting the authors on your next program!"

Talk about getting the right message at the right time! I phoned the press agent, not sure he'd talk to me. My radio program had great ratings, but it was fairly new and aired on a small station. But once I had described our style and format, the agent said, "This sounds like a perfect match. Let's book you some authors." Notice that he said "authors" plural, not singular.

That was the beginning of my *Chicken Soup for the Soul* saga. Six authors from six different sequels were booked immediately, and every interview was a roaring success. When one of the authors commented that "you feel like family," I replied, "Yes! And I want to author *Chicken Soup for the Gardener's Soul* and *Chicken Soup for the Actor's Soul*." I was vividly visualizing this actually happening, and I let people know it. Besides telling other *Chicken Soup for the Soul* coauthors about my wish, I took the next step and wrote their headquarters a query letter asking about the procedure for becoming a coauthor. Every evening before I went to bed, my desire to be a *Chicken Soup for the Soul* coauthor was part of my visualization exercise. I would actually see myself signing a contract, meeting the team, and writing a book. I visualized thousands of contributors sending me inspiring stories to be used in the book. I "saw" myself doing radio and television interviews to promote the book and reading in the newspaper that my *Chicken Soup for the Soul* book had hit #1 on the *New York Times* best-seller list. I played out every detail in my imagination as if this experience already existed.

One day, Patty Hansen, wife of *Chicken Soup for the Soul* editor Mark Victor Hansen, phoned and asked to see samples of my work. The next thing I knew, I was signing a contract to coauthor *Chicken Soup for the Gardener's Soul!* My constant visualization of my goal and the actions I took as a result had opened new doors for me.

Actors rehearse a lot. You should too. The human mind is a remarkable bio-computer, capable of incredible feats. For example, scientists assure us that our subconscious minds can't distinguish between real and imagined behavior. If you imagine an action vividly enough in your subconscious mind, your conscious mind treats that image as if it really happened. Top athletes use visualization to perfect their performance and see themselves landing the shot, making the touchdown, or crossing the finishing line.

You can use this technique in almost any facet of your daily life. Recall a useful experience in vivid detail. Concentrate on the positive aspects only. Using your inner senses and creativity while you are in this altered state of awareness activates your visual, physical, and auditory learning modes. Don't panic at the term "altered state." It just means that you're relaxed, free of distractions, and able to focus internally.

When we relax and consciously direct our thoughts, we can get our bodies, minds, and emotions to respond as if we are actually doing what we're mentally rehearsing. The rehearsed skills are stored in both the brain and the body, available to us whenever we need them. The more we rehearse, the sharper our visualization skills become, and the more we can acquire successful habits and skills.

For four years, from that day in the hammock until I signed the contract, I had talked and thought about being part of the *Chicken Soup for the Soul* team. I used the same visualization techniques that I teach my students when they want to turn their dreams into reality. There were times when I had doubts, but I kept rehearsing the values I could bring to the relationship. I followed my mantra: "Dream it! Do it!"

Chicken Soup for the Gardener's Soul is now in bookstores, and I am visualizing it being a best-seller. Perhaps by the time you read this, this goal will also have been accomplished. And I'm visualizing collaborating on another sequel, *Chicken Soup for the Actor's Soul.* Do you have a story to submit?

See It Now

Here is my visualization technique for increasing motivation, improving skills, and overcoming limiting attitudes. Start by selecting a skill you want to improve or acquire.

1. *Sit or lie in an area where you won't be interrupted.*
2. *Take three deep, cleansing breaths. (I use the belly breathing described in "The Gift of Breathing.") Imagine inhaling peace and serenity, then exhaling tension and stress.*
3. *Close your eyes and decide what activity you wish to rehearse.*
4. *Imagine going to the place where you will perform that activity.*

☆ *What do you see? Notice the colors, textures, and forms.*
☆ *What do you smell? Be aware of aromas and scents.*
☆ *What do you hear? Listen for noise, voices, music, and your heartbeat.*
☆ *What do you feel? Are you hot? Cold? What is your sense of the place?*

5. *Imagine yourself performing the activity. See yourself doing it excellently, almost to perfection. Become expert. Feel how strong and skilled you are. Your performance becomes effortless. Experience the sensation of being completely focused. You are the expert.*
6. *Appreciate your new skills. Watch yourself from outside your body. Marvel at your performance.*
7. *Complete the activity, and congratulate yourself for a job well done. Be pleased with your success.*
8. *Before you open your eyes, affirm to yourself that you will incorporate the positive effects of this mental rehearsal the next time you do the activity or experience the situation.*
9. *Look forward to experiencing the positive effects of this visualization. Open your eyes and Be the Star You Are!*
10. *Tell everyone your dream, and ask them to help you make it come true.*

You may want to make an audiotape of these instructions to guide you through your first sessions. Leave long pauses between each step. This same technique has proven successful for overcoming irrational fears, awkwardness in social or business situations, and poor concentration.

What you think about and
talk about comes about.

The Gift of
WINNING

When I signed up to play in our city's softball league, I admit I looked pretty unpromising. I was on my way to a modeling assignment in my high heels, short skirt, well-coiffed hair, and stage make-up. My fellow team members exchanged looks and fervently hoped that I planned to be their cheerleader.

Our city park system had announced that it was organizing softball leagues and had invited organizations and businesses to sponsor teams. On that first day, about fifteen people showed up who had no team affiliation. That included me and my husband. None of us knew the others, but we shared a love of softball and decided to band together. We chose to name our team "Nothing-in-Common."

I missed the initial practices, but showed up early the day of the first game. The coach sighed and put me in right field, figuring I'd do the least damage there. The opposing team smirked, smelling blood, and hammered ball after ball hard into right field.

When I play anything, I love to have fun. Having fun means playing fair, playing hard, and playing my best. The fly balls came zooming at me. I ran, I leaped, I rolled, and I caught them as fast as their guys could hit them. Three flies in a row, and their team was out.

Now it was our turn in the batting cage. Bases loaded. Two out. I was up. My new teammates were not optimistic. Everyone would have preferred that Jenny, our ace player, was at bat, but she was farther down the lineup. The pressure was on, but my confidence and focus kicked in. I have an awkward batting position, so once again, both teams underestimated me. The pitcher got two strikes on me. My team winced! But they shouted encouragingly from the dugout: "It's okay; relax, you can do it!"

The third pitch came, and I whacked it over the center fielder's head. Running, running, running. My hat flew off as I passed second. The opposing team threw to third—overthrew. I rounded third and headed for home. Everybody was yelling. The third baseman threw hard to home. I dived and slid before the catcher could catch the ball. My team went crazy. A home run, and by a girly-girl! I was covered in dirt and mud, but elated. The entire team rushed to home plate for high fives and hugs! The excitement and surprise were unbelievable.

Then the umpire yelled in the way that only umps can do, "Youuuuuuuuu're out!"

Everybody stopped in shock. "What?!" They all yelled at the same time. I had beaten the ball. I couldn't be out. "Youuuuuuuuu're out!" he shouted again, moving his arm pointedly over his shoulder to signify that I was out!

Both teams challenged the call. Both teams agreed I was safe. But the ump was right. I *was* out. In this league, the rule was no sliding at home. Nobody had bothered to read the rule book.

But all was not lost. My image as a wimp had been erased, and I became known as "the slider with the golden glove." Both sides had fabulous innings and, after a very close game, we all went out for pizza, beer, and plenty of laughs. It became a team tradition. We realized that everyone had won that night. We had all learned something new about the rules, we had played our best, and we had bonded as friends.

Over the years, my teammates have loved telling the story of how I showed up for the sign-ups looking like a glamour girl and how I blew away all their illusions in our first game. Our family goat, Mini, became the team mascot and traveled with us to all the games. The Nothing-in-Common team went on to win the city championships, and our team picture with Mini, our dogs, and our children made the front page.

We are all older now. Our babies have become teenagers. We've had lots of good times, a few injuries, and some changes in faces and careers, but we still do our personal best at every game. And we're proud to say we *do* have something in common. Win or lose, we know how to play the game.

Being a "winner" is simply being the best that you can be. The great football coach Vince Lombardi said, "Winning isn't everything; it is the only thing." I disagree profoundly. Games and sports have become such big business that the spirit of sportsmanship and fun has been lost to reverence for the dollar. As you journey through life, try to make everyone with whom you come in contact feel like a winner. When everyone feels like a winner, both personal and business relationships blossom.

I believe that when you do your absolute best, believe in your abilities, learn from your mistakes, have fun, and move on, you have already won the game. Anyone who knows me and my fierce, competitive spirit knows this is not a cop-out. When you give all you have, you are a winner, no matter what the score.

EXERCISE

Dare to Win

Apply a winning attitude to your daily routine. When you feel the rush of competitiveness, go for it!

Ask yourself:

☆ *Am I the best person for this experience?*
☆ *Do I believe in my abilities?*
☆ *How badly do I want to achieve this goal?*
☆ *Do I deserve this?*
☆ *How can I assure that everyone leaves this situation feeling like winners?*
☆ *Am I doing my best?*
☆ *Am I playing fairly?*
☆ *Are we having fun?*

Ironically, winning in life starts with believing you are a winner. But instead of thinking, "Win, win, win," think, "I win, you win, we all win!"

When everybody wins, you are truly a winner.

"If you think you are beaten, you are.
If you think you dare not, you don't
If you'd like to win, but think you can't
It's almost a cinch that you won't
For life's battles don't always go to
the stronger or faster man
Sooner or later the man who wins is
the man who thinks he can!"

—*Anonymous*

The Gift of

WISDOM

It is often said that wisdom comes with age and experience. Our elders and ancestors have much to teach us; however, we must be willing to listen to and process information before we can put it into action.

The first house my husband and I bought was located on the banks of a swift-running creek. There were several reasons we were attracted to this house. The creek, of course, would become a great playground for our flock of geese and ducks. The hillsides were covered with wildflowers and naturalized daffodils, the street offered a friendly cul-de-sac, and we were bordered by acres of open space. But the real reason I wanted the house was the gigantic avocado tree growing in the backyard.

Even before the sale was final, I dreamed of the luscious guacamole I would make from the fruit of my very own avocado tree. But spring progressed to summer, fall, and winter without a single avocado on my guacamole tree. I consulted the experts at various garden centers.

"Avocados need lots of water and well-drained soil," said the first horticulturist. "You'll need to aerate and irrigate."

"Fertilizer is the key to avocado fruiting," said another. "You need Lots of organic fertilizer."

"Sing to your tree," my holistic girlfriend announced. "It's a well-known fact that all plants love singing!" (She probably hadn't heard me sing.)

I pumped water from the creek. I rented an aerating machine. I fertilized with goose and duck manure. And I sang lullabies that only deaf trees could tolerate!

Nothing! Absolutely nothing except big, bright, shiny green leaves. The tree was obviously very happy. It just didn't know it was an avocado tree. Or perhaps it didn't want me to have my guacamole.

Cynthia Brian

One day my grandfather, Fred Abruzzini, came to visit. "What a beautiful avocado tree," he exclaimed. "When are you going to make me some guacamole?"

"Never!" I said with exasperation. "This old tree doesn't bear avocados, only pretty leaves. I've done everything—aerated and fertilized. I've even sung to it."

"No wonder you don't have any avocados," Grandpa said. "You are too nice to your tree. You have to shock it!"

"What?" I asked in disbelief.

"You have to shock your avocado tree by slapping it with sticks to get the juices flowing," he insisted. I laughed, but I figured, what the heck, nothing else had worked. So together we cut some flogging sticks and began slapping my tree. There I was with my seventy-eight-year-old grandfather, yelling, laughing, and lashing at that majestic tree. I felt like a pirate chief with the cat-o'-nine-tails in hand!

My conscience was placated, however. Sure enough, the next spring brought tiny greenish-white flowers by the hundreds followed by big delicious avocados. I was now a gifted gardener! As long as we lived there, our avocado tree provided guacamole for all our family, friends, and neighbors. The neighborhood christened me "Guacamole Mama."

I never understood why that avocado tree responded so generously to Grandpa's treatment. At the time, I thought flogging a tree was preposterous, but since, I have read of many similar prescriptions for getting trees and plants to produce, including anecdotes by James Michener and Eddie Albert. Clearly, Grandpa had more experience and wisdom than I did. After that, whenever I needed gardening advice or assistance, I knew just the expert to ask.

It has been said that age brings wisdom. When I was young, I thought I knew everything. Now I know better. As I've grown older, I have learned that wisdom is a combination of good common sense, excellent judgment, a vivid imagination, and the ability to meld all three. Wisdom comes from experience. That's why the older we get, hopefully, the wiser and more knowledgeable we become.

My grandfather only had an eighth-grade education, but he rose to be part owner and wine maker of a major California winery. His gardening and farming knowledge had been passed down to him through generations of gardeners and farmers in Italy, and his own years of experience made him wise with plants.

Wisdom stems from inner learnedness and the ability to ask others for support when the answers seem unclear. Dorothy displayed wisdom when she finally realized that she didn't need the wizard to get home. The power was within her. Yet, she needed her experiences with the Scarecrow, the Lion, the Tin Man, and the Wicked Witch to understand her knowledge. I needed Grandpa's guidance to solve my tree's conundrum.

Wisdom brings clarity to our lives, creating an inner simplicity and an outer joy. Wisdom celebrates life and all life forms. Wisdom is a deep love of ourselves.

We can turn our wounds into wisdom if we learn from our mistakes and pain. I believe my ancestors were wise and that I have inherited their ability to turn the failures and successes of my own life into wisdom. Wisdom offers doors into other people's hearts and our own. Listen to your heart, and trust your higher wisdom.

EXERCISE

Wise Choices

If you are ever in a quandary about what choice to make, ask yourself which course will bring you enjoyment and enrich others. This is your wisest choice. But what if this decision would be harmful to some? If the benefits outweigh the negatives, it remains your wisest choice. (No one ever said that wisdom was painless.)

Wisdom is the ability to think and then act.

Cynthia Brian

The Gift of
YOU

You have traveled a long way, both in this book and in your life. You still have lots of thrills, chills, triumphs, and tumbles ahead of you. Each new day is an exciting gift, waiting for you to open it. And good manners suggest that, in exchange for this present, you offer one of your own. That gift is *you!*

You were born to be magnificent. No matter who or what you are, you have extraordinary gifts to offer the world. Your skills, passions, experiences, and insights make you unique. Live in no one's shadow. Live no one else's dream. You already have all the tools you need to become the person you want to be. Take a look in the mirror. Admire yourself. You are already a *star.* You are *you.*

Cherish the past and dream of the future, but enjoy every moment of the present day. Do and be what you desire. Let your flame burn brightly within. You are an original. You have just one shot on this earth in this body, so use your talents to the maximum. The gift of life is an incredible chance to love, laugh, work, play, cry, pray, and look up at the stars.

What stories lie buried in your heart? What lessons will you share? Grab this opportunity to experience the joyfulness of being, living fully and authentically. And don't forget the rules of being the star you are:

1. You must smile.
2. You must have fun.
3. You must be willing to be wild and crazy.

Keep on daring, pushing limits, singing, dancing, and expanding your horizons. I wish you great success in living, loving, laughing, and learning to make a difference. Life is a party and you are the gift! Walk right in and enjoy the celebration!

EXERCISE

Telephone

One last exercise to pump up your energy! The telephone rings. Answer it enthusiastically, knowing that your caller has the potential to offer you something you have been dreaming of for years. How do you respond? Be prepared for greatness. It is the inevitable amalgam of your many gifts.

Pound your chest and yell at the top
of your lungs, "I am the greatest!"
Be the star you are!

THE END
IS YOUR BEGINNING!

RECOMMENDED READING

ACTING

An Actor Prepares and *The Stanislavski Method* by Constantin Stanislavski
The Audition Book by Ed Hooks
The Business of Showbusiness by Cynthia Brian
The Hollywood Walk of Fame by Samantha Hart
How to Audition by Gordon Hunt
Meditations for Actors by Carra Robertson
Reel Power by Mark Litwak
Reel Spirit by Raymond Teague
Respect for Acting by Uta Hagen

BUSINESS

The 100 Absolutely Unbreakable Laws of Business Success and *Psychology of Selling* by Brian Tracy
101 Salary Secrets and *The 101 Toughest Interview Questions* by Frances Bolles Haynes and Daniel Porot
1001 Ways to Market Your Book and *Celebrate Today* by John Kremer
The 7 Habits of Highly Effective People by Stephen Covey
Become the Brand of Choice by Jason Hartman
Borrowed Dreams and *Outrageous!* by T. Scott Gross
Dare to Change Your Job and Your Life by Carole Kanchier, Ph.D.
Getting Over Yourself by Barbara Rocha
Guerrilla Selling and *Guerilla Negotiating* by Orvel Ray Wilson
High Five! by Ken Blanchard and Sheldon Bowles
How to Get Anything You Want! and *How to Be a Great Communicator!* by Nido Qubein
How to Get Filthy Stinking Rich by Herb Kay
How to Win Friends and Influence People by Dale Carnegie
It's Not Business, It's Personal by Ronna Lichtenberg
Lessons for the Future by Andrew Dugan and David Murcott
Major in Success by Patrick Combs
Masters of Networking by Ivan Misner
The Mental Edge by Ken Baum
The One Minute Manager by Ken Blanchard
The One Minute Salesperson by Spencer Johnson
The Power of Focus by Les Hewitt
Psychology of Winning for Women and *Psychology of Winning* by Denis Waitley
Rich Dad, Poor Dad by Robert Kiyosaki
Secrets of Power Negotiating by Roger Dawson
Secrets of Superstar Speakers by Lilly Walters

The Seven Spiritual Laws of Success by Deepak Chopra
Smart Women Finish First by David Bach
Speak and Grow Rich by Dottie Walters
Success without a College Degree by John Murphy
Swim with the Sharks and *Pushing the Envelope* by Harvey MacKay
What Color Is Your Parachute? by Richard Bolles
Where Did the Money Go? and *How Much Should I Charge?* by Ellen Rohr
Why the Best Man for the Job Is a Woman by Esther Wachs

GARDENING/FARMING/ANIMALS

100 Years of Vintage Farm Tractors; This Old Tractor; and *This Old Farm*
   by Michael Dregni
Animals: A Return to Wholeness and *Animal Talk* by Penelope Smith
Are You as Happy as Your Dog? by Alan Cohen
Chicken Soup for the Gardener's Soul by Jack Canfield, Mark Victor Hansen,
   Cynthia Brian, Cindy Buck, Marion Owen, Pat Stone, and Carol Sturgulewski
Flower Essences for Animals by Lila Devi
The Well-Tended Perennial Garden by Tracy DiSabato-Aust
Wine, a Gentleman's Game by Mark Miller
You Have a Visitor by Renee Lamm Esordi

HEALTH AND SPIRITUALITY

7 Keys to Changing by Linda McNeil
Anatomy of an Illness by Norman Cousins
Age Power; Body Mind; and *Age Wave* by Ken Dychtwald
Ageless Body, Timeless Mind; How to Know God; and
   Perfect Health by Deepak Chopra
Angel Answers by Andrew Ramer
Be the Boss of Your Brain by Sherry Meinberg
The Courage to Laugh by Allen Klein
Divine Guidance by Doreen Virtue
Everybody Has a Guardian Angel by Mitch Finley
Feng Shui for Dummies by David Kennedy
Forgiveness; Love Is Letting Go of Fear; and *Shortcuts to God* by Dr. Gerald Jampolsky
Fully Human Fully Alive and *Happiness Is an Inside Job* by John Powell, SJ
Healing HIV Jon Kaiser
How to Get Your Prayers Answered by Rabbi Irwin Katsof
I Turn to the Light, A Book of Healing Affirmations Connie Bowen
Jesus, CEO; The Path; and *The Power of Positive Prophecy* by Laurie Beth Jones
Kitchen Table Wisdom and *My Grandfather's Blessing* by Rachel Naomi Remen
My Father's Voice by Alan Cohen
On the Elephant's Knee by Thomas Easley
Peak Condition by James Garrick
Prescriptions for Living and *Love, Medicine and Miracles* by Bernie Siegel

Cynthia Brian

Reflections on Life after Life by Raymond Moody
Return to Wholeness and Vital Energy by David Simon
Sacred Healing by Caroline Myss
A Soulworker's Companion by Betty Clare Moffett
Spirit Body Healing by Mary Rockwood Lane, R.N. and Michael Samuels, M.D.
The Twelve Gifts of Birth by Charlene Costanzo
When I Relax I Feel Guilty by Timothy Hansel

INSPIRATIONAL AND MOTIVATIONAL BOOKS

12 Secrets for Manifesting Your Vision, Inspiration & Purpose by D. Richard Bellamy
The Aladdin Factor and *Dare to Win* by Jack Canfield and Mark Victor Hansen
The Alchemy of Possibility by Carolyn Mary Kleefeld
All I Really Need to Know I Learned in Kindergarten by Robert Fulghrum
Anam Cara, Spiritual Wisdom from the Celtic World by John O'Donohue
As a Man Thinketh by James Allen
Be Your Own Angel by Nancy Swan Drew
Becoming a Woman of Influence by Carol Kent
Chicken Soup for the Soul (all titles) Jack Canfield, Mark Victor Hansen,
    and coauthors
Choose to Live Your Life Fully by Susan Smith Jones
The Christmas Box by Richard Paul Evans
Create a Life That Tickles Your Soul by Sue Zoglio
A Creative Companion by Sark
Don't Sweat the Small Stuff by Richard Carlson
The Greatest Success in the World by Og Mandino
How High Can You Bounce? by Roger Crawford
Inner Simplicity by Elaine St. James
It Only Takes a Minute to Change Your Life by Willie Jolley
Jonathan Livingston Seagull by Richard Bach
The Joyful Spirit by Brian Biro
Leading an Inspired Life by Jim Rohn
Let Go, Let God (tape) and *You Have the Power* (tape) by Wally Amos
The Little Prince by Antoine de Saint-Exupéry
Living in the Light and *Creative Visualization* by Shakti Gawain
The Magic Lamp by Keith Ellis
Miracle Moments for a Magical Millennium by Cynthia Brian
More of Bits and Pieces by Rob Gilbert
Papa, My Father and *Loving Each Other* by Leo Buscaglia
Permission to Succeed by Noah St. John
Power of Positive Doing and *Say YES to Life* by Ivan Burnell
The Power of Positive Thinking by Norman Vincent Peale
Powertalk (tape) by Anthony Robbins
Success Is a Journey by Brian Tracy
The Purpose of Your Life by Carol Adrienne

The Road Less Traveled by M. Scott Peck
Serendipity of Success by Joy Elise Macci, Ph.D.
Seventeen Lies That Are Holding You Back and the Truth That Will Set You Free
    by Steve Chandler
Simple Abundance and *Something More* by Sara Ban Breathnach
Success Is a Journey by Jeff Mayer
The Voice of the Master; The Prophet; Thoughts and Meditations by Kahlil Gibran
Way of the Peaceful Warrior and *Everyday Enlightenment* by Dan Millman
What Are Your Goals? by Gary Ryan Blair
Wisdom of the Ages and *Manifest Your Destiny* by Wayne Dyer

PARENTING/FAMILY/RELATIONSHIPS

The 7 Best Things Smart Teens Do by John and Linda Friel
10 Principles for Spiritual Parenting by Mimi Doe
A Return to Love by Marianne Williamson
The Ability to Love by Allan Fromme
Affairs of the Net by Michael Adamse
All Kids Need by Zimmy Zimberg
Aunties by Julienne Bennett and Tamara Traeder
Be a Goddess by Francesca De Grandis
Beyond the Pleasure Principle by Sigmund Freud
Celebrating Family by Lisa Beaver Moss
Cool Communication by Andrea and Journey Henkart
Field Guide to the American Teenager and *Uncommon Sense for Parents of Teenagers* by
    Michael Riera, Ph.D.
Girlfriends for Life by Carmen Renee
The Grief Recovery Handbook by Russell Friedman
Growing Season by Arlene Bernstein
Happily Ever After by Alan Cohen
Independent Women, Creating Our Lives by Debra Miller
Life Strategies by Dr. Phil McGraw
Life Strategies for Teens by Jay McGraw
Losing Your Parents, Finding Yourself by Victoria Secunda
Men Are from Mars, Women Are from Venus by John Gray
The New Intimacy and *Opening to Love 365 Days a Year*
    by Judith Sherven and Jim Sneichowski
No Greater Love by Loren Slocum
Orphan Train Rider: One Boy's True Story by Andrea Warren
Our Turn, Our Time by Cynthia Black
Secrets about Life Every Woman Should Know by Barbara DeAngelis, Ph.D.
Ultimate Judgment by Meg Clairmonte
The Uses of Enchantment: The Importance of Fairytales by Bruno Bettelheim
Your Erroneous Zones by Wayne Dyer

Cynthia Brian

DO YOU DARE TO CARE?

Every day, when we turn on our television sets, we are bombarded with heart-wrenching tales of violence, abuse, and a host of other obstacles to our safety. Drug use, gang violence, and unsafe sexual promiscuity threaten not only the future of our young people, but also the future of our world.

It is for this reason that I founded the charity *Be the Star You Are!* I want every individual to once again discover the uniqueness and profound gifts that God has bestowed upon us. I believe that information infused with inspiration has the power to transform and change lives. *Be the Star You Are!* is a nonprofit, volunteer organization, that runs a media library that promotes and distributes an ever-growing list of positive, informative, and empowering videos, audiotapes, books, art, and music to groups in need of hope. These materials provide tools for daily living, including

☆ Life lessons and empowering stories
☆ Guidelines for happiness, prosperity, and personal growth
☆ Promotion of self-esteem, self-growth, self-confidence, and self-worth

Be the Star You Are! acquires positive programs, commissions special productions, and promotes inspirational, educational, and informational programming through its Web site, fund-raisers, media interviews, and radio and television public service announcements.

These edutainment materials are distributed to other nonprofits, including youth groups and kids at risk, seniors, women's groups, job reentry programs, shelters and support groups, and treatment and recovery programs. Volunteers also donate their time to the charity's literacy program, Reach Out Reading.

Your contribution to *Be the Star You Are!* makes a difference. Your investment will help change the face of tomorrow from one of despair to one of hope. *Be the Star You Are!* can take people to a natural high without drugs. It can boost confidence and provide avenues for achieving a successful future.

Here are some ways you can help:

☆ Send your tax-deductible contribution. (We accept credit cards.)
☆ Advertise on our radio program.
☆ Donate your air miles.
☆ Donate goods that can be auctioned off at an event.
☆ Sponsor an event, making *Be the Star You Are!* the charitable beneficiary.
☆ Ask your company to match your donation or to make a contribution.
☆ Purchase our books, tapes, and videos.
☆ Make *Be the Star You Are!* a beneficiary of your estate or charitable trust fund.
☆ Volunteer your time.

Please join our Galaxy of Stars and support *Be the Star You Are!* Thank you for your support.

Cynthia Brian, Founder, CEO, and President
Be the Star You Are!
501 (c)(3) a nonprofit corporation
PO Box 37694556
Moraga, CA 94556

For more information:
Web site: www.bethestaryouare.org
Telephone: 925-376-7126

Sign up for a free newsletter featuring empowerment tools at www.bethestaryouare.org.

ORDER FORM

Need more copies of *Be the Star You Are!* ? We'll send them to you!

FAX ORDERS: 707-988-2454
TELEPHONE ORDERS: CALL TOLL-FREE: 877-944-STAR
Have your VISA or MASTERCARD ready!
ONLINE ORDERS: www.star-style.com, www.bethestaryouare.com,
or www.bethestaryouare.org

Please send_____copies of *Be the Star You Are!*

Company Name_____

Name: _____

Address:_____

City:_____State_____Zip_____

Telephone (____)_____

E-mail:_____

Would you like the book (s) autographed?_____ yes_____no

Please give name(s) if yes: _____

_____

Cost per book $15.95
Tax: Add 8%
Shipping: $3.00 for the first book, $2.00 for each additional book

Method of Payment:

_____Check

_____Credit Card ___VISA _____MASTERCARD

Card Number_____

Name on Card_____

Expiration Date_____

Signature_____

Start Being the Star You Are Today!
Visit the Starstyle Store online for videos and other books by Cynthia Brian
Available at http://www.star-style.com/store/index.htm

WOULD YOU LIKE TO CONTRIBUTE A STORY TO CYNTHIA BRIAN'S NEWEST BOOK PROJECTS?

PROJECT ONE

Daddy's Hands, Mommy's Heart: Children's Memories: A Tribute to Great Parents Everywhere

Were one or both of your parents role models for you? Would you like to write a short tribute to them describing why they were so wonderful or give an example of a fabulous experience with them? Cynthia is seeking stories from kids of any age anywhere around the world who want to extol the virtues of their parents. This book will compile stories from celebrities and noncelebrities, painting a portrait of what a great parent looks like as expressed through the eyes of a child.

PROJECT TWO

The sequel to *Be the Star You Are!*

Cynthia is collecting *your* stories for upcoming sequels to this first book. Sequels will focus on *Be the Star You Are! at Home, Be the Star You Are! at Work, Be the Star You Are! at School* (for teens), and *Be the Star You Are! on Vacation.* If you would like to share your story of living, loving, laughing, and learning to make a difference, here's your opportunity.

Stories for both projects should be from 200 words to 1,000 words. Please include a 50-word bio. All submissions will be acknowledged. E-mail your stories to cynthia@star-style.com or send a hard copy regular mail with a Mac disk to:

Daddy's Hands or Be the Star You Are! Sequels
c/o Cynthia Brian
PO Box 422
Moraga, CA 94556
www.bethestaryouare.com
www.star-style.com
cynthia@star-style.com

ABOUT THE AUTHOR

Cynthia Brian is constantly striving for excellence and balance as a student of life. Born on a farm in the Napa Valley in northern California, Cynthia has raised chickens and goats, driven tractors, and picked fruits, vegetables, and flowers from the garden of life for as long as she can remember.

Cynthia's passion for traveling and for people is matched by her passion for acting, which she has been doing professionally for over two decades. As an acting coach, she has guided the careers of several talk show hosts and numerous actors working in established series and in feature films.

A California-certified interior designer and professional member of ASID and IDS, Cynthia is president of her own interior and garden design firm, *Starstyle* Interiors and Designs. Her designs have been featured in several books, magazines, newspapers, and television shows. She produced *A Gardener's Calendar* and also designs furniture, including her popular *Starstyle* game table and ottoman.

She produces, writes, and hosts two television series: *Starstyle— Live Your Dreams,* an inspirational program about people who are doing what they love in life; and *Starstyle—The Business of Show Business,* an educational program about how to get going and stay going while avoiding the scams in the entertainment industry. Together with her daughter, Heather Brittany, Cynthia cohosts "Animals Cuts" segments for TV and radio about the animal kingdom.

Cynthia was heard weekly on the personal growth radio program *Starstyle—Be the Star You Are!* where she interviewed best-selling authors in personal achievement, business, and success. Her syndicated column, "Business Bytes," is read in newspapers worldwide. She is currently seeking a national radio program host.

She coauthored the *New York Times* best-selling book *Chicken Soup for the Gardener's Soul* and authored the upcoming *Daddy's Hands, Mommy's Heart: Children's Memories,* a tribute to great parents everywhere by the children who were loved by them.

To unwind, Cynthia enjoys gardening on her farm, where her favorite pastime is cleaning out the chicken coops and barns and recycling the manure into her garden. She also relishes playing with her large menagerie of animals, which include chickens, ducks, geese, goats, rabbits, horses, dogs, cats, and birds on the farm she shares with her husband and two children in northern California.

To book Cynthia as a speaker or spokesperson contact:
Cynthia Brian
Starstyle® Productions
PO Box 422
Moraga, CA 94556
www.star-style.com
925-377-STAR

To book Cynthia for commercials, TV, and film, contact:
Ed Silver ᶜ/o Stars, The Agency
23 Grant Ave., 4th floor
San Francisco, CA 94108
415-421-6272